SAINT LYDWINE OF SCHIEDAM

SAINT LYDWINE
OF
SCHIEDAM

By
J.-K. HUYSMANS

Translated from the French by Agnes Hastings

Deus carni illius sæpe dolores infligit, quatenus Spiritus
Sanctus ibi habitare possit.
Sancta Hildegardis, *Vita*, lib.ii.

TAN BOOKS AND PUBLISHERS, INC.
Rockford, Illinois 61105

NIHIL OBSTAT:

G. H. Joyce, S.J.
Censor Deputatus

IMPRIMATUR:

Edm. Can. Surmont
Vic. Gen. Westmonasterii
die 30 Novembris, 1922

Originally published in 1923 by Kegan Paul,
Trench, Trubner & Co., Ltd., London. Reprinted by
arrangement with the original publisher.

Library of Congress Catalog Card Number:
79-87551

ISBN: 0-89555-087-3

TAN BOOKS AND PUBLISHERS, INC.
P.O. Box 424
Rockford, Illinois 61105

1979

PREFACE

THE life of St. Lydwine has been written by three men of religion who were her contemporaries.

Jan Gerlac, a relation of hers, was sacristan of the Augustine monastery of Windesem. He lived many years near the Saint, even in the same house, and he tells of her daily life from observation.

Jan Brugman was a lay brother of the " Observance." He took up the work of Gerlac, translating it into Latin and amplifying it with details supplied him by Jan Walter de Leyde, the last Confessor of Lydwine.

Thomas à Kempis was sub-prior of the Augustinians of Mount St. Agnes near Zwolle. His relation is abridged from that of Brugman, but adds details gathered at Schiedam from those who knew the Saint.

Jan Gerlac had some fame as a writer, and his " Soliloquies " are still sought for. He was, according to his contemporaries, a very fervent and a very humble monk; and Jan Brugman, a friend of Denys de Chartreux, is quoted by Wading in the Annals of his order, as one of the celebrated preachers of his century ; admirable both for the elevation of his eloquence and for the number of his virtues. Thomas à Kempis, one of the presumed authors of the " Imitation of Christ," was born the same year as Lydwine and died, in the odour of sanctity, in 1471, after having written a whole series of mystical works of which several translations into French were attempted. These three who wrote the life of the Saint are thus men of good repute and worthy, on account of their position and the probity of their soul, to be believed. One may add, too, that the details of their works can be compared with the official documents drawn up, after an attentive and detailed enquiry, by the contemporary Burgomasters of Schiedam, who passed her whole life in review.

No history could therefore be presented under better conditions of good faith and certitude.

It must be owned, however, that a history of Lydwine is, thanks to them, a very difficult skein to disentangle. It is, in effect, impossible to adopt a chronological order. Brugman declares frankly " That he considered it inconvenient to do anything of the kind ; " and under the pretext of being more edifying, he groups the scenes or the life of the Saint according to the list of qualities which he wishes to impress upon us. With this method, which is equally that of Gerlac and à Kempis, there is no means of knowing whether any event which they relate took place before or after any other.

This was the fashion of writing adopted by all the hagiographers of that period. They narrate anecdotes pell-mell, only troubling to class the virtues, so as to have a store of commonplaces to draw upon in the case of any other saint. They interlarded these pious recitations with quotations from the Psalms, and left it at that.

It would seem, at first sight, that there is a means of applying a remedy to this disorder, by extracting and comparing the dates scattered here and there in the three biographies and utilizing them as clues to punctuate the life of the Saint; but this method does not secure the promised results.

Gerlac and Brugman tell us sometimes of an adventure which they relate as taking place on or about the day of such and such a saint. With these indications one can, indeed, place the day and the month, but not the year, which they forget to specify. The more precise dates which Gerlac especially records, have reference often to episodes of little importance and do not always tally with those of Thomas à Kempis. Very scrupulous when it is a question of noting liturgical feasts and fasts, this writer furnishes us with a certain number of dates, but how are we to trust them? His dates, if one looks into them, are inexact: thus he places the death of Petronille, Lydwine's niece, in 1426, and also shows her assisting in her aunt's house at a scene in which she was wounded, in 1428. One of these dates is consequently false, in this case the second, for the date 1425 given by the two other writers appears certain.

Even if the dates were correct and always agreed with one another, we should still stray about at random among various facts dated by others who are not in the least correct; and there is nothing to indicate how to class these facts. Whatever course one takes, one must, therefore, renounce all hope of chronological precision.

Moreover, in the works of the three biographers several personages appear who are the friends and nurses of Lydwine, but no details are given about them. These minor characters flit about the stage, coming one knows not whence and vanishing one knows not how; and finally, to aggravate the confusion, three of the confessors of the saint were called Jan. Now, instead of adding the surname or the name of their birthplace to distinguish them, the three men of religion give us only the Christian name, so that it is impossible to tell if the confessor Jan of whom one hears in such and such an incident, is Jan Pot, Jan Angeli, or Jan Walter.

There is, indeed, very little to go upon in this bewilderment. I do not flatter myself that I have thrown any light upon it. I have made use, in this Life, of the three texts of Gerlac, Brugman and à Kempis, completing their anecdotes by collation, and I have arranged the events according to the order which seemed to me, if not the most accurate, at least the most interesting and useful.

CHAPTER I.

THE state of Europe during Lydwine's lifetime was terrible. In France, first Charles VI. reigned, then Charles VII. Lydwine was born in the same year that Charles VI., at twelve years of age, ascended the throne of France. Even at this distance of time, the years of his reign call up horrible memories; they drip with blood and reek of licence; and in the light of the old chronicles, behind the dusty veil of history, four figures pass by.

The first is a man of weak intellect, with pale face and hollow cheeks, with eyes now dull, now full of fire. He vegetates in a palace in Paris, his clothes over-run with vermin, his hair and beard swarming with lice. This wretched being, before he became demented, had been a familiar figure, debauched, irascible and weak. It is the King, Charles VI., an imbecile taking part in the wild debauches of those afflicted like himself.

The second is an intriguing woman, eccentric, unreliable and imperious, wearing a head-dress ornamented like a devil's head with two horns, and a dress cut very low in the neck, and trailing after her a figured train of great length; she shuffles as she walks, shod in slippers with points two feet long. This is the Queen of France, the Bavarian Ysabeau, who, absorbed in the writings of some unknown author, takes her place by the side of the husband she abhors.

The third is a vain gossip whom the ladies of the Court adore, and who shows himself, at one and the same time, cordial and rapacious, affable and cunning. He oppresses the people, drains the money from both countryside and town, and dissipates it in scandalous escapades. This is the Duke of Orleans, cursed of

the people, and denounced from the pulpit by a monk
of the Augustinian order, Jacques Legrand.

The fourth, a little wizened creature, taciturn,
suspicious and cruel, is the Duke of Burgundy,
familiarly known as John the Pitiless.

All four wrangle, curse each other, quarrel and
make it up, executing a sort of devil's dance in the
decay of a country already half ruined by the insanity
of its King. France is indeed convulsed. Paris is given
over to all the atrocities of civil war, with butchers
and cut-throats as dictators, who bleed the bourgeois
as if they were beasts. The country is over-run with
bands of brigands, who overwhelm the peasants, set
fire to their crops, and cast the women and children
into the furnaces of the mills. There are the criminal
hordes of the Armagnacs, the rapacious crowd of
Burgundians, and those who stretch out their hands
to the English to help them to cross the Channel. The
English do, indeed, disembark near Harfleur, march on
Calais, and meet the French army on the way, in the
county of St. Pol, at Azincourt. They attack, and
have no difficulty in overthrowing, like ninepins, the
long files of heavy knights, prisoned, as it were, in
sentry-boxes of armour and fixed astride their horses,
which are motionless, fast stuck in the heavy clay;
and, whilst that region is invaded, the Dauphin causes
the Duke of Burgundy to be assassinated, who himself
had had the Duke of Orleans decapitated on the very
day after they had taken the communion from the
hands of the same priest, and had been reconciled
together. Queen Ysabeau, egged on by her need of
money, sold herself to the enemy, and obliged the
imbecile King to sign the treaty of Troyes; thus
disinheriting her son in favour of the sovereign of
England, who became heir to the crown of France.
The Dauphin would not accept this deprivation, but,
too weak to resist, he took to flight, and was proclaimed
King by some adventurers in a manor house of
Auvergne. The country was split into two camps,

betrayed by the one, broken by the blows of the other, and pillaged by both.   It seemed as if the kingdom of France was doomed when, at a few months' interval, the King of England, Henry V., and the King of France, Charles VI., died; but the struggle still continued between the two nations.   Charles VII., timid and thoughtless, always with his back turned towards the enemy ready for flight, abandoned himself to low intrigues, whilst the enemy robbed him of his provinces one by one.   There was really no saying how much would be left of France, when the heavens were moved and Joan of Arc was sent.   She accomplished her mission, repulsed the strangers, led her miserable monarch to Rheims for his sacring, and expired, abandoned by him, in the flames, two years before the death of Lydwine.

Thus the condition of France at the end of the fourteenth and beginning of the fifteenth century was lamentable; for as though human enemies were not enough, other scourges were added.   The black death ravaged the country and mowed down millions of her people; that disappeared and was replaced by the tac, an epidemic much feared for the terrible virulence of its cough; when this died out the plague re-appeared, and emptied Paris of fifty thousand persons in five weeks, leaving three years' famine in its train; and then again the tac returned and depopulated the towns still further.

If the condition of France was lamentable, that of England, who was torturing her, was hardly better. To the risings of the people, succeeded the revolts of the nobles.   The King, Richard II., made himself odious by his debauches and robberies.   He set out to quell the troubles in Ireland, but was deposed, and the Duke of Lancaster, under the title of Henry IV., was elected King in his place.   Richard II. was imprisoned and possibly starved to death.   The usurper's reign was passed in moderating discords and discovering plots. He burnt, on pretext of heresy, those of his subjects who had displeased him, and dragged out the feeble existence of an epileptic, tormented by the plots of his son who was eager for the succession. He died at the age of forty-seven, and this son, known till then as a drinker and a bandit, an associate of thieves and women, reveals himself, on coming to the throne, as cold and imperious, arrogant beyond measure, and of a ferocious piety. The pharisaism and cupidity of the English race are incarnate in him; he shows the harshness and prudery of the protestant, and is at once an usurer, an executioner, and a methodist parson, born out of due time. He renewed the campaign in Normandy, starved towns, falsified coinage, hanged the prisoners in the name of the Lord, and overwhelmed his victims with sermons. But this sport, in which he was to have been in at the death, grows stale when his army is decimated by the plague. He is, however, victorious at Azincourt; he massacres all those who cannot ransom themselves, and extracts enormous sums from others; and whilst their fate is in the balance, he crosses himself, mumbles prayers, and recites psalms. Then he dies at the Castle of Vincennes, leaving an infant heir some months of age. The infant's guardians—one violent and dissolute, the Duke of Gloucester; the other, vain and cunning, the Duke of Bedford—ravage France, but are completely routed by Joan of Arc, and dishonour themselves for ever in buying her, that they may throw her to the flames after a dishonourable trial.

After France and England, Flanders is taken in the flank and overwhelmed by the storm.

The history of Flanders is intimately bound up with ours, and she too was wasted by internal struggles, for the commercial rivalry between Ghent and Bruges, year after year, strewed the meadowlands with bones and made the rivers run blood.

Ghent reveals herself as a proud and obstinate city, peopled by the ultra pious and by the eternally discontented. Her trades guilds make her the bivouac of strikers, the camp in which the vile and seditious find a welcome; and all the revolutionaries of Europe are in close communication with her. Bruges seems more civilized and less opinionated, but her pride equals that of Ghent, and her love of money is even greater. She is the great emporium of Christianity, and she appropriates greedily all surrounding towns; she is the implacable arbitrator, and if it is a question of a canal which will benefit one of these townships at the expense of another, a hatred equalling that of cannibals springs up. The Count of Flanders, Louis III., tyrannical, vain and prodigal, cruel, too, and unlucky, threw himself against the people of Ghent, and tried to break their obstinacy by persecution. Their chief, Philippe d'Artevelde, marched against him, defeated him, penetrated to Bruges, and there killed for preference its richest merchants; after which he sacked the villages and despoiled the towns. The nobles of Flanders called on France for help; it was a crusade of the nobles against the working classes. Charles VI. and the Duke of Burgundy crossed the frontier, were joined by d'Artevelde at the head of an army at Roosebeke, and charged the Flemings, who had foolishly linked themselves together with chains that retreat might be impossible. The Flemings were twisted and piled one upon another, and suffocated in a very narrow space, without having been able to offer any resistance. It was a triumph of asphyxiation, a battle without injury, a massacre without wounds, a combat during which blood ran only as from casks that are tapped, from the bursting veins of their crushed faces. D'Artevelde was, happily for him, found amongst the dead, for after the victory the vilest passions were unloosed; the country was pillaged, and the women and children were murdered. Places unwilling to be destroyed bought themselves with gold: it was "your money or your life," for these nobles, who had trembled before a troop of undisciplined peasants, showed themselves inexorable. The people

of Ghent had recourse to the English, who disembarked
to aid them, but gleaned most of the booty left by the
French, so that this miserable country became a prey
both to those who attacked and those who defended
her, though neither depredations nor tortures sapped
her incredible energy. Ackerman succeeded d'Artevelde
and, supported by a troop from across the Channel,
laid siege to Ypres. Charles VI. dislodged him and took
Bergues, in which he left no soul alive: then, tired of
these orgies of murder, he called a truce. Upon
the death of Count Louis III., Philip of Burgundy
succeeded. This terrible inheritance came to him by
right of his wife. He renewed hostilities and the
massacres recommenced. Dam was reduced to ashes;
the country called Quatre Métiers became a heap of
ruins; and, as if these horrors did not suffice, religious
quarrels were added to this interminable conflict. Two
Popes were elected at the same time, who bombarded
each other with a shower of Bulls. The Duke of
Burgundy stood by one of these pontiffs and expected
his subjects to follow his guidance, but they refused,
and Philip became irritated and decapitated the leaders
of the recalcitrant party. Once more the Flemings
revolted; the churches were shut, religious offices
ceased, Flanders seemed to be excommunicated, and
the Duke, exhausted by these disputes, finally left in
peace a people he could not control and contented
himself with exacting money in exchange for their
liberty of conscience.

Such was the situation in Flanders; and if we pass
on into Holland we shall see her torn too by incessant
strife.

At the moment of Lydwine's birth, Duke Albert,
as Rudwaard or vice-regent of Hainault, governed
Holland, Zeeland, and Frisia—the provinces which
were united under the title of the Low Countries. He
replaced the real ruler, his brother, William V., who
had gone mad after his impious struggles with his
mother, Margaret of Bavaria. Whilst he was under

restraint the country had fallen a victim to a violent feud, and a desperate battle had taken place between the red caps or Hoecks, and the grey caps or Kabelljauws. These two parties, the Guelphs and Ghibelins of the Low Countries, were the result of the war between William and the Princess Margaret, the one upholding the son and the other the mother; but these hatreds survived the causes which engendered them, for we find them still active in the sixteenth century.

Directly he was named vice-regent, Albert laid siege to Delft, where he subdued the sedition in six weeks, and then took arms against the Duke of Gueldres and Bishop of Utrecht in a scandalous contest between father and son, which seems a fitting pendant to the rivalry between the mother and son of the last reign.

William V. died, and Duke Albert was proclaimed governor of the provinces. The country, worn by these dissensions, prepared to rest, but Duke Albert was under the influence of his mistress, Adelaïde de Poelgeest, and betrayed the Hoecks, whom he had Poelgeest, and betrayed the Hoecks, whom he had son William caused Adelaïde to be assassinated in the castle of La Haye, and then, fearing his father's vengeance, fled to France; but a rising in Frisia drew father and son together. Persuaded that the murderer was the only man capable of commanding his troops, Albert pardoned and recalled him. He disembarked at Kuinder, and the slaughter was renewed. Frisia ran with blood, but would not own herself conquered. In the year following she revolted anew, was subdued and rose again, this time defeating the armies of the Duke and forcing him to sign a treaty of peace. In courage and tenacity she might have been a second Ghent. This war was hardly over before another broke out; a vassal, the Lord of Arkel, declaring himself independent, at the moment of Albert's death. William VI., who succeeded his father, marched against the rebel, vanquished his garrisons, and obliged him to submit; but the Duke of Gueldres became mutinous, and the Frisians were once more in a ferment. Being very ill and at the end of his resources, William signed an armistice with them after they had captured the town of Utrecht, and died, leaving, besides many illegitimate children, one daughter—Jacqueline—who succeeded to her father's place.

The life of this singular princess reads like a romance. Her father married her at the age of sixteen to John, Duke of Touraine, Dauphin of France, who survived his marriage but a short time, being poisoned. Jacqueline then almost at once married her cousin, John IV., Duke of Brabant, a man of small intellect, who had no regard for her and insulted her by living publicly with another woman. She left him and fled to England, to Humphrey, Duke of Gloucester, with whom she was in love; obtained a decree from Peter the anti-Pope, pronouncing a divorce between her and the Duke of Brabant, and married the Duke of Gloucester. Hardly were they married when they had to return hurriedly to Holland to expel John of Bavaria, Bishop of Liége, Jacqueline's uncle, who had taken advantage of his niece's absence to invade the States. This prelate was defeated and retired, and Gloucester, who does not appear to have been very devoted to Jacqueline, installed her at Mons and returned to England. The unhappy lady had to struggle with a network of intrigue; her uncle, the Duke of Burgundy, held the threads, and she felt herself entangled on all sides. All were against her; her uncle, the Bishop of Liége, whom she had defeated, her second husband, John of Brabant, who seized Hainault when she was unable to come to its aid, and the Duke of Burgundy, who, resolved to annex Holland, imposed garrisons of his old campaigners from Picardy and Artois on her towns.

Jacqueline, who had counted at least on the fidelity of her subjects in Mons, was betrayed by them to the

Duke of Burgundy, and imprisoned in the palace in Ghent, where she remained three months; but, profiting by a moment when the soldiers who guarded her were drunk, she fled precipitately, disguised as a man, and reaching Antwerp attacked Gouda. There she believed herself safe and called on her husband for help, but Gloucester had forgotten that she was his wife, and had married again. He refused to intervene. Jacqueline decided to defend herself alone. She fortified Gouda, which the Duke of Burgundy besieged; she pierced the dyke of the Yssel and sheltered one side of the town by inundation; then, making a sortie on the other side, she fell upon the enemy and cut him in pieces. But her triumph was of short duration, for in the following year she made an unsuccessful attempt to take Haarlem by assault and her partisans dispersed, whilst, at the instigation of the Duke of Burgundy, the true Pope declared her marriage with the Duke of Gloucester null and void, and, in spite of the decree of the anti-Pope, pronounced it an adultery.

Then all turned their backs on Jacqueline, and, abandoned by those who had been faithful to her, she resolved, in order to save her liberty, to sue for pardon to the Duke of Burgundy, and at Delft she concluded a pact with him, by the terms of which she was to be recognised as his heir, yielding him her provinces during his lifetime. Her second husband having just died, she undertook not to re-marry without the Duke of Burgundy's consent; but she was hardly free before she broke her promises, for she fell in love with Frank de Borselen, Stadtholder of Holland, and married him secretly. Philip of Burgundy, who had had her watched by spies, learnt of this union. He said nothing, but drew de Borselen into an ambush and interned him at Rupelmonde, in Flanders, then informed Jacqueline that he would hang de Borselen if she did not immediately and unconditionally surrender all her rights in the Low Countries. To save her husband she surrendered all her rights in favour of the

B

Duke, and retired with de Borselen, the only man she appears to have really loved, to Teylingen. There, in this tower, the chronicles picture her sad and ill, unable to console herself in her misfortunes, amusing herself by modelling little earthenware jugs, and finally dying of consumption at the age of thirty-six, three years after Lydwine's death, without leaving any child by any of her four husbands.

Such briefly is the story of Jacqueline's life. What exactly was this strange woman? Accounts differ. Some represent her as an adventuress and libertine, others as tender and chivalrous, the victim of the ambitions of those around her; but, in any case, she seems to have been impulsive and unable to resist the emotions of the senses. A more or less accurate portrait of her in the pages of "La Flamboyante Colonne des Pays Bas" shows us a vigorous Dutch woman, something of a virago perhaps, but good-natured and energetic, though common and rough; probably imperious and headstrong, certainly versatile and brave.

Meanwhile poor Holland, under her government, had to bear the consequences of her love affairs. Sacked by the Burgundians, harassed by bands of Hoecks and Kabelljauws, she suffered cruelly, whilst inundations which involved entire villages increased her despair, and finally, to crown all, the plague appeared.

Was the rest of Europe more fortunate and happier? It would hardly appear so.

In Germany there reigned a pretentious drunkard, the Emperor Wenceslas, who trafficked in State affairs and appointments, whilst his vassals destroyed one another; and, in order to secure peace, it was necessary to sweep away both him and his concubines.

In Bohemia and in Hungary fierce war was waged between the Slavs and the Turkomans; there were also wholesale massacres of the Hussites; and the valley of the Danube was one vast charnel house, over which hovered the plague.

In Spain the natives and the Moors decimated each other, and a merciless hatred reigned between the provinces. In Castile, Peter the Cruel, a sort of maniac, killed his brothers, his cousin, and his wife, Blanche de Bourbon, and invented the most horrible tortures to torment his captives. In Arragon, Peter the Ceremonious stole the goods of his family and practised the most horrible cruelties on his enemies. The ruler of Navarre was a poisoner, Charles the Bad.

In Portugal, another Peter the Cruel, mad with vanity and persecutions, had the heart torn out of those who still breathed after being martyred. Once, in an access of frenzy, he even disinterred his dead mistress, seated her, dressed in royal ornaments and crowned with a royal crown, upon a royal throne, and forced all the nobles of the Court to pass in file before her and kiss the hand of the corpse.

Truly, the half-kindly madness of a Charles VI. seems almost reasonable when compared with the aberrations of these possessed beings.

In Italy there was civil war and plague, and in this general unloosing of scourges ruffians hacked each other to pieces in the streets of Rome. The family of Colonna and its satellites rose against the Pope, and, under pretext of restoring order, the King of Naples, Ladislas, possessed himself of the town, and, after having pillaged it, quitted it to return and pillage it again. Between Genoa and Venice there was a conflict involving ferocious reprisals; at Naples, Queen Jeanne was carried off to be suffocated between two mattresses in a castle of the Basciliate; in Milan there were all kinds of atrocities committed between the various factions in rebellion; and, worse than all, the Church herself suddenly became two-headed. If the members of her poor body—the Catholic states— languished sick and bloodless, her two heads, the one at Avignon and the other at Rome, were more than

ready to devour them. The Church was indeed
governed by the most terrible pontiffs, and it was the
epoch of the great schism in the east. The situation
of the Papal throne was as follows. The King of
France, Philippe le Bel, had at one time seated in the
Papal chair one of his own creatures, Bertrand de
Got, Archbishop of Bordeaux. After having been
consecrated at Lyons, this pontiff, instead of installing
himself at Rome, chose to live in the principality of
Avignon, and with him began that period which the
writers call the exile of Babylon. Other Popes
succeeded and died without having been able to regain
their States, until at last, in 1376, Gregory XI. retook
possession of the Eternal City, and died at the moment
when, disgusted with Italy, he was preparing to return
to France.

After the death of Gregory XI. there followed two
pontiffs, each elected by one faction and rejected by
the other. Rome named one Pope and Avignon
another, and Europe was divided into two camps.
Urban VI., the Roman Pope, the more honest, but the
more imprudent and sanguinary of the two, was
recognised by Germany, Flanders and the Low
Countries, England, Hungary, Bohemia and Navarre.
Clement VII., the Pope of Avignon, was gentle in
manner, but unscrupulous; he practised simony, sold
indulgences, bartered benefices, and trafficked in
favours. He was accepted by France, Scotland, Sicily
and Spain. The two pontiffs fought a war of interdicts,
threats and insults. They died and were replaced, and
their successors excommunicated right and left; whilst
a third Pope, elected by the Council of Pisa, hurled
anathemas at the other two.

The Holy Spirit erred and strayed about Europe,
so that it was no longer possible to know what pastors
to obey; and the confusion became such that even the
instincts of the Saints were at fault. Saint Catharine
of Sienna held for Urban VI., and St. Peter of
Luxembourg for Clement VII. Saint Vincent Ferrier

and Saint Colette submitted at one time to the anti-Pope, Peter de Lune, but eventually rallied to another tiara. It was the most absolute disorder, and Christianity had never been reduced to such chaos. GOD consented to show the divine origin of his Church by the disorder and infamy of His creatures ; no human institution could have resisted such shocks. It was as if Satan had mobilized his legions and the gates of hell were open ; the earth belonged to the Spirit of Evil, and he besieged the Church, assailing her without respite, gathering all his forces to overthrow her ; and yet she was not even shaken. She waited patiently for the Saints whom GOD should send to release her. She had traitors in high places, she had horrible Popes ; but these pontiffs of sin, these creatures so miserable, when they let themselves be led away by ambition, by hatred, by the love of money, by all those passions which are the lure of the Devil, were found infallible directly the Enemy attacked dogma ; the Holy Spirit, who was believed to be lost, returned to their assistance when it was a question of defending the teachings of Christ, and no Pope, however vile he may have been, failed in this.

It is none the less true that the miserable faithful who lived during all the horror of those unspeakable years, believed that all righteousness was crumbling away ; and indeed battlefields surrounded them whichever way they turned.

In the South, in the Christian Orient, the Greeks, the Mongols, and the Turks were exterminating each other ; in the North, Russians and Tartars, Swedes and Danes, were springing at each other's throats ; and if looking further afield, across the ravaged territories of Europe, their gaze travelled as far as the line of her frontiers, the faithful seemed to see the end of the world drawing near and the menaces of the Apocalypse about to be realized.

The boundaries of the Christian world are marked out in fire upon a lurid sky ; villages on the borders of

the heathen countries are in flames, and the zone of
the demons is lighted up.   Attila is alive again, and
the invasion of the barbarians renewed.   Like a
whirlwind the janissaries of Bajazet, the Amir of the
Ottomans, pass along, sweeping the countryside like
a cyclone and laying waste the towns.   He throws
himself on Nicopolis, against the allied Catholic forces,
and annihilates them ; the chair of St. Peter is in peril,
and all seems to be over for the Christians of the East,
when another victor, the Mongol Tamarlane, celebrated
for the pyramid of 90,000 skulls which he erected on
the ruins of Babylon, arrives with lightning rapidity
from the steppes of Asia, falls upon Bajazet, and
carries him off after having defeated his hordes in a
sanguinary battle.

Europe, aghast, looked on at the meeting of two
waterspouts, whose breaking inundated the onlookers
as in a rain of blood.

It is easy to realize the terror of simple people.
How many of those who survived the disasters of this
era, lived on with troubled souls and weary bodies,
exhausted by panic and famine, by devils' dances,
convulsions, rythmic palsies, and a sickness called by
the old chroniclers " the madness of the head," which
appears to have been meningitis, and, if not fatal, left
the sufferer insane.   In addition to all this, epidemics
appeared and re-appeared ; the black death was raging
in the East, and no region was entirely free from it.
It infested Italy and France, England, Germany and
Holland, as well as Bohemia and Spain, and was the
most dreaded scourge of all, continually over-running
Europe from the infernal reservoirs of the Levant.

Soon, in the enfeebled bodies, and in the souls
unhinged by fear, Satan entered and inspired the
impurities of nocturnal Sabbaths in the depths of the
forests.   The most execrable crimes and acts of
sacrilege were committed ; black Masses were
celebrated, and magic asserted itself.   Gilles de
Rais made away with little children and his sorcerers

plucked out their entrails, seeking in their remains the secret of alchemy, the power to turn worthless metals into gold. The people lay crushed both by what they heard and what they saw; they cried for justice and consolation among all these ills, but heard no answer to their prayers. They turned to the Church, with no better result. Their faith was shaken, and in their simplicity they said that Christ's representative on earth had no longer divine powers since he could not save them. They began to doubt the mission of the successors of S. Peter; they could not believe in them, they were so human and so feeble. They recalled the disconcerting spectacle of Wenceslas, Emperor of Germany, always drunk, going on a visit to Charles VI., King of France, who was insane, for the purpose of deposing a Pope. The Holy Spirit judged by an inebriate and a maniac.

It was not surprising, therefore, that in such a time, besides the practice of spiritism and Sabbaths, the most vehement heresies should arise and multiply from one end of the world to the other.

In England, John Wycliffe, a member of the University of Oxford and Vicar of Lutterworth, denied the doctrine of transubstantiation, affirming that the bread and wine remained, after consecration, intact. He opposed the adoration of the Saints, rejected confession, denied purgatory, and repudiated the power of the Pope. His teachings, which obtained an enormous following, united a crowd of madmen against the Church, and it was in vain that two Carmelites, Stephen Patrington and John Kinningham, struggled to oppose them. Wycliffe died, but his disciples, the Lollards, continued to propagate his errors.

They penetrated as far as Bohemia, with John Huss and Jerome of Prague. These accepted the doctrine of the Eucharist on condition that the laity were communicated under both species; they declared, however, that indulgences did not exist, that the

Papacy was the invention of men, and that the Church was the synagogue of Satan. John Huss was burned, as was also his disciple, Jerome of Prague, but their partisans, whose numbers were augmented owing to the disorders in Papal circles, set fire to churches and convents, murdering priests and monks, and the authorities attempted to reduce the Hussites to order without success. They defended themselves so bravely that King Sigismond finally signed a treaty with them to end the struggle. The Hussites broke up into numerous sects; Thaborites, who declared vengeance to be a virtue, and extolled the advantages of murder; Orebites, who were still more bloodthirsty and killed the faithful with horrible tortures; Adamites, who came from Picardie and went naked as our first parent. Later on they developed into sects less fanatic and more sociable; into Calixtins, that is to say the faithful who partook of the Chalice, and into the Bohemian Brothers, who, after having denied the Real Presence, detached themselves completely from the Church.

In Italy, the sects derived from the old heresies of the Albigensies multiplied. The remains of this heresy, which had flourished at the end of the thirteenth century, renewed the scandal of the Adamites and the Gnostics; all claimed to have obtained impeccability, and henceforth incest and adultery were permissible. It was useless to resort to destroying them by fire; they sprang up afresh. S. John of Capistran assailed them relentlessly, but in vain; they spread into Germany, where they became even more depraved, and in the fourteenth century one finds them in England, intermixed with Lollards, carrying on a hot propaganda which only increased their sufferings.

Whilst the Popes excommunicated these heretics, a confraternity of flagellation was organized in Germany, spread to Alsace, Lorraine and Champagne, and gained a footing in the south of France, at Avignon. These denied the virtue of the Sacraments, taught that blood caused by flagellation was valid matter for Baptism, and proclaimed that the power of the Vicar of Christ on earth is void.

In Flanders arose that series of errors known by the name of Walter Lollard who spread them, and extravagances were rife. A beguine, Marguerite Porette, reconstrued the abominations of the Gnostics and taught that to the creature absorbed in the contemplation of the Creator all is permitted. This woman gave audiences, seated on a silver throne, and declared herself to be escorted by two seraphim when she approached the Holy Table. She ended by being grilled alive in Paris, whither she had gone to gain proselytes, in 1310, that is to say, many years before the birth of Lydwine, but the disciples she had won still poisoned Brabant in the saint's lifetime. Another case was that of Blommardine, or Blœmardine, who died in Brussels in 1336, after having put herself at the head of the same sect and stirred up both north and south Flanders against the Church.

Ruysbroeck the Admirable, the hermit of the green valley, the greatest of the Flemish mystics, opposed them, but the virus left by the Gnostics filtered through into Belgium and the Low Countries. In 1410, when it was supposed to have worn itself out, it suddenly re-appeared, and the heresy was spread far and wide by men who called themselves " the intelligent." An unfrocked Carmelite, William de Hildernissen, and a laic of Picardy, Ægidius Cantoris, directed them. They were condemned and abjured their beliefs, but in 1428 their heresies revived with greater strength than ever. They crept into Germany and Holland, and finished by joining forces with the always active members of the Fraticellists and Lollards, who then proclaimed the reign of Lucifer, unjustly expelled from Paradise, and declared that he would now expel Michæl and his angels from Eden.

Nothing availed to eradicate these impious tenets; the Dominicans and Franciscans were baffled by the

task; the disciples of Ruysbroeck, his spiritual son
Pomerius, Gérard Groot, Pierre de Herenthals, all
tried to exterminate them, but the roots which they
tore up were reproduced with devilish rapidity, like
the fungus growths in vegetation, or those parasites
which flourish in the darkness of sewers.

Besides this more or less secret worship of the devil,
there existed, too, in the Low Countries, the influence
of doctrines corresponding to the errors of Wycliffe
and of John Huss in England and Bohemia. The
teachings of the partisans of the Reformation were
already beginning to bear fruit. Jean Pupper de
Goch, the founder of a convent for women at Malines,
admitted no authority but that of the Scriptures,
rejected the Councils of Popes, laughed at the merits
of vows, and decried the principles of the monastic
life; whilst Jean Ruchat de Wesel cried shame on
the Sacraments, contemned extreme unction, and
repudiated the Commandments of the Church. So,
too, did Jean Wessel de Groningen, from whose works
Luther later on borrowed his arguments against the
value of indulgences.

Thus was the Church sapped by heresies, and torn
limb from limb by dangerous Popes; but then, when
Christianity seemed lost, GOD raised up Saints to stop
the march of the Evil One and to save His Holy Church.

Even before the schism in the East, Our Lord had
imposed a mission upon two of His Saints to warn His
Vicars to abandon Avignon and return to Rome.

Saint Bridget was for this cause sent from Sweden
to lead the Sovereign Pontiff back to Italy. Whilst
she was striving to convince him he died, and another
replaced him, whom she also besought until his death.
The third indeed, Urban V., listened to her and
re-entered Rome, but afterwards tiring of that town
he returned to Avignon, where he died. Bridget
implored his successor, Gregory XI., to fly from
France, but whilst he hesitated she herself disappeared,
and it was only at the instance of another Saint,

Catharine of Sienna, that he determined to cross the Alps.

Saint Catharine pursued the work begun by Saint Bridget, and strove to reconcile the Pope with the Church; but Gregory XI. died, and a state of schism followed with two Popes elected, the one at Rome, the other at Avignon. The poor Saint tried in vain to combat the evil, but GOD recalled her to Himself in 1350, and she left this world in despair at the turbulent future which was preparing.

It was now that GOD in a vision commanded a pious girl, Ursula of Parma, to repair to Avignon and invite Clement VI. to abdicate. She set out on her mission, and this Pope, moved by her exhortations, was on the point of yielding, when the Cardinals who had elected him opposed the measure; they imprisoned Ursula as a sorceress, and she was only preserved by an earthquake, which dispersed her executioners at the moment they were preparing to torture her. GOD called her from the evil times on which she had fallen, and her enterprise came to nought.

Until others of the faithful could succeed her in this mission, and until the Saints under probation were old enough to follow Catharine of Sienna, a tertiary of Saint Francis, blessed Jeanne de Maille, who had already tried to liberate France by testifying in the name of the Saviour to Queen Ysabeau and Charles VI., besieged heaven with supplications, added petitions in public worship, and organized processions in colleges and cloisters in the effort to repair the ruin caused by papal disputes.

But she did not take an active part in the conflict. She seems to have been vowed more particularly to works of mercy, to the care of the plague-stricken and the leprous, and to visiting prisoners; and the true succession to Catharine fell ultimately to three Saints, Saint Lydwine of Schiedam, Saint Colette of Corbie, and Saint Frances of Romaine; a Dutch, a French, and an Italian Saint respectively.

Saint Lydwine and Saint Colette were born in 1380, that is to say, in the year that Saint Catharine passed away; and both gave their lives for the Church by suffering, in the one case passively, and in the other actively.

Although leading absolutely different existences, their lives presented some resemblance.   Both were born of poor parents, and from being fair to look upon became, by their own desire, ugly; both endured ceaseless and agonizing pain; both bore the stigmata of Calvary; both when they died recovered the beauty of their youth and had a sweet and pleasing smell. During their life they were both devoured with the same thirst for tortures; only Colette remained, in spite of all, active, for she had to traverse France from one end to the other constantly, whilst Lydwine travelled, if at all, motionless on a bed.   Finally, they resembled one another in this, that each was a saviour of her country.

Saint Colette's mission was identified with that of Joan of Arc in repulsing the English; she helped with the superhuman comfort of her tears.   Whilst Joan took the material side and fought at the head of her troops, Colette took command of the spiritual; she reformed the convents of the Clarisses, making ramparts of mortifications and prayers, threw into the struggle the penitence of the nuns, clung to the skirts of the Virgin, till she had obtained the defeat of Bedford and Talbot and the enemy had finally withdrawn.

Lydwine, by the power of her devotion and her torments, protected Holland when it was invaded by the wastrels of Burgundy, and prevented a fleet from attacking Schiedam.

Like Saint Bridget and Saint Catharine of Sienna, Saint Colette was called to combat schism in person and by visible means; she intervened with Saint Vincent Ferrier at the Council of Constance, and she tried also, some years later, to prevent the Council of

Pisa from intruding a false Pope. Lydwine did not take, humanly speaking, any share in the tribulations of her unknown sister, who struggled so valiantly against erring Cardinals and false Popes. She could hardly have known, buried as she was in her Dutch village, of the distresses of the Church, except through such knowledge as her confessors possessed; but she certainly had revelations from the Saviour; and in any case the accumulation of her sufferings was a treasure of war upon which, although doubtless ignorant of its source, both Colette and Saint Frances of Romaine drew.

The latter was specially chosen for those tasks which schism rendered necessary.

Younger than Colette and Lydwine by four years, Frances was of noble birth and allied to a husband who counted a Pope and a Saint amongst his ancestors. She differed then by her origin, her fortune, and her condition as a married woman, from the two virgins, her sisters; but if she differed from them in some points, she emulated them in others, or rather she borrowed from both of them, becoming the spiritual child, now of Colette and now of Lydwine.

She resembled the virgin of Corbie by her active life, by her vocation as leader of souls and foundress of an order, by the part she assumed in the politics of her day, by the battle she fought with the demon who assailed her; she resembled the virgin of Schiedam by her miraculous cure of the plague, by her perpetual contact with angels, by her voyages into Purgatory in quest of souls to deliver, by her special mission to atone for the crimes of the period as a sacrificial victim of the suffering Church.

By means opposed or by means identical, these three women, each bearing the stigmata, strove against the evil influences of their time, and accomplished an overwhelming task. Never indeed had the equilibrium of the world been so nearly overset; and it seemed as if GOD had never been more careful to adjust the balance between virtue and vice, and to heap up, when the load of iniquities preponderated, the tortures of His Saints as a counterbalance against them.

This law of equilibrium between Good and Ill is curiously mysterious when one thinks of it, for in establishing it the All Powerful appears to have wished to limit and put restraints on His own omnipotence. That this rule should be observed, it is necessary that Jesus Himself should make an appeal to man. As reparations for the sins of some, He claims the mortifications and prayers of others; and this is indeed the glory of our poor humanity. But, although He so respects the liberty of His children that he will not take away their power to resist Him, never has GOD been deceived. All through the ages there have been found Saints willing to pay, by their sufferings, the ransom for the sins and faults of others, and even now this generosity is difficult for us to understand.

Besides our own nature, which shrinks from all suffering, there is also the Evil One who intervenes to frustrate the sacrifice; the Evil One, to whom his Master has conceded, in this sad earthly contest, two most formidable weapons—money and the flesh. He also preys upon the cowardice of man, who knows, however, that the grace of the Saviour will avail to assure him of victory, if he only tries to defend himself. Would one not say that after the expulsion of Adam from Paradise, the Saviour, importuned by the rebel angel, had disdainfully granted him the most sure means of vanquishing souls, and that the scene in the Old Testament where Satan asks and obtains of GOD permission to tempt and try the unhappy Job, had already been rehearsed at the expulsion from Eden?

Since those times the needle of the compass has oscillated. When it inclines too much to the side of Evil, when man becomes too ignoble and kings too impious, GOD allows epidemics to be unchained, earthquakes, famines, and wars; but His mercy is such that He then excites the devotion of His Saints, enhances their merits, even practices a little deception with Himself, that His wrath may be appeased and equilibrium re-established.

Had it been otherwise, the Universe would long ago have been in ruins; but from the resources Satan has at his command, and the weakness of the souls to which he lays siege, one can understand the constant solicitude of the Church, charged as she is with the task of lightening the balance of sins and continually adding a counter-weight of orison and penitence. One can understand the need for those ramparts of prayer and citadels of supplication which she erects at the order of the Spouse; for the strictness of her pitiless cloisters and stern orders, such as those of the Clarisses, the Calvairiennes, the Carmelites, and the Trappists; and one can conceive of the incredible sum of sufferings endured by the Saints—those griefs which the Most High distributes to each one of us to purge us and to make us share a little in that work of compensation which follows the work of Evil step by step.

Now the dissoluteness of society at the end of the fourteenth and the beginning of the fifteenth centuries was, as we have said, deplorable.

The thirteenth century, which, in spite of its conflicts, appears in the mists of time so pure and blameless, with Saint Louis and Blanche of Castile, so chivalrous and pious with the faithful leaving their all to snatch the sepulchre of Christ from the hands of infidels; this century of vast cathedrals, which knew Pope Innocent III., Saint Francis of Assisi, Saint Dominic, Saint Thomas Aquinas, Saint Bonaventure, Saint Gertrude, and Saint Clair, was indeed little better than dead. Faith seemed expiring, and was destined, after dragging on through two centuries, to perish in that sewer disinterred by Paganism, and known as the Renaissance.

To sum up, if we examine the state of Europe in

the days of Lydwine, we see cut-throat nobles seeking
to destroy one another, the people reduced to misery
by war and rendered either ferocious or insane
through fear.   Most of the sovereigns were either
rogues or maniacs, like Charles VI., Peter the Cruel,
Peter the Ceremonious, and William of Holland,
unbalanced like Jacqueline, drunkards and libertines
like Wenceslas, Emperor of Germany, or cruel and
pharisaic like the King of England.   As for the
anti-Popes, they crucified the Holy Spirit, and when
we consider them we are moved with fear.

If only that were all!   But one is bound to go further
and admit that those who were consecrated to GOD'S
service were no better.   Schism was rampant, and
those to whom it had been entrusted to guide the
barque of salvation were themselves steeped in sin.
One has only to read the sermons of S. Vincent Ferrier
reproaching their turpitude, the invectives of S.
Catharine of Sienna accusing them of cupidity, pride,
and impurity, and of trafficking in the Graces of the
Paraclete, to realize the enormous weight which they
had added to the balance of Evil in the scales of
Justice.

Before such a total of sacrilege and crime, before
such an invasion of the Cohorts of Hell, it would have
seemed probable that, in spite of their courage and
devotion, S. Lydwine, S. Colette, and S. Frances of
Romaine would have succumbed, if GOD had not raised
armies for their succour.

It is more than possible that they never had any
knowledge of these armies, any more, indeed, than
the armies themselves knew of their mission; for the
Almighty is the sole master in this strategy, and He
alone sees it in its entirety. The Saints are in His hands
like pawns which He places on the chess-board of the
world at His will; their part is to abandon themselves
body and soul to Him who directs them, and to do
His will without asking to know more.

It is only when one examines the resources made

use of by the Saviour and the divers instruments which
He employed, that one succeeds in catching glimpses
of the tactics by which He subdued the hordes led
away by the rebel angels.

The number of those militants who, at the end of
the fourteenth century, took arms under Christ for the
assistance of Lydwine and the two other Saints can
hardly be estimated. Some of them are known to
us, others will probably always remain unknown, while
others again appear to have been specially occupied
in changing the scene of operations.

Without fear of mistake, however, one can name
the troops engaged in the first line, who advanced
under shelter of the prayers offered in those mystic
fortresses which were defended in France by the
Clarisses of S. Colette. In Italy the Clarisses of
S. Catharine of Bologna ; the cloistered tertiary
Franciscans of blessed Angeline of Marsciano ; the
reformed Dominicans, helped by Marie Mancini of
Pisa ; the blessed Claire of Gambacorta ; the tertiaries
of S. Dominic, who adopted the cloister under the rule
of Margaret of Savoy ; the Cistercians, whom Pope
Benedict XII. had brought back to strict rule ; the
Chartreuse sisters who still revered the memory of S.
Rosaline—all these were interceding on behalf of the
Saints.

The troops of the advanced guard were formed
by battalions of Franciscans and preaching friars.
The first marched under the orders of S. Bernardin
of Sienna, who was born in the same year as S.
Lydwine and filled a mission like that of S. Colette in
strengthening the relaxed rule of S. Francis. His
disciple, John of Capristan, who sustained him in this
task, was more especially occupied, in company with
blessed Thomas Bellacio de Linaris, in opposing the
heresies of the Fraticelles and the Hussites. S.
Jacques de la Marche, who was joined with him to
fight against the infidels ; St. Matthew of Agrigente,
who restored the ancient usages in the religious houses

of Spain; blessed Albert of Santeano, who was more
particularly charged with a war against schisms; were
also leaders of the van. Those of the second line
were led by S. Vincent Ferrier, the miracle worker,
who evangelized the miscreants; by S. Anthony of
Florence, who struggled against the works of magic;
by blessed Marcelin, whose knees, from constant
contact with the ground, had become like the knotted
bark of trees; by blessed Raymond of Capoue,
confessor to S. Catharine of Sienna, who, with John
Domenici and Laurent de Ripafratta, stimulated the
lax piety and renewed the neglected customs of the
religious; by blessed Alvarez de Cordova, who worked
for the extinction of schism and, in the same manner
as S. Vincent Ferrier, converted idolaters.

These troops, destined by the very nature of their
vocation to the labours of the apostolate, accustomed
to the task of enlightening the ignorant, and prepared
for the duties of an advanced guard, were extended
like an interminable battle front at the head of the
immense army of the Lord, of which the two wings
spread far and wide. One, composed of the seasoned
regiments of the Carmelites, was commanded by their
Prior, John Soreth, who quickened the fervour of his
declining order and created the institute of the
Carmelites; by S. Anthony d'Offen and blessed
Stanislas of Poland, who were martyred; by Jean
Arundine, Prior of the House of Bruges; by Ange
de Mezzinghi, who helped to reform the rule in
Tuscany; by Bradley, raised to the Bishopric of
Dromory in Ireland, whose austerities were famous.
The other wing was composed of the serried masses
of the Augustinians, who had been rallied and reformed
in Italy by Ptolomée of Venice, Simon de Cremona, and
Augustin of Rome; in Spain, by John d'Alarcon,
who introduced into Old Castile convents of strict
obedience; while their third order had just blossomed
out into a flower of the Passion, blessed Catherine
Visconti.

And these newly drilled regiments enclosed detachments that were weaker and badly armed; the Camaldules who, in the disorder of their ranks, could still count a learned monk, Ambrose Traversari, and two Saints, Jerome of Bohemia, the apostle of Lithuania, and the oblate Daniel; Brigittins, both monks and nuns, hardly born into the religious life and badly prepared to serve in a compaign; the Servites, whose discipline was being strengthened by Anthony of Sienna, and whose standard-bearer was a tertiary, blessed Elizabeth Picenardi; the Premontarians, whose rule, like that of the convents of Fontevrault which Marie of Brittany was soon going to remodel, was so relaxed that their power to help was almost negligible.

Between these two wings, behind the advanced line of the children of S. Francis and S. Dominic, spread a mass of resisting strength, the bulk of the army, the dense and massive centre of the most flourishing order of the Middle Ages, the order of S. Benedict, with all its great divisions. First there were the Benedictines proper, directed in Germany by the Abbot of Castels, Otho, who restored the ancient use of the order, and by Abbot Jean de Meden, who converted the dissolute customs of one hundred and forty-seven abbeys; in Italy, by Louis Barbo, Abbot of S. Justine of Padua, who re-subjected numerous monasteries to the severe rule of the order, amongst them that of Mont Cassin, the cradle of Benedictine rule; in France, by the Abbot of Cluny, Odo de la Perrière, the cellarer, Etienne Bernadotte, the Prior, Dom Toussaint, a nephew of S. Colette, who was, by reason of his virtues, compared to Peter the Venerable; by William of Auvergne, cited in the chronicles as having been a veritable Saint; by blessed John of Ghent, Prior of Saint Claude, who interposed between the King of England and the King of France to try and induce them to make peace. Then came the Cistercians, led by the blessed Eustace, first

Abbot of Jardinet, and by the venerable Martin of
Vargas and Martin of Logroño, who re-organised the
Bernardine houses of Spain; the Celestins, who
delegated one of their most holy monks, Jean Bassand,
to be confessor to S. Colette, and were all well
reputed and much relied on in France; the Olivetains,
well seasoned and led to the assault by the venerable
Hippolite of Milan, Abbot of Mount Olivet, by brother
Laurent Sernicolaï de Perouse, by the lay brother,
Jerome of Corsica, who died in the odour of sanctity
at the convent of San Miniato at Florence, by the
venerable Jerome Mirabelli of Naples, and by the
blessed Bernard de Verceil, who founded two convents
of the order in Hungary. Finally there were the
Humiliates, in whose cloisters we find the oblate
blessed Aldobrandesca, famous at Sienna for her
miracles.

In enumerating this army the chosen legion of
recluses must not be omitted, those women who lived
a hermit's life, which S. Colette herself had lived at
Corbie for four years, the female anchorites buried
in the deserts of the East or voluntarily walled up in
the towns, and to whom a little bread and a jug of
water were passed through an opening in the door.
The names of some of these holy recluses are known
to us, such as that of Aliz de Bourgotte, interned in a
cell in Paris; of blessed Agnès de Moncada, who, by
the teaching of S. Vincent Ferrier, betook herself, as
did Madelaine, to weep on the sins of the world in a
grotto; of blessed Dorothea, patron Saint of Prussia,
who sequestered herself near the church of Quidzini,
in Poland; of blessed Julie della Rena, who incarcerated
herself at Certaldo, in Tuscany; of Perrone Hergolds,
a tertiary of S. Francis, who bore the stigmata and
retired into a hermitage in Flanders; of Jeanne
Bourdine, walled up at La Rochelle; of Catherine Van
Borsbecke, a Carmelite, who buried herself in a sort
of cave near a sanctuary outside Louvain; of another
daughter of Carmel, Agnès, who was found some

years after the death of Lydwine still walled up in a
retreat near the Carmelite chapel at Liége. These
were the flower of the servants of Jesus, the guard
of honour of Christ, from whose ranks sprang S.
Catharine of Sienna, S. Lydwine, S. Colette, S. Frances
of Romaine, and blessed Jeanne de Maillé—all victims
most particularly pleasing to GOD, the living effigies
of the Passion, the standard-bearers of the Lord, the
stigmatized!

In Germany there was a tertiary of the Franciscans,
Elizabeth the Good of Waldsec, and the Clarisse,
Madeleine Beurler; in Italy, a tertiary of S. Francis,
Lucie de Norcie, a Clarisse, Marie de Massa, a widow,
blessed Julienne of Bologna, an Augustinian, S. Rita
de Cassie, and the ecstatic Christine, of whom the
name, although without details, has been preserved
by Denys the Carthusian. In Holland, there was the
Dominican Bridget, and the Beguine Gertrude of
Oosten; and who can say how many more, lost in the
ancient annals or fallen into complete oblivion?

To these active troops may be added the soldiers
attached to no regiment, who fought as partisans in
their own countries, such as blessed Peter, Bishop of
Metz and Cardinal of Luxembourg, or S. Laurence
Justinian, Bishop of Venice. These inflicted on
themselves incredible mortifications to expiate the sins
of their times, and among them were Jean de Kenty,
the apostle of charity, in Poland, S. Jean Népomucène,
the martyr of Bohemia, and blessed Marguerite of
Bavaria, a friend of S. Colette. Finally there was a
reserve corps recruited amongst voluntary laics and
priests, or monks who had not been carried away by
the assaults of the devil.

Thus at the entry of this vast army into the war,
marching under the banner of Christ, the scales
regained their equilibrium between good and evil.

At first sight this army was imposing, but on closer
inspection it was evident that if the chiefs who led
were admirable, the troops placed under their command

were wanting in cohesion, irresolute and feeble. The bulk of the contingents were furnished by the monasteries and convents, and, as we have just seen, disorders and factions were rife in the cloisters ; rules were dying, and the greater part of the statutes were dead.   The phalanx of those serving had consequently no enduring piety and were hardly exercised in the first steps of the mystic way. It was therefore before all necessary to reform the squadrons, to recall the religious to the forgotten use of their arms, to equip them with new offices, to teach them once more the practice of mortifications, and to restore their knowledge of the wiles of sin.

The Carthusians were the only exceptions to this general deterioration. They were divided into two camps, but discipline was, nevertheless, intact. They had amongst them clever strategists and powerful Saints : Denys de Ryckel, called the Carthusian, one of the greatest mystics of the period ; Henri de Calear, Prior of the monastery of " Bethlehem Maria " at Ruremonde and master of Gerard Groot, one of the writers to whom the " Imitation of Christ " has been attributed ; Etienne Maconi, the beloved disciple of S. Catharine of Sienna ; blessed Nicolas Albergati, who became Cardinal after having been Prior of the Ascetics at Florence ; Adolphe d'Essen, the apostle of the Rosary, who was director of blessed Marguerite of Bavaria ; and many others.

The Carthusian companies formed a nucleus of old soldiers, accustomed to the fire of infernal battles, and they served as rear-guard, sheltering with the rampart of their prayers the transport corps of the army, screening the garrisons of pupils, the young recruits who had just been assembled, and giving them time to strengthen themselves and make themselves fit for the struggle. Amongst these recruits who composed the battalions of reinforcement may be noted the handful of oblates of S. Bennet, founded by S. Frances of Romaine, and, above all, the group of new

Carmelites raised for the service of mystic places by
Saints like S. Angela of Bohemia, who was cloistered
in the monastery of Prague; venerable Agnes Correyts,
foundress of the Carmel of Sion at Bruges; venerable
Jeanne de l'Emeuv, who created the monastery of
Notre Dame of the Consolation at Vilvorde, and was
one of the first spiritual daughters of John Soreth;
blessed Jeanne Scopelli, Superior of the monastery of
Reggio; blessed Archangele Girlani, Prior of the House
of Mantua, whose incorruptible body had the power to
heal women attacked by cancer of the face or breast.

Lydwine herself raised no army, was attached to
no corps, and led no cloister to the attack of the
miscreants; she fought in solitude, like a lost child,
from her bed; but the enormous weight of the assaults
which she endured was almost more than can be
possibly conceived. She alone was worth a whole
army, an army which had to face the enemy at all
points.

Like other Saints of her century, she gave herself
in expiation for the souls in Purgatory, for the
abominations of schism, for the excesses of clerks
and monks, for the delinquencies of kings and people;
but besides this sacrifice, by which she undertook to
atone for the sins committed from one end of the
universe to the other, she also bore the burden of
scapegoat for her own country.

As her biographers observe, whenever GOD sought
to chastise Holland, it was to her He first addressed
Himself; it was she who received the first blows.

Was she alone in the Batavian region to bear the
burden of punishment for sin? Was she not aided
by other Saints in that special mission to the Low
Countries, as she was in her mission as expiatrice for
the world in general? It seems almost beyond doubt
that she was.

The stigmatized whom we have mentioned, Gertrude
of Oosten and Bridget, no longer existed when she
began thus to suffer by proxy, for the one had died

in 1358 and the other in 1390; thus they did not intervene in the propitiatory work which she undertook; they began it without knowing who would finish it, and Lydwine was simply chosen to be legatee of their goods. She took their place as she had already done that of a Saint of the preceding century, a martyr of compensation whose existence presents singular analogies to her own—S. Fine of Tuscany, who also passed her life on her bed and was covered with ulcers which exhaled the sweetest perfume.

It is impossible to enumerate those persons in Holland alone whose merits lightened Lydwine's task; all that we know (but we know it by very sure means, that is to say, by the chronicles of the monasteries of Windesem and Mount Saint Agnes) is, that GOD saw fit at this time to raise up in the southern provinces of the Netherlands an admirable company of mystics.

There then existed a school of practical ascetics, the outcome of the teachings of Ruysbroeck, and it flourished in the region of Over-Yssel, more particularly at Deventer.

A man of this latter village, who, after being converted by the Prior of the Carthusians at Monnikhuisen, near Arnhem, became famous by reason of his sanctity and his science, was Gérard Groot or the Great, translator of Ruysbroeck, who preached at this time at Campen, Zwolle, Amsterdam, Leyden, Zutphen, Utrecht, Gouda, Haarlem, and Delft, and fired the masses by his eloquence. The churches could not contain the crowds that he attracted, and he preached to them in the wind-swept cemeteries, effecting numerous conversions and filling the abbeys with his recruits. He, with his pupil, Florent Radewyns, priest of Deventer, ended by founding the institution of "the brothers and sisters of communal life," which rapidly pushed its roots into the Low Countries and Germany. This order, which one would like to qualify with a title which it never bore, " the oblates of S. Augustine," was a veritable centre of study and prayer. The men were housed in Radewyns' house, and occupied themselves with transcribing the manuscripts of the Bible and the Fathers; and the women, residing with Gérard, a kind of beguine foundation, devoted themselves to needlework when not engaged in prayer.

Gérard died in 1384, at the age of 44, while nursing the plague-stricken of Deventer. After his death, Florent Radewyns and the other brothers, faithful to his recommendations, erected a monastery at Windesem, under the rule of S. Augustine; and this village, until then little better than an osier bed, gave birth in Holland to eighty-four monasteries for men and thirteen convents for women.

These congregations of the " communal life " were Cistercians and Carthusians, the only religious bodies who recognized their primitive constitutions, and they often averted the wrath of the Lord, whom the dissolution of the orders must have particularly angered, for, if we believe Ruysbroeck, Denys the Carthusian, and Pierre de Hérenthals, the disorder among the monks of the United Provinces and Flanders was frightful.

It is certain that the mystic school at Deventer supported by its prayers the work of Lydwine, which it knew and loved, for two of the Augustinians who belonged to it, Thomas à Kempis and Gerlac, wrote biographies of the Saint; and they tell us that, not content with submitting herself to be chastised as a substitute for the crimes of the universe and of her own town, she also consented to take upon herself the sins of persons whom she knew, and the corporal maladies which they found insupportable.

This insatiable desire for self-sacrifice loaded her with ills. She was at one and the same time the tireless danaïd of suffering, the vase of sorrows, which she forced herself to fill without ceasing, the good farmer of Jesus, experiencing the torments of His

Passion, and the charitable suppliant who would, during thirty-eight years, discharge by the magnitude of her sufferings, the debts of health and of carelessness, which others hardly cared to pay.

She was, in a word, both a general and a special victim.

This life of expiation would be incomprehensible if one had not indicated the causes and shown the number and nature of the offences whose reparation was in some sort the cause of her sojourn here below; but the foregoing sketch of the history of Europe at the end of the fourteenth and the beginning of the fifteenth centuries explains the multitude of tortures which was unique in the annals of the Saints. They surpassed indeed, by their duration, the sufferings of those of the elect, to whom, after perhaps short torture, the more glorious death of the martyr was allowed.

CHRIST THE PRIEST

CHAPTER II.

LYDWINE was born in Holland, at Schiedam near the Hague, on Palm Sunday, the day after the feast of S. Gertrude, in the year of Our Lord 1380.

Her father, Pierre, was town watchman by trade, and her mother Petronille, came from Ketel, a village in the neighbourhood of Schiedam. They were both descendants of families which had become poor after enjoying some prosperity. Pierre's ancestors, who should have belonged to the nobles, were, according to à Kempis, valiant soldiers. We possess no other precise details of their lineage, for the historians of the Saint tell us only of the father of Pierre, Joannes, who is described to us as a pious man, praying night and day, eating meat only on Sundays, fasting twice a week, and contenting himself on Saturdays with a little bread and water. He lost his wife at the age of forty years, and was obstinately assailed by Satan. His dwelling underwent all the phenomena connected with haunted houses; the Devil shook it from top to bottom, drove away all the servants and broke the crockery, without however, as Gerlac very quaintly specifies, upsetting the butter contained in the broken pot.

His son Pierre had by his wife, Petronille, nine children; one daughter, Lydwine, who was the fourth child, and eight sons, of whom two have been more particularly mentioned by the biographers, one simply by his name of Baudouin, the other, William, as appearing several times in his sister's history. He married and had a daughter who bore the ancestral name of Petronille, and a boy who was called after his uncle Baudouin.

If we further mention a cousin, Nicolas, who appears twice in the background of our picture, and another relative, Gerlac, the biographer, who, though we cannot tell why, lived for a long time in the Saint's house, we have given, I think, all that the early writers tell us of the family.

The day Lydwine was born, her mother, who did not think she was on the point of being delivered, had gone to High Mass, but her pains came upon her and she had hurriedly to return home, where her child was born at the moment when, on this Feast of Palms, they were singing in the church the Passion of Our Saviour according to S. Matthew. Her delivery was painless and easy, although at the birth of her other children she had suffered greatly and nearly died.

The child received at the Font the name of Lydwine, Lydwyd, Lydwich, Liedwich, Lidie or Liduvine, a name which, under all its differences of spelling and sound is derived from the Flemish word "lyden," to suffer, or would signify, according to Brugman, "great patience" in the German tongue.

The biographers observe that both her name and the moment of the festival at which the child was born, were prophetic.

If we except an illness, of which we shall have to speak, we have no detail of her infancy worthy of note. Gerlac, Brugman, and à Kempis fill the interval with edifying notes on the devotion of the child to the blessed Virgin of Schiedam, represented by a statue of which the history is as follows :—

A little before the birth of Lydwine, a sculptor, according to Gerlac and à Kempis, a merchant according to Brugman, came to Schiedam with a virgin in wood, which he had either carved himself or bought, and proposed to go and sell it at the fair held about the date of the Assumption at Antwerp. This statue was so light that a man could easily handle it, yet, when placed in the boat on which it was to be carried from the one town to the other, it became suddenly so heavy that it was impossible for the vessel to quit the port. More than twenty sailors tried to draw her from her moorings, while the people, who were looking on at this spectacle from the quay, laughed and jeered at their impotence. Mortified and exhausted, they ceased their efforts, never having known anything so annoying, and asking themselves whether this effigy of the Madonna might not possibly be the cause. Anyhow, they wished to be quit of it, and the merchant, threatened with a ducking, had to take back the statue, which immediately became light in his hands, and disembarked it amongst the acclamations of the crowd, whilst the boat, thus lightened, sailed gaily away.

All cried, therefore, that the virgin had only acted in this way because she wished to place herself amongst them, and that, in consequence, they ought to keep her. They went to fetch the priests of the parish and the members of the trade guilds, who immediately acquired the statue and placed it in the church, where they founded a guild in its honour.

It is not surprising that Lydwine, who had certainly been rocked to sleep to the recital of this adventure, had from her earliest years loved to pray before this statue. Not being able to go and see it in the evening, when they sang canticles and hymns on their knees before the Altar of Our Lady, she arranged to visit it during the day, though not as frequently as she desired, for her life was a busy one.

Indeed, at seven years of age she filled the office of servant to her mother, and it was difficult for her to find time to pray and meditate. Thus she profited by the mornings when Petronille sent her to carry the morning meal to her brothers at school, to acquit herself as fast as possible of her commission and find time on returning to say a Hail Mary in the church; and once when she was late and her mother, displeased, asked her which road she had taken, she replied quaintly: " Do not scold me, mother dear, I went to salute Our Lady the Virgin, and she returned my greeting with a smile.''

Petronille became thoughtful; she knew her child incapable of lying and of so pure a soul that GOD was pleased to inspire her and preserve her thoughts from illusion, so she was silent, and in future tolerated her slight unpunctualities without too many black looks.

Her infancy was passed in helping her mother who, with eight other children and the little money her husband's trade brought in, had much difficulty in making both ends meet. As she grew older, she became a clever housewife, and at twelve years she was a serious girl, hardly caring to join in the games of her friends and neighbours, or to share in their amusements and dances, but only really happy when alone. Without insisting, without yet emphasizing His touch upon her, without revealing Himself in the language of the spirit, GOD drew her to Himself, letting her dimly understand that she was His alone.

She obeyed without understanding, without even suspecting that life of agony which stretched before her, and on which she must soon enter.

One incident happened which threw a light on her future when more than one young man of the village asked her in marriage. She was then pleasing to look upon, well made, and endowed with that special beauty of the fair Fleming, whose charm lies chiefly in the candour of the features, the gracious sweetness of the laugh, and the expression of tender seriousness in the eyes. Some among the aspirants were of fortune and family superior to her own. Pierre, her father, could not help rejoicing at this unexpected good fortune, and insisted on his daughter making her choice; but suddenly she understood that she must vow her virginity to Christ, and she flatly refused to listen to her father, who soon became angry.

'' If you wish to force me,'' she cried, '' I will obtain some repulsive deformity from my Saviour that will put all these suitors to flight!''

As Pierre, who did not like to own himself beaten, returned again to the charge, the mother intervened and said: " See, my dear, she is too young to think of marriage and too pious for it to suit her; as she wishes to offer herself to GOD, let us at least give her with a good grace."

In the end they resigned themselves to her wishes, but she remained uneasy at the knowledge of her own beauty, and until she became ugly, as she wished to be, she went out as little as possible. She felt that all love which is bestowed on a creature is a fraud committed against GOD, and she implored GOD to help her to love Him alone.

Then He began to cultivate her, to root out all thoughts which could displease Him, to hoe her soul, to rake it till the blood flowed. And He did more; for as if to attest the justice of the saying of S. Hildegarde, at once so terrible and so consoling: " GOD dwells not in bodies that are whole," He attacked her health. This young and charming body with which He had clothed her seemed suddenly irksome to Him, and He cut it in all directions, that He might better seize and mould the soul it contained. He enlarged this poor body by giving it the terrible capacity of assimilating all the ills of the earth, and burning them in the furnace of its expiatory sufferings.

Towards the end of her fifteenth year she was hardly recognisable, for then, like an eagle of love, GOD precipitated Himself upon His prey, and S. Isadore's legend of the eagle which seizes its young in its claws and flies with them towards the sun, where they must gaze without flinching at the fiery disc under pain of being dropped, was verified in Lydwine. She faced without flinching the sun of justice; and the symbol of Jesus, fisher of souls, replaced her gently in His eyrie, where her soul grew and flourished in its shell of flesh, which was destined to become, before burial, something monstrous and without form.

Behind her is outlined on the far off heights, the

grand figure of Job weeping on his dung-hill. She is his daughter; and the same scenes are carried down the ages from the confines of Idumea to the shores of the Meuse, scenes of irreducible sufferings borne with inexhaustible patience and aggravated by the discussions of pitiless friends and by the reproaches even of her own people. There is this difference, however, that the trials of the Patriarch ended during his life, while those of his descendant ceased only with her death.

CHAPTER III.

TILL her fifteenth year, Lydwine seems to have been fairly healthy. Her biographers record that when of tender age she was attacked by stone; but neither Gerlac, nor Brugman, nor à Kempis, tell us of any infantile affections that she had to undergo. It was not, indeed, till towards the end of her fifteenth year that the fury of the love of her heavenly Spouse fell upon her.

Then she had an illness which did not indeed endanger her life, but left her in a state of weakness which none of the nostrums prescribed by the apothecaries of that epoch succeeded in curing. Her cheeks became hollow and her flesh melted away; she became so thin that she was only skin and bone; the comeliness of her features disappeared in the protuberances and hollows of a face which, from pink and white, became of a greenish hue, and finally ashen. Her wishes had been granted; she was as ugly as a corpse. Her lovers rejoiced that they had been dismissed, and she no longer feared to show herself abroad.

However, as she could not succeed in recovering her strength, she was confined to her room, where, some days before the Feast of the Purification, some friends visited her. It was freezing hard at the moment; the river Schie, which runs through the town, and the canals, were frozen over; and in this wintry weather all Holland was skating. These young girls invited Lydwine to skate with them, but, preferring to be alone, she made the bad state of her health a pretext for not going with them. They insisted so much, however, reproaching her for not taking more exercise and assuring her that the open air would do her good, that, for fear of annoying them, she finally, with the consent of her father, accompanied them on the frozen water of the canal behind which the house was situated. She was just starting, after having put on her skates, when one of her comrades, going at a great pace, threw herself against her before she was able to get out of the way, and she was dashed against a piece of ice whose edges broke one of the lower ribs on her right side.

Weeping, they took her home, and the poor girl was stretched on a bed which she hardly ever left again.

This accident was soon known throughout the town and everyone thought it his duty to give advice. Lydwine had to endure, like Job, the interminable chatter of those whom the misfortunes of others render loquacious; but some who were wiser, instead of reprimanding her for having gone out, thought that GOD had, without doubt, some special reasons for treating her thus.

Her afflicted family were resolved to try all means to heal her. In spite of their poverty, they called in the most renowned physicians of the Low Countries. They dosed her heavily, but the trouble only grew worse, and as a result of their treatment a hard tumour formed in the fracture.

She suffered agonies, and her parents were at a loss to know what Saints to invoke next, when a famous practician of Delft, a very charitable and pious man, Godfried de Haga, surnamed Sonder-Danck because he invariably replied "No thanks, please," to all the patients he treated gratuitously, came to see her in consultation. His ideas on therapeutics were those which Bombast Paracelsus, who was born some years after the death of Lydwine, expounds in his "*Opus paramirum.*" Amongst all the incoherent clap-trap of his occultism, this astonishing man had seized the idea of divine equilibrium when he wrote on the subject of the essence of GOD: "you must know that all

sickness is an expiation and that, if GOD does not consider it finished, no doctor can interrupt it......
the doctor only heals if his intervention coincides with the end of the expiation determined by the Saviour."

Godfried de Haga then examined the patient and spoke thus to his assembled colleagues, who were most curious to know his verdict : " This sickness, dear friends, is not under our jurisdiction; all the Galens, Hippocrateses and Avicennas of the world would here lose their reputation."   And he added, prophetically : " The hand of GOD is on this child.   He will work great marvels in her.   Would to GOD she were my daughter ; I would give willingly a weight of gold equal to the weight of my head, to pay for that favour, if it were to be sold."

And he departed prescribing no remedy.   Then all the quacks lost interest in her, and she gained, at least for a time, the privilege of not being obliged to swallow useless and expensive remedies, but the trouble increased, and the pain became intolerable.   She could get no ease, either lying, sitting, or standing.   Not knowing what to try next, and being unable to remain a moment in the same position, she asked to be lifted from one bed to another, thinking thus to quiet her acute tortures ; but these movements only exasperated the ill.

On the Vigil of the Nativity of S. John the Baptist her torments reached their culminating point.   She sobbed on her bed in a state of terrible abandonment, and at last she could bear it no longer; her pain increased and tore her so that she threw herself from her couch and fell upon her father's knees, who was seated weeping at her side.   This fall broke the abscess, but instead of bursting outside, it broke within, and the pus poured from her mouth.   These vomitings shook her from head to foot and filled the vessels so quickly that they had hardly time to empty them before even the largest was overflowing again.

Finally, she fainted in a last effort, and her parents believed her dead.

However, she regained consciousness, and then the most unhappy life imaginable began for her. Unable to support herself upon her legs, and always teased by the craving for a change of position, she dragged herself on her knees, rolled on her stomach and held on to the chairs and the corners of the furniture. Burning with fever, she was obsessed with vicious tastes, and drank dirty water or tepid water when she could get it, which her stomach rejected. Three years passed thus, and to perfect her martyrdom, she was abandoned by those who until then had come from time to time to visit her. The sight of her agony, her groans and cries, the horrible mask of her face, furrowed by tears, drove her visitors away. Her family alone helped her; her father's kindness never failed, but her mother was less resigned to her lot as sick nurse, and, weary of hearing her constant groaning, was often harsh with her.

The grief she experienced, feeling so wretched already and being obliged to submit to tirades and reproaches as well, would no doubt have ended by killing her, had not GOD, who until then seems to have been in a state of doubt about her, suddenly intervened on her behalf, shewing her, by a sudden miracle, that He would not desert her, and at the same time teaching a lesson of mercy to her mother.

The circumstances were as follows:—

One day two men were quarrelling in a Square, and one of them, drawing his sword, fell upon the other, who, being either disarmed or less courageous, took to flight. Seeing the door of Lydwine's house open at the corner of the street, he burst in. His adversary, who had not seen him enter, suspected, nevertheless, that he had taken refuge there, and seeing Petronille looking at him in terror on the threshold, he cried, foaming with rage: "Where is he, this son of death? Do not try to deceive me, he must be hidden with you!" She assured him, trembling, that he was not; but he

did not believe her.   Pushing her aside and uttering
the most terrible threats, he penetrated right into
Lydwine's room and commanded the sick girl not to
deceive him.

Lydwine, incapable of lying, replied: "He whom
you are pursuing is indeed here."

At these words Petronille, who had slipped in behind
the man, could not contain herself and boxed her girl's
ears, crying: "How now, miserable fool, you give up
a man who is your guest when he is in danger of
death!"

The furious man, however, neither saw nor heard
anything of this scene.   Blaspheming aloud, he searched
for his enemy who had become invisible to him, but
who was standing before him in the middle of the room.
Not discovering him, he rushed out to recover his
traces, whilst his antagonist decamped in the other
direction as quickly as his legs would carry him.

When they had gone, Lydwine, who had received
this correction without complaint, murmured: "I
thought, mother, that the fact of telling the truth
would suffice to save this man"; and Petronille,
admiring her daughter's faith and the miracle which had
rewarded it, was filled with the most kindly sentiments
and in future bore the trouble which Lydwine's
infirmities caused her with less resentment and
bitterness.

It must be admitted that she had some excuse for
her bitterness.   The good woman had incessant
difficulties and harassing work, and if the infirmities
of her child already seemed excessive, they were
nothing to what were coming upon her.

Soon Lydwine could not even drag herself about on
her knees and clutch the coffers and chairs, but had to
crouch down in her bed, this time for ever.   The wound
under her rib, which had never healed, swelled up,
and gangrene declared itself.   The putrefaction bred
worms, which moved under the skin of the stomach
and spread over three ulcers, large and round as the

bottom of a bowl. They multiplied in the most alarming manner, and, according to Brugman, swarmed so that they appeared to boil. They were as large as the end of a bobbin, their bodies were grey and watery and their heads black.

The doctors were summoned again, and prescribed that plasters should be applied to these nests of vermin made of fresh flour, honey, and the fat of capons, to which they counselled the addition of cream or the fat of boiled eels, the whole sprinkled with the flesh of beef dried and reduced to powder in an oven.

These remedies, which demanded some care in their preparation—for it was remarked that if the flour had been ever so little too cool the worms would not feed upon it—eased her and were the means of drawing from the wounds one or two hundred worms in twenty-four hours.

About the plaster made with the fat of capons, Lydwine's biographers tell us this anecdote.

The Curé of Schiedam was then one P. André of the Order of Premontarians, detached from his convent in the Island of S. Marie, and this priest had a truly degraded soul. Gluttonous and rapacious, caring only for his own well-being, he wished at the approach of Lent to entertain the clergy of the parish, and killed some capons which he had taken care to fatten. Now at that time he was due at Lydwine's house to shrive her, and knowing of his plans and of the fowl that were prepared, she asked him to give her the fat of one of them for the making of her ointment. He replied with anger that he could not; his capons were thin, and the little gravy that ran from them was used by the cook to baste them. She insisted, and even offered butter in exchange equal in weight to the fat; but as he still refused, she looked at him and said:

"You have refused what I asked as alms in the name of Jesus; well, I now pray to our Saviour that your chickens may be devoured by the cats."

And so it happened. When, on the morning of the

feast, the larder was inspected, instead of capons ready for the spit only scattered fragments of bones were discovered.

If this adventure, as we shall see by the sequel, did not have the effect of making this priest less selfish and sordid, it served at least to render him more sagacious and less churlish on a similar occasion, for Gerlac relates this further episode:

Besides the plasters of flour and lard, Lydwine sometimes used slices of apple freshly cut, laid on the wounds to allay the inflammation. Now the Curé possessed an abundance of apples in his garden, so the Saint begged some of him for this purpose. He began to grumble and declare that he had none left, but when he got home he remembered the lost capons and immediately sent some apples to his penitent, saying: "I offer them to you for fear that this time it will be the squirrels that eat them."

But truly these medicaments were only palliatives and did not heal. A doctor of Cologne who had heard of Lydwine, perhaps through his friend Godfried de Haga, was at first more successful, though when everything is taken into account he seems to have made matters worse in the end. He applied to these virulent centres poultices steeped in a mixture which he prepared by distilling certain plants picked in dry weather in the woods at dawn, when they were still covered with dew. This mixture, added to a decoction of centaury or millflower, little by little dried up the ulcers. This doctor was a good man, and to make sure that Lydwine should not be deprived of her remedy if he predeceased her, he charged his son-in-law, an apothecary of the name of Nicolas Reiner, to send her after his death all the flasks of the mixture that she needed to close the wounds.

But the moment arrived when all these palliatives became useless, for the entire body of the patient was alive. Besides these ulcers in which colonies of worms fed without destroying them, a tumour appeared on the shoulder and putrified. This was the dreaded plague of the Middle Ages, the fire of the burning ill, which attacked the right arm and consumed the flesh to the bone. The nerves all twisted and broke, except one which retained the arm and prevented it from becoming detached from the trunk. It was from now onwards impossible for Lydwine to turn herself to this side, and only her left arm remained free to raise her head, which was also attacked. Violent neuralgic pains assailed her, which bored into her temples like a gimlet and beat like a mallet with constant blows on her skull. Her forehead was cleft from the roots of the hair to the centre of the nose; her chin dropped under the lower lip, and her mouth swelled; her right eye was extinguished, and the other became so tender that the least light caused it to bleed. She suffered also from violent toothache, which raged sometimes for weeks and rendered her half mad; and finally, after a quinsy, which suffocated her, she lost blood through the mouth, ears, and nose, with such profusion that the bed was running with it.

Those who stood by wondered how such a quantity of blood could flow from a body so completely exhausted, and poor Lydwine tried to smile. "Say," she murmured, "you who have been in the world longer than I, whence can that sap come which in spring swells the vine, so black and bare in winter?"

It would seem that she had endured every possible ill. After reading the descriptions of her biographers, which I have somewhat modified, one feels that one has been in a hospital watching a succession of deadliest diseases and most unbearable tortures.

Soon, in addition to other infirmities, her chest also was involved; her nose was filled first with a livid humour, then with inflamed sores; the stone which had tortured her in her infancy returned, and she evacuated a calculus the size of a small egg. Next the lungs and liver decayed; then a cancer devoured her flesh; and finally, when the pestilence ravaged Holland, she was the first victim, and was afflicted with two abscesses. "Two, that is well," she exclaimed, "but if it pleases Our Lord, I think three in honour of the blessed Trinity had been better!" and a third abscess formed in the cheek.

She would have been dead twenty times over if these affections had been natural; one alone would have been enough to kill her; and besides there was no hope of a cure, nothing to try, nothing to do.

But the fame of all these ills so strangely united in one person, who continued living and was yet mortally attacked in every part of her body, soon spread abroad; and if it brought her quacks, who had sometimes aggravated her ills with doubtful panaceas, it brought her also another visit from that good Godfried de Haga, who had attended her after her fall.

He arrived at Schiedam, accompanied by the Countess Marguerite of Holland, one of his patients, who wished to verify for herself the case of this extraordinary person, of whom she had often heard the nobles at the Court speak. She wept with pity on seeing Lydwine, so unlike a human being was she in appearance.

Godfried, who had already prognosticated the divine origin of these ills, could only reiterate his lack of power to heal them by his art; but, believing that he might succeed in easing the patient, he removed the intestines, separated them, and after having cleaned them, replaced those that were fit for use. His diagnosis was that she was afflicted with a putrefaction of the marrow, which he attributed to the fact that Lydwine did not eat salt with her food, and he added, on leaving, that a new malady, dropsy, would shortly declare itself. His forecast was correct, and dropsy appeared directly the ulcers, dressed with the poultices ordered by the Cologne doctor, were healed. When they no longer suppurated, the sufferer began to swell, and regretted the exchange of one evil for another, and that a worse.

This incredible assault of physical calamities she endured for thirty-eight years, without enjoying an instant's respite or a single easy hour during that time.

It is as well to draw attention to the fact that amongst the miseries which she endured were two out of the three scourges which came from the East and desolated Europe during the Middle Ages : the burning ill, a sort of gangrene, burning like a hidden fire in the flesh of the limbs and splitting the bones, until death ended the torture; and the black death, which, according to the observation of a contemporary doctor, " declared itself by continuous fever, external tumours and carbuncles, frequently under the armpit, and caused death in five days."

There remained the third scourge, which also was the despair of these centuries, leprosy.

This was missing from the list of torments experienced by this poor girl. GOD, who, in His Scriptures and in the lives of His Saints, appears to interest Himself in a special manner in the " mesel " or leprous, whom He cured and from whom He borrowed the repulsive figure to try the charity of His Saints, did not see fit to put His servant to this last trial; and the motive for this exception, which at first surprises us, is easily understood on reflection. Leprosy would have counteracted the Saviour's designs and rendered the development of Lydwine's holiness impossible.

It is well to remember that, during the Middle Ages, lepers were considered incurable, for all the pharmacopœia of the doctors, the hellebore, sulphur baths, flesh of vipers, used since ancient days, and arsenic, tried by Paracelsus, had failed to cure even one. They were shut up, for fear of contagion, in hospitals, or isolated in small houses in districts which they were forbidden, under menace of severe penalty, to leave. They had even to wear a distinctive dress, a sort of grey tunic or prison dress, and to shake in their hand, which was always gloved, a rattle called a " tartavelle," to prevent people from approaching. The leper was a pariah, dead in law, separated for ever from the world, and buried at his decease in a place apart.

The liturgy was terrible towards him. The Church celebrated in his presence, before his sequestration, a Mass of the Holy Spirit with the prayer " pro infirmis," and then conducted him processionally to the hut or sick quarters, if such existed in the country. The frightful prohibitions, which cut him off from the number of the living were read to him, three pellets of earth taken from the cemetery were thrown on the roof of his hut, a cross was planted before his door, and that ended the " mesel."

In certain districts of France the ritual used was still more sinister. The wretch afflicted with the malady of " Monsieur Sainct Ladre " entered the church on the day fixed for his ordeal stretched on a bier and covered with a black cloth, as if he had been dead. The clergy chanted the " libera " and carried off the corpse. The leper did not stand till he arrived before the lazar house or hut which was to shelter him; with bent head he listened to the reading of the sentence which enjoined him not to set foot outside, to touch no one, and even to pass to windward of healthy persons if by chance he should come across them.

The rules of leprosy have been everywhere the same in most details, and the customs of the county of Hainault, which was in the fourteenth century one of the provinces composing the domain of the Low Countries, include a series of ordinances of this kind. It is therefore certain that, had Lydwine been attacked by leprosy, she would have been taken away from home and practically buried alive; she would not have been tended by her father and mother, or, after their death, by her nephew and niece, who would have been separated from her for fear of spreading the disease; she would, from that time onward, have remained unknown, since no one would have been able to visit her, and the example which GOD desired her to set would have been totally useless.

It must be noted, too, that this question of the care which was given to her appears to have been considered in a very special manner by Our Saviour. He overwhelmed her with torments; He disfigured her, substituting for the charm of her clear countenance the horror of a face swollen out of all shape, a sort of lion's muzzle, ravaged by channels of tears and streaks of blood; He transformed her into a skeleton, and raised on this wasted frame the dome of a stomach filled with water; He made her, for those who look only on the outward appearance, hideous; but if He heaped upon her all these misfortunes, He intended that the nurses charged with dressing her wounds should not be disgusted and tired of their charitable offices by the odour of decomposition, which must perforce accompany such wounds.

By a constant miracle He made of these wounds veritable censers of perfume; the plasters which they took off, teeming with vermin, sweetly scented the air; all that came from her had a delicate aroma; and He wished that from her body there should always emanate an exquisite atmosphere of shells and spices of the East, a fragrance at once keen and sweet, something like the smoke of cinnamon and spices.

CHAPTER IV.

SPEAKING incidentally of Lydwine in his biography of Sister Catherine Emmerich, who was, in the nineteenth century, one of the direct inheritors of the Saint of Schiedam, a German monk, P. Schmöger, draws a comparison between her afflictions and those which the Church then endured. For example, he likens her ulcerations to the wounds of Christianity torn by the disorders of schism, suggests that the pain of the stone which she suffered symbolized the state of concubinage in which numerous priests then lived, that the swelling of her breast signified the children "deprived of the milk of holy doctrine," and so on. The truth is that these analogies are singularly wanting in logic, and that it would be both more exact and more simple to make the general statement which we have already suggested, that Lydwine expiated by her maladies the faults of others.

But her soul in this torn envelope, this vestment riddled and eaten of worms, was it invariably firm? Was it sufficiently fervent and robust to endure without murmuring the measureless weight of her ills? Was Lydwine a Saint from the moment that her infirmities prostrated her?

Not at all; the few details which have been left us affirm the contrary. She did not at all resemble those lovers of GOD who possessed, so they said, all the virtues without the trouble of acquiring them. Her biographers, so vague on some points, have not misled us as so many of their colleagues have done, whose histories present to us women who are not women, heroines impeccable but false, beings who have nothing living, nothing human, about them.

She broke down under the pain and wished to fly when she found herself captive on her bed. She cried till she had no tears left, and very nearly fell into despair. How could it have been otherwise? She was not prepared to climb the hill of Calvary in such terrifying stages. Till the day when she broke her rib, life had been for her full of work, but easy; her childhood did not differ from that of many little girls of the people whom poverty ripened young, for it was necessary when they came out of school that they should help their mothers with the other children. She was, however, happier than her school comrades and her neighbours, for she was beloved, as none of them were, by the blessed Virgin, who condescended to animate her statue and to smile to give her pleasure; though Lydwine, who knew nothing of the mystic way, could not guess that these attentions were only the prelude to frightful torments. She imagined in her simplicity that these indulgences would continue and that it would be with her as it was with all those whose souls Jesus seized for the forge of Love and poured, when melted, into the nuptial mould of His Cross; but she was going to learn that the marriage of the soul consummates itself more often when the body is reduced to a state of dust, to the condition of a rag. Suddenly these initial joys ceased, for as soon as she had weaned the soul, the Madonna put it out of her arms on the earth, and it had to seek its own nourishment and walk alone without leading strings. In fact, it followed the ordinary route before beginning to tread any strange paths.

During the first four years of sickness she believed herself veritably damned, and all consolation was refused her. Having overwhelmed her with blows, GOD turned from her and appeared no longer to know her. Her situation was certainly then as sad as that of all others whom sickness confines to their bed.

After these foretastes of suffering, which stimulated prayer with the hope, if not of an immediate cure, at least of some ease to the acute pain, discouragement claimed her when she saw none of her petitions granted, and her prayers became more feeble as her miseries increased.   She was unable to absorb herself in devotion; her pitiable lot entirely engrossed her; it was impossible to think of anyone but herself, and the time was passed in deploring her misfortunes.   Those prayers which were continued by force of habit, by a secret impulse from heaven—prayers which one would judge to be the most regarded, as they are the most meritorious, for they cost so much—degenerated in a moment of overwhelming distress into mere expressions of resentment, into demands upon GOD to fulfil the promises of His Gospels, into bitter repetitions of the "ask and it shall be given you," and concluded in lassitude and disgust.   The question of the value of her prayers insinuates itself little by little, and when, in a moment of fervour, the wish to pray returns, the power is gone.   Invocations which do not come from the heart, fall to the ground, and it is unthinkable that Christ should stoop to pick them up.   The temptation to despair then commences; and whilst He stirs the brasier of tortures, the spirit of Malice becomes plaintive, and the sufferer falls back on herself exhausted.

The horizon becomes black and the distance is blotted out.   GOD, whose presence still dominates, appears only as an inexorable miracle worker who could heal you, if He would, by a sign, but will not. He is no longer even indifferent, He is an active enemy; we ourselves should shew more mercy than He manifests were we in His place!   Should we allow people to suffer thus when we could so easily relieve them?   GOD appears as a bad Samaritan, an unmerciful judge.   It is useless to say to ourselves, in the light of good sense, that we have sinned, that we must expiate our offences; we believe that the sum of our transgressions is not great enough to warrant the imposition of so much pain, and we accuse our Saviour of injustice, daring to point out to Him that there is a disproportion between the sin and its punishment. In this disorder we make no attempt at consolation except self pity and complaint at being the victim of injustice. The more we groan the more we fall into self-love, until the soul, turned awry by these querulous adulations of its own being, is thrown back upon itself, and the sufferer finishes by turning his face to the wall, turning indeed his back to GOD, not wishing to speak to Him, desiring, like a wounded animal, nothing but to suffer in peace hidden in a corner.

But this desolation has varying degrees of intensity, and the impossibility of surmounting fate turns the poor soul, which cannot always keep the same position, towards its Maker. Then we reproach ourselves for our contumely; we implore His pardon, and a softness is born of this reconciliation. Little by little ideas of resignation to the Saviour's will plant themselves within us and take root, if the Devil, always on the watch, does not intervene to extinguish them, if, for instance, a visit made in charity and in the hope of affording comfort does not completely miss its aim, throwing us back into sentiments of regret and envy, one of the special miseries of a sick bed. If solitude weighs on the patient, visitors overwhelm him. If no one comes he says he is abandoned, neglected by those on whose friendship he relied, and if they come they cause a relapse into misery by contrasting their own lot with that of their friend. We must have already advanced very far on the road to perfection not to suffer from this comparison, and Lydwine must have known well these despairs of the lacerated soul.

We know positively that when she heard the laughter of her comrades at play in the street she melted into tears and asked GOD why she, apart from all others, should be so hardly treated.

We have to believe, however, that she was already fitted to bear the most terrible calamities, for GOD took no heed of her tears and, instead of alleviating, increased them.

To these bodily tortures, to these torments of the soul, was shortly added the horror of mystic darkness. Whilst she tried to stand up against discouragement, she entered the wine-press of the expiatory life and was there immersed; for then, besides the obsession of her own impotence, there began a spiritual ataxy which made the soul waver until all the faculties suffered paralysis. As S. John of the Cross observes, GOD plunged the understanding into darkness, the will into indifference, the memory into the void, and the heart into bitterness. And to these periods of spiritual abandonment Lydwine was subject for years. She thought herself cursed by the Heavenly Spouse, and the apprehension that this state would continue indefinitely augmented her anguish.

No human creature could have resisted such assaults if she had not been under divine surveillance and constantly sustained. GOD, however, concealed His aid from Lydwine during this period of purification; He withdrew all tangible consolations; He did not even lend her the aid of a priest, for it is very certain that this Curé of Schiedam, this man of capons, was quite incapable of helping her in her desolation. Neither does it appear that the balm of the afflicted, the sovereign medicine of the soul, the communion, was very often administered to her, for Gerlac and Brugman note that at the time when she could still drag herself about, her parents led her to church on Easter Day, where she knelt as best she could at the altar rail.

They tell us further that when she was confined to her bed the quinsy, by which she was afflicted, often prevented her from consuming the sacred elements; indeed à Kempis, more precise, declares distinctly that she only communicated when she was well, at the feast of the Resurrection. Then, he adds, when she could no longer leave her room, she obtained permission to receive the body of the Lord once more;

and finally, a long time after she was completely bedridden, they brought her the Eucharist six times a year. At this period, it is true, the Sacrament was distributed at fairly regular intervals, but may we not trace the spiritual anæmia which overwhelmed her, in part to this privation of the sole cordial powerful enough to re-animate her?

To sum up, never did woman appear so abandoned by Him whose caresses seemed changed into bitter deceits and hard rebuffs. Her case would seem to be almost unique. The other Saints knew certainly the same trials; they passed, like her, through the experiences of the purgative life, but they did not, for the most part, undergo at the same time the tortures of hell and physical suffering. The soul might be bleeding, but the body would be in health to sustain its companion to the best of its power; to tend it like a sick child whom one cradles in one's arms; to lead it into churches; to sooth its agony by distraction. Or else, on the contrary, the body failed but the soul remained active and raised her acolyte by the force of spiritual energy. With Lydwine, alas, the soul and its shell were equally afflicted; both were worn and unable to help each other; both were on the point of falling, when suddenly the Saviour, whom she thought so far off, affirmed Himself in power, showing, by the man who was made invisible, that He was watching there at her side and that He indeed thought of her.

Judging that the darkness had lasted long enough for the poor girl, He tore it aside in this light of grace. Then he confided to a human intermediary, to a priest named Jan Pot, the care of explaining to her her vocation and of consoling her.

Who was this Jan Pot, her confessor at the same time as Dom André, the Curé of Schiedam? Gerlac and à Kempis speak of him as being that ecclesiastic who came to communicate her when she had obtained permission to partake of the Lord's Supper twice a year. He does not appear to have held the Curé in

very great esteem, for it was he who announced to
Lydwine—with joy, says Gerlac—that the cats had
eaten the capons. Where did he come from? What
was his position in the town? How did he know the
Saint? To all these questions we have no answer.

However, if we compare two passages, one in Gerlac
and the other in Brugman, both relating to a Schiedam
magistrate's temptation to suicide, of which we shall
speak further on, we may perhaps gather that Jan Pot
was the curate of the parish. Anyhow, we can feel
assured that he was truly sent by GOD to explain
Lydwine's mission to her and to direct her.

After having one day spoken the ordinary commonplaces suitable to the sick, he concluded simply :—

"My daughter, till now you have neglected to
meditate sufficiently on the Passion of Christ. Do so
in future and you will see that GOD'S yoke of loving
suffering will become easy. Accompany Him to the
Garden of Olives, to Pilate, to Golgotha, and say to
yourself that when death prevents His further suffering,
all is not finished, that you must further, like a faithful
widow, accomplish the last wishes of your Spouse, and
supply by your sufferings what are still necessary to
His."

Lydwine listened without really understanding what
these words meant. She thanked him for having been
so kind to her, and when he was gone she tried to profit
by his advice and pondered over it. But it was in vain
that she tried to represent to herself the scenes of
Calvary; her thoughts wandered, and her own torments
interested her more than those of Jesus. She tried to
get the better of herself by adopting a method which
Jan Pot had briefly indicated to facilitate the practice
of this exercise; she forced herself to rally her thoughts
and concentrate them on the Saviour; but they quickly
returned to herself. Then she completely lost her
head. When she had recovered a little she summoned
all her strength to apply blinkers to the eyes of the
spirit, so as to prevent her looking to one side or the

other, and to force herself to follow only one track;
but neither did this meet with any success, for the soul
obstinately refused to advance.   This effort to control
her thoughts utterly exhausted her, and this she very
frankly confessed to Jan Pot when he visited her again.

"Father," she said, "I wish to obey you, but I
do not understand anything at all about meditation.
When I struggle to consider the tortures of Christ I can
think of nothing but my own.   The yoke of Christ has
not, as you assured me it would, become lighter.   Ah!
if you knew its weight!"

Jan Pot did not appear the least surprised at this
result.   He praised Lydwine for her attempt and
patiently explained to her that her parched condition,
her want of energy, the wandering of her thoughts,
her inability to concentrate on one sole point, were
nevertheless graces.   He made her understand that
prayer recited by compulsion may be the most
agreeable that GOD can receive, seeing that it is the
only one that costs the utterer dear.   He said to her,
with S. Gertrude, that if the Saviour always accorded
inward consolations they would be harmful, for they
would render the soul tender and diminish the powers
it had acquired; and it is probable that, after this
preamble, he firmly tore away the veil which hid the
future, and revealed to her her vocation as a victim
on earth, illustrating his meaning by S. Paul's phrase,
"to complete the sufferings of Christ."

He certainly explained to her the law whereby we
are all sharers in the evil of the world, and the law
that out of evil may come good; that, as all are
partakers in Adam's sin, so also all are partakers in
our redemption by Our Saviour.   In other words, each
one is, up to a certain point, responsible for the faults
of others, and ought also, up to a certain point, to
expiate them; and each can also, if it so please GOD,
attribute in a certain measure the merits which he
possesses or acquires to those who have none or who
will not acquire them.

These laws have been put forth by the Almighty, and He has first observed them in applying them to the Person of His Son.   The Father consented that the Word should take the sins of the world to Himself and should pay the ransom for others.   He willed that His satisfactions which could not benefit Himself, since He was innocent and perfect, should profit the miscreants, the guilty, all the sinners whom He had come to purchase.   He willed that the Saviour should be the first to present the example of mystic substitution, of the reparation of Him who owes nothing for him who owes all; and Jesus wished that certain souls should inherit the succession to His sacrifice.

Indeed the Saviour cannot suffer again Himself, having ascended to His Father and the joy of Heaven; His task of redemption was accomplished with His blood, His tortures finished with His death.   If He is still to suffer here below, it can only be in His Church, in the members of His mystic body.

Those souls given to reparation who re-act the anguish of Calvary, who nail themselves to the empty place of Jesus on the Cross, are in some sort the counterparts of the Son.   They reflect His suffering face in a mirror of blood.   They do more, for they alone give this all powerful GOD something He would otherwise lack; the possibility of suffering again for us.   They satisfy this desire which has survived His death, for it is as infinite as the love which engenders it; they dispense to this marvellous Poor the alms of tears; they restore to Him in His joy that sacrifice which is denied Him.

Jan Pot, explaining all this to Lydwine, added, "And if these souls, capable like their Creator of being chastised for the crimes of which they are not guilty, did not exist, it would be with the universe as it would be with our own country without the protection of the dykes.   It would be engulfed by the tide of sins like Holland by the flow of the waves.

"They are then, at one and the same time, the benefactors of Heaven and Earth.

"But, my daughter, when a soul reaches this height, the manner of suffering changes. GOD in some way intermingles the extreme sensations of beatitude and grief, so that they amalgamate. Where is the one, and what remains of the other? One cannot say; it is the incomprehensible fusion of an excess and a lack of moral energy, and the soul would burst under the pressure if the pain of the body did not intervene to permit it to recover breath so that it may the better rejoice. In short, it is by the steps of suffering that one makes the ascent of joy.

"At the actual moment your spiritual being is inflamed, but you suffer because you do not wish to suffer; the secret of your distress lies there. Gather up and offer to GOD that suffering which causes you to despair, and He will lighten it! He will reward you with such compensations that the moment will come when you will cry: 'But I have cheated Him! He has contracted with me on false terms! I offered myself to expiate by the most terrible chastisements the transgressions of the world, and He fills me with a measureless joy, a happiness that knows no bounds. He exiles me, He dispossesses me, He disembarrasses me of myself, for it is He who laughs and weeps, it is He who lives in me!'

"When this happens, I will say what I say now. Do not be uneasy. Our Saviour knows very well that He has lent Himself to this fraud, but He only loves those who feel thus.

"Your vocation is clear; it consists in sacrificing yourself for others, in making reparation for faults you have not committed, in the practice of a sublime and truly divine charity.

"Say to Jesus: 'I wish to place myself of my own will upon your Cross, and I wish it should be you who drive in the nails.' He will accept this office of executioner, and the Angels will aid Him. He, your

Saviour, will take you at your word! They will bring Him the thorns, the gimlet, the cords, the sponge, the vinegar, the lance; but when He sees you stretched on the gibbet, suspended between heaven and earth, as He was upon the wood of the Cross, not yet able to attain the firmament but no longer touching the earth, His heart will melt with pity and He will not wait till His justice is satisfied before taking you down. Like Nicodemus and Joseph of Arimathea, He will support your head whilst the blessed Virgin lays you on her knees; but there will be no more tears; Mary will smile, Magdalen will weep no longer and will embrace you gaily like an elder sister!"

Lydwine's eyes were opened; she began to understand the causes of the incredible sufferings she endured. She accepted willingly this mission which the Redeemer had called her to fulfil; but how should she proceed?

"In following the advice which I have given you," said the priest, "to meditate ceaselessly on the Passion of Christ, it is necessary that you should not be discouraged, and because you did not succeed at the first attempt in being carried away outside yourself, you must not renounce an exercise which will lead you without fail, when you are accustomed to it, to lose your own will and follow that of the divine Spouse.

"Do not imagine, either, that your trial is longer and more bitter than that of the Cross, which was relatively short, and that after all many martyrs suffered torments more barbarous and more lasting than those of Our Saviour when they suffered the wheel, grilling, or flaying with iron combs, when they were forced into red-hot helmets, boiled in oil, sawn asunder, or slowly ground between the millstones. For nothing is more untrue, and no torture can compare with that of Jesus.

"Think of the prelude to the Passion in the Garden of Gethsemane, of that inexpressible moment when He put His divinity in some manner in suspense, despoiled Himself of His power of becoming insensible, so that He might the better debase Himself to the level of His creatures and to their mode of suffering. In a word, during the drama of Calvary, humanity predominated in the GOD man, and this was exquisite pain.   When He felt Himself become suddenly weak under the terrible burden of iniquities which He was called upon to bear, He trembled and fell on His face.

" The darkness of night overtook Him and formed a great frame for pictures lighted by who can tell what lurid colouring.   On a background of menacing light the centuries defiled before Him, bringing with them the idolatries and incests, the sacrileges and murders, all the old misdeeds perpetrated since the fall of the first man—and they were saluted, acclaimed as they passed by the evil angels!   Overcome, Jesus lowered His eyes.   When He raised them these phantoms of past generations had vanished, but the wickedness of that Judea which He had evangelized teemed before Him and filled Him with anger.   He saw Judas, He saw Caiaphas, He saw Pilate, He saw Saint Peter, He saw the debased creatures who were going to spit on His face and crown Him with drops of blood.   The Cross rose ominous on the disordered heavens, and groans were heard from out of Limbo.   He rose, but seized with vertigo He swayed and sought an arm to sustain Him.   He was alone.

" Then He dragged Himself to His disciples, who slept, and woke them.   They looked at Him alarmed and fearful, asking themselves if this man with agitated gestures and eyes full of emotion was indeed that Jesus who had been transfigured before them on Mount Tabor with His visage resplendent and His robe as of snow on fire.   The Saviour smiled in pity; He only reproached them because they had not watched, and after having returned to them twice, He left them whilst He agonized alone, apart.

" He knelt to pray, but now it was no longer a question of past or present; it was a question of the future which was even more to be dreaded. The future centuries succeeded each other, showing territories which changed, towns which developed, even seas changed in form, and continents which were no longer recognizable. Only men remained the same, under a different dress; they stole and assassinated, they persisted in crucifying their Saviour to satisfy their lusts and their passion for gain. In surroundings varying with the ages the same golden calf was erected and reigned. Inebriate with grief, Jesus sweated blood and cried: ' Father, if Thou wilt, take away this cup.' Then he added, resigned: ' Thy will, not mine! '

" Here then, my daughter, you see that these preliminary tortures surpass all that your imagination is capable of conceiving; they were so intense that the human nature of Christ would have been broken and He would not have reached Golgotha alive if angels had not come to console Him; and yet the climax of His sufferings was not yet attained. That was only reached upon the Cross. Without doubt His physical torture was horrible, but how small a thing it was when confronted with those others! For on the Cross it was the assault of all the united ignominies of all time, the opprobrium of past, present and future, melted and concentrated into a sort of corrosive essence, in which He was overwhelmed. It was something like a charnel-house of hearts, a pestilence of souls who threw themselves on the wood of the Cross to infect it. This cup which He had accepted to drink poisoned the very air! The angels who had assisted the Saviour in the Garden of Gethsemane did not any longer intervene; they wept, cast to the ground before this abominable murder of GOD; the sun vanished, the earth uttered horrible groanings, the terrified rocks were on the point of opening. Then Jesus uttered a loud cry: ' Father, why hast Thou forsaken me? '

" And he died.

" Think of all that, Lydwine, and assure yourself your sufferings are as nothing compared with those.

Call to mind the unforgettable scenes in the Garden of Gethsemane and of Golgotha ; look at the head of the Spouse insulted by blows and crowned with thorns ; put your steps in His footprints, and the stages will become easy, the forced marches light.''

And the good man left her, having promised to come again. Lydwine was generous, she gave herself without reserve as a beast of burden to carry the load of sins ; but this oblation did not free her, nor lighten any of her pains.   When she would stop in meditation at the halts of the stations, she stumbled like one who has had his eyes veiled and cannot, when first released, walk straight.   She quitted once more the road to Calvary to wander in little paths which insensibly led her back to her point of departure, her own sufferings. GOD considered her in silence and made no movement. Naturally she was agitated ; she believed that Jan Pot had inflicted an impossible task upon her and melted again into tears.   She was ready to sink under despair when Easter burst upon the liturgical cycle of the year. Then the good Jan Pot took with him the Saviour under the elements of the Sacrament, and said :

'' My child, till now I have talked of the martyrdom of Jesus.   I need no longer do so, for it is He Himself who will knock at the door of your heart and speak to you.''

And he communicated her.

Immediately her soul was stirred and overwhelmed by love, by a fiery stream surrounding as with a nimbus the sweat-covered Face, which she contemplated in the most profound depths of her being as the very source of her personality.   Carried away with grief and joy she no longer took count of her wretched body ; the groans which her tortures had wrung from her disappeared in her cries of hosannah.   Drunk with a divine inebriety, she wandered in mind with no further consciousness of self than to collect a bouquet of her sufferings and offer it to the divine Host in the hope that it might find acceptance.   Then her tears flowed for two entire weeks in a rain of love which at last saturated the arid and almost dead soil.   The celestial gardener spread His seed and at once the flowers of the Passion arose.   Those meditations on the death of the Redeemer, which had so harassed her, now never tired her; the sight of the divine Spouse in agony took her into His very presence and outside herself.   What she now yearned after was not the jubilant health of her comrades, but the silent tenderness of Veronica, who had been so fortunate as to wipe the blood from the face of Christ.   Ah! to be Magdalen; to be the Cyrenean, the man to whom was reserved that unique privilege, that unique glory, of helping GOD to transport the sins of the world with His Cross!

She would have wished to be amongst them, making herself useful in some way, in passing the water to the holy women, the herbs, the basin, the sponge to wash the wounds; she would have wished to be their servant, to render them humble service without being seen.   It seemed to her now that she was placing her feet in the footsteps of the Son; that in suffering she carried away a part of His griefs and thereby diminished them; and she was ambitious to snatch them all from Him, reproaching Him for keeping too many.   She complained of the inadequacy of her tortures, of the parsimony with which He afflicted her; and without ceasing she moved forward an assiduous pilgrim on the road to Calvary.   In imitation of the Psalmist she prayed seven times a day.   She created canonical hours for her own use; she divided the day into seven parts and the drama of the Passion into the same number, and she seemed to have a time-piece in the spirit, so exact was she in meditating on the subject corresponding with the hour without ever being a minute in advance or a second behind.

And yet her bodily torments were increasing.   Her toothache had become so violent that her head trembled, and fever racked her with alternating heat and cold.   When the access was most violent she spat up a red-coloured water and fell into such weakness that it was impossible for her either to speak a single word or hear anyone talk; but instead of abandoning herself to despair, as was formerly her habit, she thanked GOD for thus slaking the thirst of His tortures.

They asked her sometimes if she was always desirous, as formerly, to be healed, and she replied: " No, there is but one thing now that I desire; it is, not to be deprived of my discomforts and pains."

And bravely she took a further step, and addressed herself to Christ.

The Carnival was near, and thinking of the increase of sins it would cause at Schiedam because of the indulgences of the feast, she cried: " Lord, revenge Thyself on me for the additional offences which these feasts will inflict on Thee!"   And her prayer was immediately answered; she experienced such an acute pain in the leg that she was silent and asked for nothing more.   She endured this martyrdom heroically, which ceased indeed only on the day of the Resurrection, and repeated to those whose pity took the form of complaints that she would very willingly submit to such sufferings for forty years and more, if she knew she would obtain in exchange the conversion of one sinner or the deliverance of one soul from Purgatory.

CHAPTER V.

AFTER she had entered the way of mystic substitution and had, of her own free will, offered herself as the scapegoat for the sins of the world, Jesus threw His dominion upon her and she lived that abnormal existence wherein griefs serve as a means of procuring joy. The more she suffered the more she was satisfied and the more she wished to suffer. She knew that she was not alone now, that her tortures had but one aim, that they tended to the good of the Church, and that they palliated the offences of the living and the dead. She knew that it was for the glory of GOD that the perfumed flower-bed of her wounds raised both humble and magnificent flowers. She could verify, by her own experiences, the justice of a reply of S. Félicité to the railleries of an executioner who was jeering at her cries, when she lay in prison before being thrown to the wild beasts in the arena.

" What will you do when you are being devoured by the beasts? " asked this man.

And the Saint replied:

" It is I who suffer now, but then, when I have been martyred, it will be another who will suffer for me, because I shall suffer for Him."

It is very difficult to analyse this life, so different from ours during the greater part of which small tortures and joys were intermingled. Both our exultations and our pains are indeed moderate and of small account; we live in a temperate climate, in a zone of tepid piety, where vegetation is stunted and nature feeble. Lydwine herself had been uprooted from an inert soil to be transplanted into the ardent soil of mysticism; and the sap, till then torpid, boiled over in the fierce fire of Love.

She panted, twisted herself, ground her teeth, or lay half dead, and all the time she was in a state of ecstasy.   She was always either in one extreme or the other; her intense joy compensating for her intense suffering.   She expressed it very simply.   " The consolations which I experience are proportionate to the trials I endure, and I find them so exquisite that I would not change them for all the pleasures of man."

Nevertheless, the sum of her maladies continued to overwhelm her and she was attacked by a furious recrudescence of disease.   Her stomach finally burst like a ripe fruit, and they had to apply a woollen cushion to press back her entrails and prevent them from leaving the body.   Soon, when they wished to move her to change the sheets of her bed, they had to bind her members firmly with napkins and cloths, for otherwise her body would have fallen to pieces and come away in the hands of those who tended her.

By a miracle evidently intended to certify the superhuman origin of these ills, Lydwine no longer ate food, or scarcely ate any.   In thirty years she only ate as much as a healthy person is accustomed to consume in three days.

During the first years of her life as a recluse her only food from morning to night was one round of apple of the thickness of the Sacred Host, which they toasted for her at the end of a little pair of tongs; and if she occasionally attempted to swallow a mouthful of bread steeped in beer or milk, she was only able to do so with great difficulty.   After a time the slice of apple became too much for her and she had to content herself with a drop of wine and water flavoured by a dash of spice of muscade, or by a morsel of date.   Next she sustained herself solely on wine and water, wetting her lips with it rather than drinking it, and absorbing about half a pint in a week.

Very often, as spring water was dear in Schiedam,

they gave her river water from the Meuse, which was either salt or fresh according to the ebb and flow of the tide, for the Meuse runs into the sea quite near the town. Lydwine preferred to have it drawn for her just at the flow, when it was bitter and salt, as she could then herself convert it into a most acceptable drink.

When she was reduced to taking only liquid food, sleep, which was already rare, completely forsook her, and the nights were endless, implacable, as she remained motionless on her back, of which the skin was raw. Those attending her reckoned that she had not slept as much as three good nights in thirty years!

Finally she ceased to take any food at all, and even the wish to sleep, which was only, according to her biographers, a temptation of the devil, also disappeared. A sort of lethargy indeed overcame her each time she prepared to meditate on the Passion of Christ, and she struggled in vain against this drowsiness.

"Give up these exercises and sleep," said Jan Pot to her, "you will come back to them later."

She obeyed, and this state of irresistible torpor ceased.

This want of nourishment and this perpetual insomnia caused her to be subjected to the most cruel humiliations and base insinuations. All the town talked of the singular case of a young girl who neither ate nor slept yet remained alive, and the fame of this marvel was widespread. To many her story seemed impossible; they ignored the numerous facts of this kind recorded in the biographies of Saints who were predecessors or contemporaries of Lydwine. Attracted by curiosity, many visited her and explored her house relentlessly, and she had to submit to an inquisitorial enquiry into her life. Her detractors were not four only, as in the case of the friends of Job; they were legion! Most of them saw only a head riven from forehead to nose; a face furrowed like a melon;

a body whose flesh had to be compressed like that of a mummy by the interlacing of bandages; and disgust overcame them at the sight of so many infirmities! Their curiosity was deceived. They had only discovered a gorgon's mask, where they had expected to find a more or less comely face which would have moved them, or a physiognomy, more or less bizarre, at which they could have gibed. They only saw the surface; they distinguished no ray of light under the horn panels of this broken lantern set in the shade in a corner; and yet the soul shone through, for Jesus filled it with His love and gilded it with His radiance!

They revenged themselves for their disappointment by accusing her of deceit. They said that she did not really observe the diet; that she ate greedily when she was alone, and that she drank at night. They pestered her with questions, prepared pitfalls for her, tried to lead her to contradict herself. To all their interrogations she answered simply:

"I do not understand you. You believe it is impossible to subsist without the help of food; but GOD is master I presume, and can act as He wishes. You affirm that my maladies should kill me; but they will not kill me till the Saviour wishes it." And she added, for those who tendered hypocritical pity: "I am not to be pitied. I am happy as I am; and if the recitation of a Hail Mary would avail to cure me, I would not recite it."

Others went further still and brutally abused her, crying: "Make no mistake, my beauty, we are not duped by you! You pretend to live without nourishment and you feed secretly. You are a pretty cat, and as deceitful as can be."

And Lydwine, a little surprised at this violence, asked them what interest she could possibly have in lying like that. "Besides," she said, "to eat is not a sin and not to eat is not an act of glory, so far as I know."

Embarrassed by the good sense of these replies they

changed their mode of attack and charged her with
being possessed. The devil alone was capable of
working such magic; and these deceits were the result
of a pact with him. Rare, indeed, were those who
believed her to be neither charlatan nor sorceress, but
understood what she was in reality, a victim ground
in the mortar of GOD, a pitiful emblem of the suffering
Church.

Little by little, however, the truth prevailed. Annoyed
at these conflicting accounts, the burgomasters of
Schiedam resolved to get at the facts of the case.
They subjected Lydwine for months to incessant
surveillance and were compelled to recognizes that she
was a Saint whose abnormal existence could only be
explained by a particular design from on high; a fact
which they promulgated in a legal document sealed
with the seal of the city. They met on the 12th
September, 1421, to verify the testimonials concerning
Lydwine's life; the privation of all nourishment and
of sleep; the state of the body reduced to a heap
of shreds; one portion of the entrails amputated,
the other teeming with parasites and yet exhaling a
sweet perfume; in short, all the details that we have
enumerated. The legal document is inserted at length
in the volume of the Bollandists at the head of the
second life by Brugman.

One ought also to add this fact stated by all her
biographers, that Lydwine's parents preserved in a
vessel fragments of bone and strips of flesh which had
detached themselves from their child's limbs, and that
these remains exhaled a sweet perfume.

Some gossips, who had heard of this prodigy, ran
to assure themselves of its veracity; but Lydwine,
whom these visits incommoded, implored her mother
to bury these poor remains, and to satisfy her
Petronille did so.

It seems that after this proclamation of the
burgomasters and municipality of Schiedam, Lydwine
was left in peace, as her good faith was of public

F

notoriety.   Four years later, however, when Philippe
of Burgundy, after having invaded Flanders, left a
corps of occupation at Schiedam, the commandant of
the place, who was a Frenchman, wished to assure
himself that the phenomena attested by the town
manifesto were correct.   He gave as a pretext his
desire to protect the Saint from possible outrage, and
quartered on her house a troop of six soldiers, whom
he chose from amongst the most honest and most
religious.   Then he removed her family, who had to
camp in another part of the town, and ordered his
subordinates to relieve each other, so that they should
not lose sight of their prisoner by day or night, and to
prevent any food or drink from reaching her.   They
executed these orders to the letter, inspecting even the
pots of ointment to be sure that they did not contain
any substance that could comfort her.   No one, except
a widow of the name of Catharine, was admitted to
tend her, and she was searched before she entered the
room.   They mounted guard thus round her bed for
nine days, and during that time they saw Lydwine a
prey to extravagant tortures, dissolved in tears, but
smiling, lost in ecstasy, enwrapped, as if outside the
world, in waves of joy.

As for herself, it is doubtful if she perceived their
presence; GOD so snatched her away, far from her
dwelling place, sparing her the irksome spectacle of
these men whose eyes never left her.   When their
duty ceased they certified shortly that their captive
had lived, as they had been told, on air alone without
taking any food.

This surveillance, therefore, only went to prove once
more Lydwine's honesty and the authenticity of the
unusual existence which she underwent.

Indeed, this repetition of investigation was very
unnecessary.   The challenge of a little town always
on the watch, the rage for espionage in the province,
made the whole affair very public.   Lydwine would not
have been able to swallow a mouthful of bread without

all Schiedam knowing it; but if GOD willed that these facts should be closely examined into and proved, it was that no doubt should remain and that such graces should not be relegated to the place of mere legend.

Indeed, it must be admitted that He constantly acts in this way. Did He not act in the same manner in the nineteenth century with Catharine Emmerich and Louise Lateau, two stigmatised Saints whose lives present more than one analogy to that of Lydwine?

CHAPTER VI.

Up till now it was principally her mother who had tended Lydwine, but Petronille fell ill in her turn, worn out by age and the cares of an existence which was always striving to make both ends meet in her poor household. The fatigue which Lydwine's infirmities caused her and the grief which she felt at seeing her pestered by gossip and lies, and abused even in her bed, finally proved too heavy. She took to her bed and did not again leave it; but she was conscious and, knowing that she was dying, she trembled to recall the follies of her youth with its acts of weakness and hours badly employed. Perhaps she reproached herself with having been too hasty with her daughter; in any case she confessed her fears to her and begged her to obtain mercy from the Saviour.

Lydwine, who wept bitter tears while listening to her, consoled her as best she could and promised to gratify her as far as might be possible through the merits acquired by her long sufferings. She made this sole condition, that the dying woman should resign herself to leave this life and abandon herself in all confidence to the indulgent tenderness of her Judge.

Petronille, who knew what funds of grace her child possessed, was reassured and passed away in peace; But Lydwine, persuaded that she now possessed nothing, since she had given all to her mother, hastened to make up for her loss. She sold the furniture and the clothes that she could do without, and distributed the money to the poor. Then she decided that her bed was too soft and sold it to her nephew and niece, who were installed as her nurses. She then ordered them to lay a plank, taken from the side of a barrel, on the damp floor of her room and to cover it with straw; and this straw, which quickly became an abominable dung-heap, was henceforth her sole bed. The task of moving her to it was, in spite of all their precautions, a terrible one. They had to bind her up in order that she should not break in pieces, and in raising her up they were forced to tear up the flesh which adhered to the sheet.

She felt that even this was not enough and in order to rub the skin raw she obtained a belt of horsehair which she never took off.

She was then twenty-eight years of age. Winter set in—a winter so long and so intense that the oldest people never remembered to have endured one like it. It became known as the great winter, and Thomas à Kempis says that all the fish perished in the frozen waters. Now in this shivering season she lived in a room without light and without air, deprived of fire, clad simply in a little woollen shirt spun for her by the sisters of the third order of S. Francis at Schiedam, and wrapped in a bad blanket, even though her wounds and her dropsy rendered her more sensitive than others to the cold.

At night she wept tears of blood which froze on her cheeks, and in the morning they had to detach these stalactites from her face, rough and blue with frost. As for the rest of her body, it was almost paralysed, and her feet were so stiff that they had to rub them and wrap them in warm cloths to re-animate them.

She continued, however, to live in this state worse than death; and there was rarely a sou in the house! The few charitable persons who had helped her until then now forgot to do so; she no longer had enough linen to dress her wounds, and she would have died of misery and cold if a Franciscan of the name of Werembold, a native of Gouda, who was for several years rector and confessor of the sisters tertiary of S. Cecilia of Utrecht and minister general of the third order of S. Francis, had not come to visit her.

They each knew the other by a vision they had both had at the same hour on the same day, when they were celebrating the Feast of the Annunciation, and from that moment this priest, who was a veritable Saint, had desired to see her with his own eyes.

He undertook the journey for this purpose and found her in such distress that he burst into tears and was not able to speak.   He gave her all he possessed—thirty Dutch pieces—that they might, at any rate, buy her a pair of sheets, and, indignant at the hardness of heart of the people of Schiedam, he mounted the pulpit and reproached them in such a way that several persons, whose zeal for this work of mercy had cooled, repented.

And this good Werembold did more than assure her of the necessaries of life for some time; he continued the lessons of Jan Pot, and pointed out to her the mystic way.   He was a clever strategist in divine warfare; he knew how potent a fertilizer suffering is for the flower of the soul, and he admired the loving wisdom of blessed Tortionnaire, who always arranged that the griefs which he could not prevent should be changed without delays into joys.   There must have been some singular conversations between these two elect, and if one may believe à Kempis, they talked chiefly of their death.

Werembold hoped to be summoned to the future life after Easter, but his companion undeceived him; she assured him that he would linger until Whitsuntide, and indeed he died in the year 1413, on the vigil of this feast, on Saint Barnabas' day.   He, too, was a prophet, declaring that she must resign herself to endure yet a long time her lamentable fortune; for there remained as much for her to undergo as she had already suffered, and she survived him, indeed, for twenty years.

She was present in the spirit at his agony.   On the day on which he died the sisters tertiary of Schiedam announced to Lydwine that they were setting out for

Utrecht in order that they might have news of Werembold, whom they knew to be very ill. "Make haste, make haste," said she, and throwing back her head she let them understand that they would be too late. When they reached Utrecht that evening they knew by the tolling of the bell that the Saint had not deceived them.

After the death of Petronille, her husband, old Peter, his son Wilhelm, and his two children Petronille and Baudouin, relieved each other in tending Lydwine; but there was a great lack of skill now that the mother was gone.

One accident after another occurred, which afflicted the poor Saint still further. Her father's sight was failing; during the great winter he had had the great toe of his right foot frozen and had been obliged to give up his post as night watchman. This caused a return of black poverty. He would not, from delicacy of feeling, consume any of the alms which his daughter received, and so he lived only on scraps and odds and ends.

At this time Duke William VI., Count of Holland, passing through Schiedam with his wife, the Countess Marguerite, and several persons of the Court, heard talk of the poverty of the Saint's father. He had compassion and said to the old man:

"How much does it cost you to live here? Name the sum, and, in consideration of the virtues of your daughter, I will pay it to you."

Pierre assured the Count that twelve French crowns a year would amply supply his needs.

Wilhelm paid them at once, and considering that the request was too modest, promised to double the amount if it became necessary. This money was at first faithfully paid; but as generosity very easily tires, especially with rich people, the good man at last received nothing and did not think he had the right to claim anything.

Meanwhile, whilst he was profiting by his short spell

of good fortune, he wished to gratify his desire to frequent the churches, which he had never been able to realize for want of time; but he was nearly blind and so weak on his legs that the slightest touch upset him.   Thus, when he was out, Lydwine nearly died of anxiety; and she had reason to be uneasy, for they picked him up one day nearly suffocated.

It was Whitsun Eve and Pierre had left the house to go and hear vespers, when he met a man who proposed that they should take a walk outside the town till the hour of the office.   He agreed, and they went as far as a place called Damlaën, conversing together. There he felt tired and stopped, whereupon his companion caught him round the waist, threw him into a deep ditch full of water, and disappeared. He was drowning when a carter, coming along the road, saw him, extricated him from the mud and brought him back in his cart to his daughter.

She indeed thought him dead and was weeping, for someone who had seen the old man stretched motionless in the cart, had come in haste to warn her that they were bringing back her father's corpse.

This adventure, to which the biographers assign a diabolical origin, so terrified the Saint that she devised all kinds of means to keep old Pierre at home in future, but having become a little childish, he escaped directly he felt that he was not being watched, and as he never left the house except to go to church, his daughter had not the courage to reprimand him.

Indeed, he was more an anxiety than a help to her; and his son William does not seem, in spite of his good nature, to have been much more apt than Pierre in looking after Lydwine.

He it was who nearly roasted her alive.   One morning, before going to work, he went into his sister's room to assure himself of the state of her health and put the candle which he had lighted on a shelf above his sister's head.   Then he went out, leaving her alone in the house, for the father also was

out hearing Mass.   Now the candle fell over and set
fire to the straw on which Lydwine was laid.   She was
meditating on the Passion of Our Lord and did not
perceive it at first, but the crackling of the straw
roused her from her trance, and with the only hand
which she could move—the left hand—she pressed the
flames and extinguished them without being burnt.
When her father returned she no longer lay on a bundle
of straw but on a heap of ashes.

This brother, who was so imprudent, appears to have
been an excellent man and devoted to his sister, but
was married, unfortunately, to a foolish and wicked
woman, who believed she had the right to do anything
she wished, probably because she gave her children
to Lydwine's service.   The Saint endured without
complaint the foolish gossip and ill-judged remarks of
this virago, who could not open her mouth without
bawling and indulged in paroxysms of shouting for no
apparent reason.

But if Lydwine took all these trials quietly others
found it more difficult to accept them, as, for instance,
the Duke of Bavaria, who came to Schiedam to consult
the Saint on a case of conscience.   The crimes which
he had committed and the apostasy which he made in
putting off his bishop's robes in order to marry, no
doubt tormented him.

He had himself announced under a borrowed name,
but Lydwine, divinely warned, was not deceived.

Hardly had he sat down by her when the woman
entered and stunned them with her foolish remarks
and cries.

He was much annoyed and said to Lydwine, " How
can you endure this harpy?   When she is here it must
be impossible to live in the house."

And the Saint answered, smiling, " Monseigneur,
what would you have?   It is a good thing to suffer
the impertinences and weaknesses of such people, were
it only to correct them by patience and to teach oneself
not to get irritated."

Being a practical man, the Duke hit on another solution; he bought the woman's silence for the time being, and, delighted to pocket a sum of money, she remained quiet whilst he was there.

Lydwine's nurses were, indeed, not worth very much; the father was more of an encumbrance than a help, the brother was busy away from home, his wife was insupportable, and there remained only the two children, Baudouin and Petronille, who happily did not resemble their mother and were much attached to their aunt, but were too young to be of much assistance. Besides, owing to the nature of the sick woman's infirmities she could only be decently tended by women. GOD watched over her.

Some pious neighbours made themselves responsible for dressing her wounds and changing the linen, amongst whom figures a woman who was an intimate friend of Lydwine's and appears often in her history.

Who was this Catherine Simon, whom we have already seen near Lydwine when she was kept constantly in sight by the six soldiers, and who ended by living with her altogether?

Gerlac calls her Catherine, wife of Maître Simon the barber; Brugman describes her sometimes as a servant, sometimes as a widow, sometimes as the faithful companion of the Saint; Thomas à Kempis speaks of her as a woman of quality and says she was not the wife or widow, but the daughter of Sieur Simon, whose profession he does not mention.

Are these Catherines and these Simons one and the same? One of the translators of à Kempis distinguishes between two different Catherines, the one a daughter of Simon and the other a widow of someone unknown.

In any case it is certain that this woman loved and cared for Lydwine as a daughter, and that she compensated her for all that she had to endure from the Curé of Schiedam, the man of the capons, who did not forbear to persecute the Saint in the most atrocious manner.

CHAPTER VII.

BEFORE narrating the wicked machinations of this man, it is well to repeat once more that the Church was then driven before the wind; the Popes were given up to a warfare of Bulls, the monasteries were rotten to the core, heresies raged, and Europe was in a state of dissolution. There was no reason why Holland, ruled first by a Prince capable of murder and then by his eccentric daughter, the Countess Jacqueline, should be spared by the Demon more than any other country, so the mean character of both the regular and the secular priests ought not to excite surprise.

Moreover, Lydwine was singularly exposed to outrages and seemed endowed with the sad privilege of attracting to her all the rogues and fools. Many came to visit her without apparent motive, glared at her insolently, and left her after loading her with abuse. On one occasion a madwoman who had insulted her, was so enraged at her silence and calm that she spat in her face and had to be forcibly ejected; but Lydwine sent her a little present, saying to the person whom she charged with this commission:

" That dear sister has done me a great service, for she has helped me to purify myself; it is less a present than the payment of a debt, and I shall be obliged if you will take it to her."

Her humility and patience never failed her; she endured the vulgarities of her sister-in-law, and the ill-treatment of the intruders without flinching. At these times her thoughts dwelt upon Our Saviour insulted and buffeted, and she thanked Him for allowing her to pick up the crumbs of His sufferings.

Stretched like Job on his dung-heap, she did not dispute like the Patriarch but withdrew within herself and trod the path of Calvary.   She loved humiliations as others love honours; affronts did not agitate her any longer, and it became necessary, in order to cause her real suffering, that she should be subjected to more serious abominations than those she had hitherto endured.

It was Dom André who accomplished this task.

Lydwine, as we have said, only approached the Sacraments at rare intervals during the first years of her maladies; but afterwards, when her infirmities increased, she experienced the necessity of receiving the body of the Lord more frequently, and she asked permission to communicate on the principal feasts of the year.

The Curé of Schiedam, then an ecclesiastic or monk whose name we do not know, consented, but he soon disappeared—history does not tell us how—and it was the Premontarian, Dom André, who succeeded him.

As soon as he had taken possession of the parish Lydwine begged him to treat her in the same manner as his predecessor had done, but he scolded her.

She returned to the charge, pointed out to him that her situation was exceptional, that she was sacrificed for others, that to deprive her of the Eucharist was to deprive her of all consolation and all help.   He persisted still more brutally in his refusal.   She then tasted the bitterness of that truth which her last descendant, one of the stigmatized of the nineteenth century, Marie Putigny of the Visitation of Metz, formulated for souls of the reparation: " To desire to communicate is to invite suffering! "

His denial crucified her and she wept bitter tears, without, however, moving this man.   She ended by keeping her grief to herself, but as her nurses observed, when the bell of the church announced the elevation at the Mass, or the tinkle of the bell warned her of the passage of the Viaticum in the street, she raised herself eagerly on her couch and then fell back and seemed to be at the point of death.

Some friends intervened on the occasion of a solemn festival, but they obtained no success; the Curé did not deign to give them any explanation. The truth is that he was obstinate and became more hostile from day to day. As he had to imagine some excuse for his conduct, he tried to persuade himself that Lydwine was in league with the Devil. Under pretext of unmasking her frauds, and urged also, no doubt, by pride in the thought that he was going to prove himself more clever than his colleagues, he resolved to employ a subterfuge which would confuse Lydwine, proving that she had lost the gift of insight into hidden things which people who were acquainted with her life attributed to her.

Consequently he appeared to relent, and on the vigil of the Nativity of Our Lady he confessed the Saint and promised to bring her the Holy Species on the next day.

She continued sad, for an angel had said to her immediately: "A new storm is preparing; this Curé will give you unconsecrated bread; GOD wills that I warn you, that you may not be deceived."

He arrived the next day and, before a certain number of Lydwine's friends, raised the Host from its surroundings and made her solemnly adore it. Then he communicated the sick woman, who, seized with nausea, rejected it.

Dom André feigned indignation and cried: "How, miserable and foolish woman! Do you dare to vomit the body of the Lord?"

"It is easy for me to distinguish between the body of Jesus and a simple wafer of unleavened bread," replied Lydwine. "If this Host had been consecrated I should have swallowed it without the least difficulty; but that one has not been; my whole nature revolts against consuming it. I must reject it."

The Curé trembled but brazened it out, swore that the Redeemer was there present under this Appearance, and, in order to impose on those present, insisted on re-transferring the Host solemnly to the church.

In consequence of this adventure Lydwine was much afflicted. Where was the learned and pious Jan Pot? Had he quitted Schiedam because of disagreements with the Curé? Was he occupying the post of chaplain or curate in another town? Was he dead? The biographers are silent. The fact remains that this priest, who might have aided the sick woman or even have communicated her, was not there. He had served as a link between the Saint and GOD; his mission had been no doubt fulfilled, and, if he was still in this world, the Saviour was probably employing him on other duties; but poor Lydwine, deprived of his assistance, wept night and day. It was all she could do not to relapse into despair, when suddenly Jesus intervened.

One day when, ruminating on her misfortunes, she lay and groaned on her bed, an angel appeared and said to her: " Cry no longer, my sister, you are going to be consoled in your affliction. The Well-beloved is near, you will see Him with your own eyes."

She believed it her duty to warn Dom André, so that he should not impute to a demoniacal intervention the favour which she prepared herself by prayer to receive. He shrugged his shoulders and laughed in her face.

When evening fell, such a light illuminated her chamber that her relations, who were conversing in another room, ran in, thinking she was on fire.

" Do not be alarmed," said she, " there is no fire here and consequently no danger. Leave me alone and be sure to shut the door."

It was when her relatives had left her, between eight and nine o'clock, that GOD permeated her to the very depths of her being. Her sufferings left her; her griefs no longer existed; her soul knelt in the rags of her couch and stretched eager arms towards the Spouse; but her eyes, which she had shut, were opened; a star sparkled above her bed, and near her shone an angel resplendent in his tunic of pale fire.

He touched her lightly and for some instants her wounds disappeared; her plumpness and the colours of health returned. A forgotten Lydwine, healthy and young, emerged from this yellow chrysalis that lay streaked with blood on its rotten straw.

And the angels entered. They held the instruments of the Passion, the Cross, the nails, the hammer, the lance, the column, the thorns, and the scourge; one by one they ranged themselves in a semi-circle in the room, leaving an empty space around the bed.

They flamed in draperies of fire bordered by shining orphreys, and flowers of fabulous gems flashed upon the moving fire of their robes. Then suddenly all bowed; the Virgin advanced, accompanied by a magnificent following of Saints crowned with flaming nimbi. Blessed Mary, dressed simply in white flames, carried gems in the tresses of her hair, whose facets, unknown amongst the jewels of earth, burnt with dazzling light. Any other than Lydwine would have been unable to bear the overpowering brightness. And the Virgin smiled, whilst the Infant Jesus advanced and sitting upon the edge of the bed spoke tenderly to Lydwine.

Suddenly the soul of the Saint was melted with excess of joy; but the Holy Child extended his arms and was transformed into a Man. The face was disfigured; the hollow cheeks were furrowed with livid scars; the crown of thorns rose above the forehead, and red drops ran down from the points; the feet and hands developed wounds, and a bluish halo encircled the feverish marks. Calvary succeeded the stable of Bethlehem without perceptible transition, and Jesus crucified was substituted in an instant for Jesus the Babe.

Lydwine was beatified, ravished and harrowed; ravished to be at last in the presence of the Well-beloved, harrowed that He was martyred in this way;

and she laughed and cried at one and the same time, when the wounds of Christ darted upon her luminous rays, which transpierced her feet, her hands, and her heart.

At the sight of the stigmata she groaned, thinking immediately that men would conceive a better idea of her and show her more deference, and she cried: " Saviour, my GOD, I implore of you, take away these signs, that this may be between you and me; your grace is sufficient for me!"

" Marvellous to relate," says Michel d'Esne, Bishop of Tournai, " a little skin immediately covered these wounds, but the pain and the bruise remained." And indeed, in accordance with her desire, the pain of these divine imprints lasted to the end of her life.

Then the blessed Virgin took respectfully from the hands of the angels the instruments of the Passion, and made Lydwine kiss them one after the other; and immediately her mouth had touched them they vanished away. Then Jesus again changed and became again an infant, but He was always nailed to the Cross, of which the size had diminished with His own stature. Lydwine was fainting with grief, but the Holy Child was transfigured and smiled upon her, so that she cried: "I thank you, my Saviour, that you have condescended to visit your poor servant!"

Her father, listening in the next room, was curious to know to whom she was speaking and crept to the door. Then Lydwine the young and beautiful wrapped herself again in the chrysalis of horror; the glorious body of the blessed Virgin and her angels vanished; Jesus rose and began to become invisible, when, afflicted at His departure, the Saint cried:

" Saviour, if Thou art truly He whom I believe, prove to me before Thy departure that I am not the victim of an illusion; do not abandon me without leaving me a sure indication that it is Thou and not another who is here!"

At these words Jesus clothed Himself in a new form, and Lydwine perceived floating above her head the Sacred Host. At the same instant a white cloth descended upon her pallet and the Sacred Host gently placed itself there.

Old Pierre, who continued to listen at the door though he understood nothing that was passing, at last entered and sat himself by the side of the bed.

"Kneel, father," said she, "for my Saviour, Jesus crucified, is here."

Stupefied, the father knelt and indeed saw the Sacred Host. He ran to fetch his children and Margaret, Agatha, and Wivina, good women, his neighbours, who were seized with surprise and fear in gazing upon the body of Christ thus fallen from the heavens. All discerned a wafer a little smaller than that supplied for the priests' use and a little larger than that reserved for the faithful; all recognized that the circumference was edged with luminous rays and that in the centre was designed the image of a child crucified, who had bleeding wounds in his feet and hands, and, near his heart, a drop of blood of the size of a small pea. Certain details, however, were only seen by some of them; thus old Pierre and his son William distinguished five wounds and the neighbours could only discover four. One of them, Catherine Simon, noticed that the blood still flowed from the side and the right foot, whilst it seemed to have dried up at the other wounds; and, finally, to the Saint the celestial oblation seemed raised a little in the air, but to the other spectators it appeared to repose upon the cloth.

Although the night was well advanced, William went to rouse the Curé so that he could examine this marvel with his own eyes. He arrived with his hands dirty, says Gerlac, and addressed himself in an arrogant tone to Lydwine:

"Why do you allow me to be disturbed at this hour?"

"Do you not see this miracle?" replied she, showing him the Sacred Host.

"I see only an imposture of the Devil!" cried he.

She assured him that it was not so.

He looked at this apparition of the bread very closely and discovered there, as the other persons present had done, a bleeding body. He was aghast, but recovered his assurance, ordered everyone out of the room, and, shutting the door, tormented Lydwine, adjuring her, by the judgment of GOD, never to speak of this prodigy.

He pressed her and tried to force an oath from her, but though she refused this, she kept silence till the day she was interrogated by the Ordinary.

Lydwine's refusal exasperated him.

"After all," he said, "what do you intend to do with this Host?"

This question embarrassed Lydwine. "If I deliver it over to him," she thought, "he is capable of misusing it; if I keep it, Jesus will no doubt depart from it." She reflected, and a sudden inspiration decided her.

"I beg that you will communicate me with it," she said.

"How, you ask to be communicated with the Devil."

"No," she said sweetly, "it is not Satan, but truly my Saviour Jesus who is hidden under the aspect of this bread, which I implore you to give me."

"If you insist absolutely on receiving the Sacrament, I will go and fetch a Host from the tabernacle in the church, for I have no idea where this one comes from, and once more I counsel you not to put your faith in this."

Finally, understanding that she would not yield, he inserted it into her mouth, murmuring: "Accept this fraud of the Demon, but may it operate on you according to your faith."

Lydwine swallowed it without difficulty, and, like

the other consecrated wafers, it entered into her soul and quickened it.

Dom André left her lost in her ecstasy and returned home irritated and unquiet.

The next day, which was the vigil of S. Thomas, he brooded over his adventure, and, fearing that it would be noised abroad in the town, he resolved to be beforehand. When the faithful were assembled in the church, he mounted the pulpit and said:

"Dear brethren, Lydwine, the daughter of Pierre, whose intelligence is weakened by illness, was snared last night by the Malicious One; the temptation was at once subtle and perilous; I ask you to pray for her, and to recite an 'Our Father' on her behalf."

At the moment of entering the Saint's house, he turned to the spectators, whose number had greatly increased, and said:—

"Know you that the Evil Spirit has insinuated himself into this dwelling. He has deposited with Lydwine, assuring her that it contained the Lord's body, an empty species, a simple round of wheaten bread. I can assure you of this and I am willing to be burnt alive if I lie; but if this Host was a fiction, that which I bring to her is not. Jesus Christ is there present, for it has been transubstantiated by the power of the priest. If then any should talk of what occurred last night in this dwelling, let him attribute these acts to the malice of the Evil One, who, the better to deceive us, transforms himself sometimes into an angel of light. That she may the better resist his illusions, I concede to her the Holy Eucharist, and do you of your charity pray for her."

So saying he saluted the faithful and entered the sick woman's house with his head erect.

Lydwine had heard all. She received Dom André with her habitual gentleness, but exclaimed:

"O Father, you did not give the facts accurately; I have not been seduced by a snare of the Devil, and who should know that better than yourself, since I warned you beforehand that GOD had prepared this grace for me? Did you not also observe that I absorbed the wafer without the smallest difficulty, whilst the smallest crumb of ordinary bread would have choked me! Also, are you not my confessor, from whom I have nothing secret? Do you indeed consider me a daughter of perdition?"

She was silent, then resumed:

"Nevertheless, I will pray to the Lord that He may not impute this to you for sin."

He was beside himself with rage, and cried: "Am I to communicate you or not?"

She replied that he must do as he wished, and he communicated her.

But whilst this strange priest flattered himself that he had got himself out of a difficulty in persuading his parishioners that he had acted mercifully in succouring one possessed, Lydwine's friends did not hesitate to tell all who wished to hear of the miracle which they had witnessed. They were reasonable people and pious, and one would judge them incapable of lying. There was a general movement in Schiedam against this Curé, whose dishonesty was but too well known. Trembling before the angry crowd at his door, he took refuge in the church, where he felt himself protected by ecclesiastical immunity, and the magistrates, frightened by this rising of the populace, hastened to join him there.

"Be open with us," they said, "confess the truth, so that we may be able to quiet this rabble which opposes you."

"But," replied he, "the truth is that which I proclaimed this morning when I announced to the faithful that the so-called favour of which Lydwine boasts was a lie and an execrable temptation: I have nothing to add."

"Well," asked one of the burgomasters, "but where is this Host?"

He did not dare own that he had yielded it to the Saint, and he replied: " I no longer have it."

" And what have you done with it ? "

He lied once more, declaring that he had destroyed it.

" Where? In what place? Show us the ashes that we may examine them."

Dom André refused, and being unable to get any more out of him, the magistrates withdrew.

However, as the tumult increased and the fury of the populace became more and more menacing, they returned a second time to the church and resumed their interrogations.

The Curé was disconcerted and contradicted himself. Importuned with questions, he replied that he had got rid of the diabolical wafer by drowning it.

They pressed him further and wished to know the place, the receptacle in which he had immersed it.

Quite distracted and losing his head, he stammered: " I have put it down a sewer, so as to prevent people from being guilty, through it, of the crime of idolatry."

When the crowd learnt that he had buried in a sewer a Host reputed miraculous by people worthy of faith, it raged and was ready to tear this wicked priest in pieces as soon as he should emerge from his refuge.

The burgomasters, more and more uneasy at the turn events were taking, returned a third time and implored the Curé no longer to mock them with his lies.

" Reflect," they said, " and beware, for the indignation against you is such that were you to leave this refuge we could not be answerable for your life."

Dom André hung his head, but it was impossible to extract a word from him.

Then the magistrates, after a consultation, determined to have recourse to the Bishop and despatched a messenger to beg him to come to Schiedam and restore order. Heaven had already warned Monseigneur

Mathias, assistant bishop of Utrecht, in whose jurisdiction lay the parish of Schiedam, that his presence
was necessary. He set out in great haste, accompanied
by his vicars general and by the judges of the diocese.
The Curé heard of this and the little assurance which
remained to him fled.   Fearing to leave the church, he
sent a friend to implore Lydwine to have pity on him.

"I know that I have been at fault," he pleaded,
"but your charity reassures me; do not, I implore
you, charge me before the tribunal, but minimize the
importance of the charges laid against me as much as
possible.   I will not conceal from you that without you
I am lost."

Good Lydwine promised, on condition that he
understood that she could not falsify the truth, to
make light of the accusations brought against him,
and, in any case, to ask the prelate to deal gently with
him.

The Bishop and his suite arrived at the Saint's house,
bringing with them the weeping Curé.   Then the
miracle became the subject of a canonical examination
and the witnesses against Dom André were heard; but
when it came to Lydwine's turn, she expressed the
desire that, out of respect for the sacerdotal character
of the accused, the laymen should be ordered to retire.
They acquiesced; but, before replying to any precise
questions which might be put, she said:

"Monseigneur Bishop, I implore of your grandeur
two graces."

"Speak,   my   daughter,"   replied   Monseigneur
Mathias, "speak with confidence, I will grant you
anything that does not pervert the spirit of justice."

"I implore then first," she said, "liberty to express
myself; my pastor has in some sort bound himself to
me, in spite of myself, by a promise that I cannot break
without your permission; I beg you, therefore, to be
clement and not to strike either his person or his
goods."

The Bishop released her from an oath to which she

had not indeed consented, and promised on the second point that he would consider her recommendation.

Then she related in every detail the miracle of the Sacrament. "The sight of the Host descended on my couch aroused in me," she said, "the desire to consume it; and I asked that Dom André should communicate me with it. He consented; but if he sinned in that by his good nature, I am alone guilty, and it is only right, Monseigneur, that I should conjure you by the love of GOD to spare him."

What sentence was finally passed? The biographers tell us that there was none, but that the Bishop consecrated for the service of the altar the cloth on which the Host had reposed; and that they ended this incident by praising Lydwine for having been so lenient towards a priest whom they pronounced to be harder than Nabal and more cruel than Lamia.

Anyhow, it is certain that this wretch was not sent back to his convent. He remained Curé of Schiedam and dispensed the Holy Eucharist to Lydwine in future without much grumbling; but he did it, no doubt, more through fear of exciting new trouble than from a sense of duty, for he did not mend his ways, and became neither less grudging nor more charitable to the poor than heretofore. Moreover, he made a bad end.

At the time when the plague broke out at Schiedam, Lydwine, as we have noted above, was attacked by it and prayed the Curé to bring her the Viaticum. He came trembling, for he anticipated death, and from fear of contagion he shut his mouth and stopped up his nose.

Lydwine saw this, and said to him:

"It is all right, Father, my ill is not one of those communicated by smell or by taste; it is, indeed, not of human origin."

Dom André was at first silent and confused. Then, feigning a courage which he had not, he cried: "Please GOD, Lydwine, I shall live to assist at your death!"

"You will not assist at it," replied the Saint

gravely; " it is I who will see yours, and, since we are on this subject, listen to me.   Put your affairs in order as quickly as possible; be ready to appear before GOD."

He frowned and as usual laughed at her; but some days after he fell ill, and recalling the prediction of his penitent, he deputed someone near her to ask her pardon for his railleries.

" I pardon him with all my heart," replied Lydwine, " but do not let him deceive himself; he is condemned. Tell him to confess himself and make restitution without delay of those goods he has misappropriated, for death is at his heels."

At the word restitution, when it was repeated to him, Dom André had a fit of rage and sent to declare tc the Saint that he had nothing with which to reproach himself, as he had never taken anything unjustly.

She was alarmed at the obstinacy and blindness of the priest, but nevertheless, made one more attempt to save him.   She called a person of confidence, specified the objects stolen formerly by this man, and despatched him to invite the sinner to restore them; but this request only infuriated him, and he died with foam on his lips in an access of anger against the Saint.

CHAPTER VIII.

THE successor of Dom André in the curacy of Schiedam was another Premontarian from the same monastery in the island of Saint Marie, Jan Angeli of Dordrecht, or Jan the son of Angeli, as à Kempis calls him. He was a debauched creature, not less ignorant than his predecessor of the phenomena of mystic asceticism, but he had a good heart and was charitable and complaisant.

At first he knew nothing of Lydwine's case, but amongst his penitents was a young girl who was very devoted to the Saint. They talked often of her and he could not but wonder what pleasure this young girl found in staying for hours near a bedridden creature whose appearance filled him personally with disgust.

One day he wished to clear up the mystery and questioned her.

As she was very shy, she did not dare to answer him at first; but presently, worried by his insistence, she could not avoid crying out: " If any one has the right to be astonished, it is I, Father, for after all, you are her confessor. How is it you have never felt anything of what I feel every time I approach her? "

" Bah! " exclaimed Jan Angeli. " What is it you feel that is so extraordinary when you are in her presence? "

" I do not know; I cannot explain it. I feel as though I were no longer here below when she is near. I cannot explain myself, but this I can assure you, if you knew her soul you would visit her more frequently."

" I'll be hanged if I understand a word of what you are saying! "

" Well, Father, you have to go to her to-morrow to

confess her, look at her hand and perhaps then you will understand."

The Curé went indeed to Lydwine's house the next day, and his first care was to try and catch sight of the Saint's hand, but it was buried under the blankets, because she had not, as she usually did, put on her glove. The truth was that if he had examined the palm of her hand very closely, he would have discovered the bruise of the stigmata; but she had never spoken to anyone of those imprints.

Only one woman, the widow Catherine Simon, had noticed them and had pressed Lydwine with questions, but she, neither wishing to own the truth nor to lie had kept silence. Once, however, when hard pressed, she had exclaimed while joyously squeezing her friend's hand: "Oh head, oh head"—which meant, according to Brugman, "Silence, my secret is my own!"

Anyhow, she did her best to conceal her left hand, the only one of which she could make use; but what she could not succeed in hiding was the pervading perfume of spices which arose from it.

This was, according to Gerlac, perceptible to the taste, and when one breathed it, one also tasted in some sort the celestial dainties which the perfume recalled. It was like a precious and fleeting taste of wine, the feverish scent of wallflowers, the pungent warmth of ginger, or, above all, the fragrant smell of cinnamon.

Resolved not to leave without having satisfied his curiosity, Dom Angeli said:

"Dear mother Lydwine, please give me your hand."

From obedience she stretched it out to him and the room was perfumed.

"Ah," cried he, "why have you never revealed to me that you had at your disposal the lost odours of Eden? How did I not myself discover, when I confessed you, that you were one of those souls whom Jesus loves to fill with his graces!"

"Recall the conversations we have had, Father,"

replied Lydwine. " I have often hinted that my pains were only the counterparts of my joys, and if you did not better divine my meaning it was doubtless because GOD so desired."

He exclaimed: " Your words have been for me like roses offered to a pig!"

And he was honest in thus abusing himself, for this odour which flowed from the sick woman's fingers not only reached his smell and his taste, but also penetrated to his innermost consciousness and stirred up remorse for his horrible sins. He could no longer bear it, but sighed and burst into tears, saying:

" Listen to me; I feel that the Saviour orders me to confide in you; I have committed transgressions without name, horrible sins."

He threw himself on his knees, but, seized with shame and frightened at the foulness of his confessions, he dared not complete the list of self-accusations, and became silent.

At first Lydwine was horrified at this scene, but quickly perceiving that she alone had enough influence over this unhappy being to reform him, she examined his soul to its very depths and extracted a sin which he had concealed.

" Let us see," said she, " do you not commit this sin of adultery frequently?"

Trembling with shame, he denied it, swearing that he did not.

The Saint appeared to believe him and did not insist.

He left her, worried by his lie, and after a time returned.

" Why have you lied?" she said roughly to him. " I have seen you since our conversation, on such a day, at such an hour, and such a place, again alone with this woman. Is this true?"

" Who has been able to reveal my misdeeds to you?" he cried in confusion, and choked by his tears he left the room and took refuge in the little garden attached to the house, to weep at his ease.

When he was relieved he came in and promised Lydwine to amend his ways.

After that he really loved Lydwine, and she was not, as we shall see, ungrateful.

This Jan Angeli, who was not for very long Curé of Schiedam, and seems indeed only to have held the post temporarily, was a mere passer-by in Lydwine's life. Another priest, a holy man this time, Jan Walter of Leyden, was more especially designed by Providence to exhort her.

Who was this Walter, whose three step-sisters were friends and nurses of the Saint? Was he attached to, or chaplain of one of the convents in the town? Did he belong to that order of the sons of S. Norbert, who administered the parish in those days? I do not know. Historians tell us of the death of Dom André, which took place in 1426, but they are as silent about his successor as if he had never existed.

On the other hand, did Walter fill the post which Jan Pot had filled towards Lydwine in the days of Dom André? Yes, Gerlac expressly affirms that he did. As Lydwine died in 1433, one can compute that he began to exercise his ministry towards her in 1425, for Brugman attests that he was her confessor for the last eight years of her life. He thus overlapped Dom André by one year only, since Dom André died, as we have just said, in 1426.

What we can be quite sure of is that this sacerdotal hatred, which had so tortured Lydwine, ceased with the death of Dom André. She could receive the consolation of the altar as often as the needs of her soul required. At one time Jan Angeli and Jan Walter accorded it her every other day; but sometimes the quinsy from which she suffered and the fevers which devoured her so dried her mouth and contracted her throat, that they had to pour a little water between her lips to enable her to swallow the Host; and the effort of deglutition which she had to make was so painful that she nearly fainted.

GOD then spared her further torments from bad priests. Certainly many crowded round her, but to these she owed no obedience and they had not the right either to annoy her or to command her.

She had, besides, enough tortures without that, for her ills increased continually.

No part of her body was whole; her head, neck, chest, stomach, back, and legs decomposed, and day and night wrung cries from her. Only her feet and her hands remained almost intact, and they were devoured by the dull fire of the stigmata. One of her eyes which was not quite dead but could not tolerate any light, became still more tender and bled even in the half light. They had to hide her behind curtains, groaning and motionless; and when they tried to move her to change the linen, her wounds became inflamed by the rough spiked ends of the straw.

She was no longer able to look out of the narrow window opposite her bed and see those charming skies of the Low Countries, those heavens of a marvellously tender blue, on which float knots of silver and flakes of golden vapour. The shadows of the passers-by, the boughs of the trees shaken by the wind, the masts of barques sailing on the neighbouring canals; all these signs of life which, moving before her window-panes, had served at times to distract her, were lost to the half-blind creature which she had now become.

In the winter, too, when the sky, heavy with snow, seemed to rest on the eaves of the houses, or, on rainy days, blurred the outlines of the buildings, she had still been able to enjoy that cheery gaiety within the houses of the poor which is so typical of Holland. In her more peaceful moments she had found distraction in the cheerful fireside, in the great chimney, which the cold had brought to life again, with its shining hook on which the singing kettle swung in a cloud of blue smoke. On the sooty firebacks the crackling sparks clung and the twigs of vine and white wood ash fell, whilst under the mantelpiece, which projected into the room, and near the pokers which lay on the tiles of the hearth, the high iron fire-dogs, on their standards with rounded ends fashioned like baskets, supported the dishes placed there to be kept hot.   The flickering fire lighted up the cinders, the copper kettles, and the cauldrons, and flashed upon the utensils hanging on the wall—spoons, long two-pronged forks, frying-pans and strainers, spits and grills and graters, all the utensils that figured in the humblest houses in those days.

This little amusement of watching the ashes, the hide-and-seek of the flames reflected on the rounded flanks of the vessels, the clouds framed in the leaded tracery of the window-panes, all those trifling things which occupy the mind of a sick person and distract it for a moment or two, were for the future denied her. When she emerged from her divine inebriety it was darkness that met her gaze, for the sight of a glowing coal would have pierced her eye like a point of red-hot metal, and the meals for the little household had, therefore, to be prepared in another room, which for her meant a great deprivation.   This low, damp room in which she lay in perpetual night would have moved anyone but her to suicide.   She was already buried in a tomb, and yet she had not the compensation of solitude, for the curious continued to flock around her.

Whether these visits were abusive or simply idle, they crucified her, for they deprived her of those of the angels with whom she lived as a sister.

At what moment did she enter into close relation with these pure Spirits?   It is impossible to tell, for, according to her biographers, she did not confide her secrets even to those most intimate with her.   Neither can we follow, as we can with others of the elect, each step of her progress in the mystic way, for no chronology of the graces which were imparted to her exists, and it can only be affirmed that when she suffered too much GOD sent His angels to console her. She talked with them as with elder brothers, and when, to prove her, Jesus withdrew Himself from her, she called to them, weeping: "Where is He? How can He afflict me and not have pity upon me; He who has so insisted that I should be merciful to my neighbours? I shall never act towards them as He is acting towards me. Ah! if I exercised towards Him the power of attraction which He exercises over me, I should draw Him to my arms, I should cause Him to penetrate to the bottom of my heart, or rather I should penetrate His and entirely submerge myself therein."

She implored them to go and seek Him, to bring Him to her at all costs, and would end by weeping and crying: "I am mad, I do not know what I say."

Then the angels comforted her, and smiling, brought back the Divine Spouse to her side.

Whilst her contemporary, S. Françoise de Romaine, saw the angels chiefly under the aspect of children with golden hair, Lydwine saw them under the form of adolescents marked on the forehead with a resplendent cross so that she could distinguish them from demons, who are forbidden, when personating angels of light, to display this sign. But her angel was less vigorous than that of the Italian Saint, who boxed her ears in public when she committed the smallest fault. Lydwine's simply left her and only returned when she had been shriven, thus making her understand that it is impossible to converse with men or with women, even when animated by the best intentions, without falling into some imperfection, or, at least, uttering an indiscreet word; and that though conversations have sometimes some good in them, silence is always better.

This flight of her celestial confidants, when people were with her, caused her most passionate grief.

One fête day, at mid-day, she begged her confessor and one of her relations called Nicholas, who had been dining in the house after Mass, to leave her alone for the space of three hours that she might rest. Nicholas went for a walk, but the confessor—whose name the biographers omit—returned secretly to the house and stayed watching behind the door of Lydwine's room. The guardian angel, whom the Saint expected, appeared, but contented himself with hovering about the bed without approaching her. She asked him if she had been guilty of any sin.

"No," he replied, "if I leave you it is because of him who spies upon you there behind the door."

Lydwine began to sob.

Puzzled by the noise of her complaints, the priest came out of his hiding place and confessed his fault; but when she saw that it was her confessor who had annoyed her good angel in this way, she wept yet more bitterly.

"Ah! Father," said she, "why do you act thus towards me? You must doubt my honesty, since you wish to verify for yourself what I tell you."

These relations with the pure Spirits that she wished to keep concealed were noised abroad, for certain facts could not escape being known, especially those which took place before witnesses.

Every year, on the Wednesday after Quinquagesima Sunday, Jan Walter brought the ashes. Now, one year he could not get to her at the hour arranged, and while Lydwine was wondering if he were indisposed or had forgotten, an angel appeared and shrived her in his place.

"It is done," she said when Walter arrived at last, my brother angel has been before you."

Walter opened his eyes in surprise, thinking his penitent mad, but on leaning over her he distinguished a cross of dust very clearly traced on her forehead, and he approached his own to it, in order to bless himself also with this powder of palm consumed in Eden.

"How happy you are, dear Lydwine!" he cried, clasping his hands; and she smiled, telling him that after the ceremony her angel had declared that in such cases the faithful would do well to present themselves at the altar with a lighted candle, in order to affirm their faith by the wax, their charity by the flame, and their mortification by the Cross.

Another day a pious widow, who nursed her and was aware that the angels revealed themselves to her friend under a visible form, begged that she would show her one.

Lydwine being grateful to this woman, who was very probably widow Catherine Simon, for many kindly offices, implored the Lord, and, after being assured that her prayer was granted, said to the widow:

"Kneel down, my dearest, here is the angel whom you desire to know."

And the angel appeared in the room under the form of a young boy whose dress was woven of threads of white fire. This woman was so enchanted that she was unable to utter a single word to express her joy.

Then Lydwine, rejoiced to see her so happy, asked:

"My brother, will you authorize my sister to contemplate the splendour of your eyes, if only for a moment?"

And the angel looked at her, and the woman was so taken out of herself that for some time she continued to groan and weep for love, without being able to sleep or eat.

Lydwine sometimes said to her intimates: "I know no affliction, no discomfort that a single look from my angel does not dissipate; his look acts on grief like a ray of sun on the dew of the morning, dissipating it altogether. Think then with what joy the Creator fills His elect in heaven, since the least sight of His angels avails to disperse all ills and to plunge us into jubilation which surpasses by a great deal all that we can expect here below."

Then she added: "We ought to love and venerate these pure Spirits who, although very superior to us, consent to protect and serve us"; and she gave an example to her friends by reciting before them this prayer:

"Angel of GOD and well-beloved brother, I trust

H

myself to your beneficence and implore you humbly to
intercede for me with my Spouse, so that He may
forgive me my sins, strengthen me in well-doing, help
me by His grace to correct my faults, and lead me to
Paradise, there to taste the fruition of His presence
and to possess eternal life.   Amen.''

This guardian angel, whom she thus besought, was
pleased to come and lead her, in spirit, for a walk.

Gerlac, who lived near her, noted that when the
soul left its carnal sheath for the first time, Lydwine
suffered terrible anguish.   She was suffocated and
thought herself dying; and when the soul had left the
body it became cold and insensible, like a corpse.

But, little by little, she accustomed herself to this
detachment from her shell, and it was afterwards
effected without her feeling it.

The route followed on these excursions was usually
as follows: The angel stopped first before the altar of
the Virgin in the parish church, then he guided her into
the festal gardens of Eden, or, more often still, into
the horrible wastes of Purgatory.

She wished to visit the souls detained in these sad
prisons, for no one was more devoted to these souls
than she; she wished, at any cost, to diminish their
torments, to shorten their captivity, to change their
misery into glory; and thus, although each of these
voyages caused her incomparable tortures, she
willingly followed her companion when he led her to
this terrible waiting-place.

There she perceived souls tortured in the centre of
storms of fire, and she passed through this whirlwind
of flame when the angel showed her this means of
relieving them.   GOD allowed her to see with her own
eyes the pains inflicted on certain of these tortured
ones; and she saw them, as did S. Françoise de
Romaine, under a bodily form, roasted on brasiers,
heaped up on a red-hot grid, torn with bronze combs,
transfixed with spits of red-hot metal.

'' Whose is that soul that endures this frightful

martyrdom?" she asked one day, turning in consternation to her guide.

"It is the brother of that woman who has recently asked your prayers; ask that it may be relieved and it will be."

Lydwine hastened to follow this advice, and the soul was withdrawn from that particular prison to another less terrible one, common to all souls which had not to be purged of any special sin.

When she had come back from this voyage, the sister of the dead man worried her to know her brother's fate. Lydwine was embarrassed and said: "If I told you what I know, you would lose your head." But the woman assured her that she would not be troubled by it, so the Saint told her of her brother's change of gaol, and added: "To liberate him completely you must renounce those delicate dishes you are so fond of. You are preparing for your meal a capon, but you should deprive yourself of it and give it to the poor."

The woman followed her advice, and at dawn the next day she caught sight of a troop of demons, one of whom, after having seized the capon, boxed her ears with it and Lydwine's also. She was horribly afraid, but GOD saw fit to add to her trials such violent pain that the wretched woman cried for mercy. Then Lydwine interceded with the Saviour, bore the rest of the trial in her place, and the soul was at last released.

Another time, during the night of the feast of the Conversion of S. Paul, Lydwine saw in a dream a man unknown to her who was trying to scale a mountain, but fell back at each effort. Suddenly he perceived the Saint and said to her: "Have pity on me, carry me to the top of this mountain." She put him on her shoulders and climbed painfully to the summit, where she enquired his name. He replied, "I am called Baudouin du Champ"; and thereupon she awoke.

Her confessor, having come to ask after her in the morning, remarked that she could hardly breathe and was exhausted with fatigue. As he was distressed at her condition, she told him her vision of the night.

"Baudouin du Champ?" said the priest. "The name seems familiar to me, but I cannot remember where I have heard it." Now three days after, having gone to celebrate Mass at Ouderschie, a village about two kilometres from Schiedam, he learnt that the sacristan was called Baudouin du Champ, and that he had died the very night he had appeared to Lydwine.

She was consumed with anguish for these souls and sought on all sides to procure Masses for them, praying, "Saviour, chastise me, but spare them!" and Jesus listened to her and bruised her under the millstone of her woes.

She was besieged also with supplications by those condemned souls beyond the tomb; especially by the souls of bad priests, who surrounded her sleeping and waking, and drew upon her an avalanche of torments!

These, after their death, were the most assiduous of her tormentors.

One of them called Pierre, whose life had been a sink of iniquity, had repented, but had died before he could expiate his faults on earth. Lydwine, under whose exhortations he had been converted, prayed very often for his soul, of whose end she was ignorant. Now twelve years after the death of this ecclesiastic, whilst she was still imploring divine mercy for him, her angel led her to Purgatory, where she heard a lamentable voice which cried for help from the bottom of a well.

"It is the soul of that abbé for whom you have addressed so many petitions to the Lord."

She was horrified to know that he was still in that gehenna.

"Will you suffer to save him?" proposed the angel.

"Yes, certainly," she exclaimed.

Then he conducted her to a torrent which poured down a ravine, and commanded her to cross it, but she recoiled, deafened by the noise of the waters and frightened by the depth of the abyss. She panted, seized with giddiness, and could hardly keep from fainting; but her guide comforted her, and at length she threw herself into the gulf, rolled in the seething waves, clung to the edges of the rocks, and finally reached the other shore, whereupon the soul of her protégé bounded from the well and flew all white to heaven.

In the same manner she delivered that miserable Angeli, who had been carried off in a few days by the plague at Schiedam.

As we have said, this priest, after having confessed himself with tears to Lydwine, had left her, full of firm resolutions, but soon fell a victim again to his sensual desires. Lydwine begged him to change his mode of existence, to separate from this woman who led him into evil, and he promised, but was so feeble that he could not resist. At last the Saint's earnest entreaties succeeded in drawing him from his vice, but he was attacked by the plague eight weeks afterwards.

He dragged himself to Lydwine's house and asked her if he ought to prepare himself for death by extreme unction.

" Yes," she said.

He hesitated and waited; but feeling still worse, and being now unable to leave his bed, he sent a messenger, who repeated the question. This time she replied that he should swallow a little beer and bread; if he could retain them for the space of an hour he would not die, but if not . . . . . . He followed this prescription, and during three-quarters of an hour felt no nausea. He thought himself already cured, when, as the hour struck, vomiting began.

He called a priest in haste, received the last Sacraments, and died on the day of the Nativity of the Blessed Virgin.

Lydwine, who was uneasy about his soul, prayed

without ceasing, inflicted on herself severe tortures, and endeavoured by all the means in her power to buy him back.

Finally she asked her angel where he was, and by way of reply he led her into a most horrible place.

" Is it Hell? " she asked, trembling.

" No, it is the district of Purgatory which is near to it. Hell is there; are you curious to visit it? "

"Oh no!" she exclaimed, frightened by the howlings, the noise of blows, the clank of chains, the crackling of fire which she heard behind the immense black walls, stretching like a curtain of soot. Her companion did not insist, but continued to walk with her in the domain of the souls who had stopped half-way there.

A well, on the edge of which an angel was sadly seated, arrested her attention. " Who is it? " she said.

" It is the guardian angel of Jan Angeli; the soul of your former confessor is imprisoned in this well, see "—and her guide raised the lid. She recognized her friend's voice and called to him. He emerged on fire, throwing out sparks like metal at white heat, and, with a hardly audible voice, he named her, as was his custom when alive, " my dear mother Lydwine," and implored her to save him.

This soul on fire, this inarticulate voice, so upset her that her cincture of hair burst, and she came to herself.

" Ah! " said she to the women who were watching and were astonished to see her shuddering and depressed, " ah! believe me, it is only the love of GOD which could induce me to descend into such horror; without that, I should never consent to look upon such terrible scenes! "

On another day a good priest, showing her a vessel full of mustard seed, said: " Indeed, I should be happy not to undergo more years of Purgatory than there are seeds in that pot! "

" What is that you are saying! " she cried. " Do you not then believe in the mercy of the Messiah? If you knew what the torments of that place were, you would not speak like that!''

Now this ecclesiastic died some time after and several persons, who had been present at this conversation, enquired of Lydwine for news of his fate.

'' He is well,'' she said, '' because he was a worthy priest; but it would have been better for him if he had had a firmer faith in the virtue of the Passion of Christ, and if he had had during his life a greater fear of Purgatory!''

Meanwhile, she knew so well how to apply the merits of her sufferings to the unfortunate Angeli, that she succeeded in delivering him.

She was consulted from far and near as to the destiny of dead persons, but frequently refused to reply.

'' You are very reserved, and make a great favour of it,'' said one woman to her; ''I myself have often talked before his death with a Saint who did not make such a fuss about informing people.''

'' That is possible,'' said Lydwine.   '' It is not for me to judge if the Saint did right or wrong in acting thus.''   And at the same instant her angel instructed her that the so-called Saint was suffering in Purgatory for the very reason that he had intermeddled in things which did not concern him.

It was necessary that she should be truly instructed by the Saviour before she concerned herself with such questions, since it was so much worse for the indiscreet if the answers, instead of consoling, alarmed them. This happened to the Countess of Holland after the decease of William, her husband.   Rumour reported that Lydwine had been dead some three days, but had just been resuscitated and had brought back news of the Count from the other world, saying that he was enjoying the endless bliss of the just.

The Countess immediately sent one of her officers to Schiedam.

" You may well believe," said Lydwine to him, a little troubled by this message, " that if I had been dead three days I should at this hour be entombed. As to the soul of your prince, permit me to point out to you that if it had entered directly into heaven, I, who have been sick so many years, should perhaps have the right to be surprised and to weep at the length of my exile, whereas I now make no complaint."

On another occasion, to uproot the evil instincts of a sinful priest, she obtained leave from Heaven for him to contemplate Hell. This ecclesiastic, Joannès Berst or de Berst, who had rendered her some little services in connection with some family affairs, frequented the house of a lady, Hasa Goswin, who kept open house and was especially attractive to libertine and gluttonous priests. Lydwine had frequently exhorted him not to set foot again in this evil haunt, but he had never listened to her counsels. When Hasa Goswin died, de Berst returned to see the Saint, and was desirous to know what had become of the woman.

" GOD may grant you grace to see her," said Lydwine sadly.

She prayed, and some days afterwards they both saw Hasa Goswin tortured in frightful fortresses by demons, confined in chains of fire, broken by unspeakable torments in Hell.

Joannès de Berst was terrified and promised Lydwine to change his conduct; but after a time he laughed at this vision, persuaded himself that it was only the result of a nightmare, and continued to go from bad to worse. The Saint reprimanded him seriously, but at last said in despair: " I can no longer turn the justice of GOD from this man "; and he fell suddenly ill and died.

Lydwine, unfortunately, had no Clement Brentano near her, as Sister Catherine Emmerich had, to write down her visions in the rare moments when she consented to speak of them. It is possible, however, with the different details given us by her biographers, to reconstruct the story of her voyages into the territory beyond the tomb.

In truth, her conception of Hell and Purgatory and Heaven is identical with that of all Catholics of her time.

GOD almost always adapts the form of His visions to the comprehension of those for whom they are intended. He takes count of their character, their turn of mind, their habits. He does not change their temperament to render them capable of considering the spectacle which He judges it necessary to show them; on the contrary, He adjusts this spectacle to the temperament of those whom He calls upon to contemplate it; but the Saints whom He favours see these pictures under an aspect inaccessible to the weakness of the senses. They see them intense and luminous in a glorious atmosphere, which words cannot express; and then, of necessity, they belittle and materialise their vision by trying to interpret it in human language and thus reduce it to the level of the crowd.

Such appears to have been the case with Lydwine.

Her visions of Hell and Purgatory, with their dungeons with barred windows, their high, soot-coloured walls, their horrible prisons, their rattling of chains, their suffocating wells, their cries of distress, hardly differ from those of Françoise de Romaine, and we find it thus represented in the statues and pictures of her century.

It is thus portrayed to us on the entries and porches of the cathedrals in their representations of the Last Judgment, it appears on the wood-carvings preserved in our museums, in those of the German, Stephen Lochner, at Cologne, to cite one of the best known.

They are, indeed, the same scenes of torture in the same surroundings; the damned howl or groan, are attached by chains or handcuffs and struck by devils armed with forks, and they roast in castles, whose windows are barred with hot iron. But in these representations of punished malefactors, the artists who only had their own imaginations to rely on, seem to have begun, like Lochner, unconsciously to discover a comic side, which was afterwards developed intentionally—when faith was less lively than in Flanders—by Jerome Bosch and the two Breughel.

As to Paradise, Lydwine sometimes saw it after a Flemish ideal, of which the painters of the fifteenth century made use, under the aspect of a festal hall with magnificent arches ; the viands served on cloths of green silk in basins of gold, and the wine poured into goblets of crystal and gold. Jesus and His Mother were present at these love feasts ; and amongst the elect seated at this table, Lydwine distinguished those who were priests when alive, clothed in sacerdotal vestments and drinking from chalices.

One day, says Brugman, she recognized in one of these companions of Christ, whose chalice was upset, one of her dead brothers, Baudouin, who had been destined from birth by their mother, Petronille, to the priesthood. He had indeed a vocation but had deserted it, for, although a very pious man, he had fallen in love with a woman and married her.

The most habitual conception Lydwine had of Eden was not, however, that of a festival organised in a palace ; it was that of a garden with lawns always green and trees always in flower ; a marvellous garden, in the walks and paths of which the Saints sang of the glory of the Lord in an eternal morning of radiant springtime.

She often ran there, under the guardianship of her angel, who talked and prayed with her and raised her into the air when she could not succeed in making her way amongst the overgrowth of roses and lilies or the dense clumps of trees.

The description of this garden, which her biographers only reveal to us in portions here and there, is narrated at length and shown to us in its entirety in the paintings of artists who were her contemporaries, for instance in the "Adoration of the Lamb" of Van Eyck, which is preserved to-day in one of the chapels of S. Bavon at Ghent.

The central panel of this work represents Paradise itself under the form of an orchard and meadow planted with orange trees in fruit, myrtles in flower, figs and vines; and this demesne extends into the distance, bounded by an horizon pale and luminous, retaining, in full day, the aspect of a sky at dawn, against which rise belfries and gothic towers, the pinnacles and turrets of a celestial Jerusalem, altogether Flemish in conception.

Before us, in the foreground, springs the fountain of life, whose falling jets adorn with white bubbles the great black circles of the basins, and, on each side on the grass starred with daisies, groups of men are assembled, kneeling or standing. On the left are the patriarchs, prophets, and other personages of the Old Testament who prefigured or taught the people of the birth of the Son; sturdy people hardened by preaching in the desert, showing skins tanned by the sun and burnt by the refraction of heat from the sand; all bearded and clothed in dark stuffs draped in long folds; all meditating or re-reading the texts, now verified, of the promises they had announced. On the right kneel the apostles, also sunburnt by all climates and drenched by rains; and behind them stand the popes, the bishops, the abbots of monasteries, the laics, the monks, the personages of the New Alliance, draped in splendid copes dyed with purple and broidered with flourishes of gold; the popes crowned with shining tiaras, the bishops and abbots with golden mitres, sparkling with the interlacing fire of gems. These carry the Cross, rich with enamel and inlaid with jewels, and are either praying or reading those prophesies which they had seen fulfilled during their lives. Except the apostles, who are bearded, all are newly shaven and of white complexion; and those who do not bear the Roman tiara or the mitre have the head encircled with a monastic crown or arrayed in sumptuous fur caps, such as those worn by the rich burghers of Brabant and Flanders at the date of S. Lydwine's sufferings.

In the space left void above them, in the centre of the grass sown with daisies and bordered on the right by a vine, on the left by clusters of gladiolus lilies an altar serves as a pedestal to the Lamb of the Apocalypse, a Lamb from whose breast a stream of blood flows into a chalice placed under His feet and surrounded by a white garland.

Higher still, where the plain ends and the trees begin, two processions, the one above composed of personages of the Old Testament, the other of personages of the Gospels, advance slowly from the dark, almost black, trees, and stop behind the altar in a sort of diffident and fearful joy. On the left, waving palms, are the martyrs, pontiffs and others, with the pontiffs at the head clothed in sparkling mitres and in dalmatics of a dull and sumptuous blue, stiff with embroideries which seem to be hung with pearls like drops of water; on the right, also bearing palms in their hands, are the virgins, whether martyrs or not, and the holy women, their hair loose and crowned with roses, amongst whom in the first rank stand S. Agnes with the lamb, and S. Barbara with the tower, all dressed in light-coloured garments of tender blues, peach flower pink, pale green, tinted lilac, and palest yellow.

One can picture Lydwine mingling with them in these orchards, speaking, as also did her angel, to all these members of the Communion of Saints, admitted as a friend and sister by these elect, who recognized her as one of themselves.

One sees her kneeling with them and adoring the Lamb in this sweet scene, under the festal sky, in the midst of a silence which may be heard, an imperceptible murmur of prayers welling up from these souls at last liberated from their terrestrial prison; and one can easily picture these pure women and young monks, with the faces of young girls, taking pity on the distress of their sister, still chained to her carnal prison, approaching and comforting her, and promising to implore the Saviour to shorten her days.

And some of them—she told her confessor—said, to encourage her to support her ills with patience: "Consider our condition; what remains now of all those torments we suffered on earth for the love of Christ? See the infinite joys which have succeeded our brief tortures!"

When she emerged from her ecstasy and found herself in her poor dwelling on her couch of straw, Lydwine wept for joy at having been so well received by the Saints of Paradise; but despite her resignation, she could not avoid tears of regret at being separated from the Lamb and parted from these friends by the years which she still had to live.

CHAPTER IX.

THESE travels on which her angel conducted Lydwine did not confine themselves entirely to the magnificent or hideous regions of the other world; very often, without making her leave this earth, he led her far away to the countries sanctified by the death of Christ, or else to Rome, that she might visit the seven churches, or even simply to the convents of the Low Country.

Like Sister Catherine Emmerich, she followed in Palestine the footsteps of the Redeemer from the crib of Bethlehem to the Mount of Calvary. There was no place in Judea which she did not know. One day, when her confessor, whom later she obtained permission to take with her, manifested some doubts as to the reality of these excursions, Jesus said to Lydwine:

" Will you come with me to Golgotha ? "

" O Saviour," she cried, " I am ready to accompany you to that mountain and to suffer and die there with you ! "

He then took her with Him, and when she returned to her bed, which corporeally she had never left, they saw ulcers on her lips, wounds on her arms, the marks of thorns on her forehead and of splinters on all her limbs, which exhaled a very pronounced perfume of spices.

On returning home with her, her angel said:

" The Saviour wills that you should carry back with you visible and palpable signs, so that your director may be assured that your excursion to the Holy Land has not been imaginary, but real."

On another journey, when she was climbing behind her guide in a ravine, she sprained her foot, and when she came to herself her foot was indeed dislocated and she suffered with it for a long time.

There was, therefore, also a material side to these wanderings of the spirit, and she did indeed penetrate with her angel into the cloisters when he transported her thither.

Once the prior of the monastery of S. Elizabeth, situated near Brielle in the Island of Doorne, came to see her, and she gave him a description so exact and so detailed of the cells, the chapel, the chapter house, the refectory, the porter's lodge, and all the rooms in the house, that he was astounded.

"But how can you know all this?" he exclaimed, when he had recovered from his stupefaction, "you have never been there!"

"My father," replied she, smiling, "I have been there frequently when I was in ecstasy, and I know all the monks' guardian angels there."

This power, which seems incredible, of duplicating herself, of being simultaneously in two different places, has been accorded before and after her to many other Saints.

Bridget of Ireland, Marie d'Oignies, S. Francis of Assisi, S. Anthony of Padua, all appeared in tangible bodies in two places at once. The Benedictine, Elisabeth de Schonan, although she was in a town sixteen leagues distant, was present at the consecration of a church in Rome; the presence of S. Martin de Porres was vouched for at the same time at Lima and Manilla; S. Pierre Régalet adored the Holy Sacrament in one town, whilst he was praying at the same moment, in the sight and hearing of all the world, in another; S. Joseph de Cupertino talked with different people simultaneously at two different places; S. Francis Xavier did the same on a ship and on a sloop; Marie d'Agréda converted the Indians in Mexico, whilst seated in her own convent in Spain;

Blessed Passidée was present both at Paris and Sienna; Mother Agnés de Jesus visited M. Olier at Paris without leaving her convent at Langeac; Jeanne Bonomi was seen during four days communicating at Jerusalem, although she had not left her abbey at Bassano; Blessed Angelo d'Acri tended a dying person in her own house and preached at the same moment in a church; S. Alphonso of Liguori consoled the last moments of Pope Clement XIV. at Rome, whilst he sojourned in flesh and blood at Avinzo; and the gift of ubiquity was also bestowed on a lay brother of the Redemptorists, Gérard Najella.

This gift of the Lord is not confined to past centuries. It still exists in full strength in our own days. Catherine Emmerich, who died in 1824, is an example of it, and a stigmatized Saint still nearer our own times, for she did not die until 1885, Catherine Putigny, the sister of the Visitation, was seen in two parts of Metz at one and the same time.

The case of Lydwine is thus not an isolated one; neither is it surprising that miracles of another kind abounded in her life, for her relation with the angels continued, and she lived as much with them as with the people who surrounded her.

Evidently she had very close companionship with Saints during her journeys in Eden, but she does not seem, as so many other Saints did, to have kept up relationship with any particular Saint; at least her chroniclers do not tell us of it. Once we hear of her contemplating, more especially in Paradise, S. Paul, S. Francis of Assisi, and the four pre-eminent doctors of the Latin Church, S. Augustin, S. Jerome, S. Ambrose, and S. Gregory. On another occasion we surprise her receiving a visit at her own home from these same four doctors, who urged her to warn Jan Walter to persuade one of his penitents at Ouderschie to have recourse to the bishop or the grand penitentiary of the diocese, in order to obtain absolution for an unconfessed sin which he, personally, was unable to remit; but those are, I believe, the only occasions on which they were specially concerned with her.

Indeed, without neglecting the auxiliary cult of angels and of saints, Lydwine was before all things possessed by the divine Spouse, who, when He did not intervene in person, employed by preference angels rather than Saints to serve as interpreters to her.

This impatience which consumed her to go and rejoin the Well-beloved in heaven, did not prevent her from being the most attentive of women to the things of the earth, the most charitable towards the poor and afflicted.

She was reduced to live on alms and yet she distributed these alms amongst the poor. Condemned never to leave her bed, she charged widow Catherine Simon and other friends to distribute them for her, and recommended them to buy the finest fish and to cook them with tasty sauces, in order to give pleasure to the suffering members of Christ.

Widow Simon, who chiefly occupied herself with these commissions and distributions, acquitted herself of them with such devotion that, after having prayed Jesus to reward her, Lydwine said to her one day, when she returned from the market:

"The Lord is very pleased with you, my dearest; tell me the grace you most long for and I will intercede that it may be granted you."

"If you will obtain for me pardon for my sins and the grace of final perseverance, I would look upon you as the best of sisters and mothers," replied the good woman. "For the rest, I leave it to your charity."

"You don't ask much," said the Saint, smiling. "However, I charge myself to present your supplication, which cannot be displeasing to GOD. As to the rest that you leave to my charity, the Lord will provide. Go you then to church and pray for me."

And this woman, who had entered sad and pre-occupied, left joyously, knowing well that the prayers of her friend would be listened to.

I

At other times widow Simon and her companions contrived, in the interests of the sick woman herself, not to obey her strictly.   Distressed at her condition, they arranged to take toll of the sums she confided to them and to abstract the fraction necessary to supply her wants, but she perceived these friendly deceits and complained.

"I know," she said, "your good intentions, but I wish it had pleased GOD that you should be more docile, for these wretched folk whom you have defrauded will one day be kings in heaven, and it is wanting in the respect due to them to make them wait in this manner."

In other things she was sagacious and far-sighte When she had hoarded a little money in winter, she ᴠalted down meats, and sent them in summer, with ᴜer benediction, to the beggars she relieved.   At other times she offered eggs, beer, butter, bread, and grilled fish, and, when her means permitted, she added a little milk of almonds or wine for the sick children.   This far-sighted charity was rewarded by numerous miracles.

One day, when they had taken from the pot a quarter of salted beef, and divided it into thirty parts, for as many families, the quarter was found intact.

"Well," she said, to her astounded intimates, "what are you astonished at; is it not written in the gospels 'ask and it shall be given you'?"

This miracle was known by the whole town, and wealthy people wished from devotion to taste this dish.

Another day, Lydwine, who manifested a preference for the honest poor and for those who had seen better days and had come down in the world through reverses of fortune, was puzzled to know how she could help certain families.   Her provisions were exhausted, her purse empty, and her protégés literally dying of hunger; so she appealed to the generosity of a good man, who immediately cooked a leg of pork and brought it to her.

This man was truly merciful, for he was himself in want, and he condemned himself, by giving away this joint, to living on bread alone. He was not a little amazed when, returning home, he saw hanging in his kitchen another leg of pork, much larger than the one of which he had deprived himself, although it had been impossible for anyone to have entered his house.

Upon another occasion an epileptic beggar, whose seizures were frequent, strayed down the town, was seized with a fit in the open street and dragged herself, when it had passed off, to Lydwine's dwelling. She was consumed with thirst, and drank all the Saint's reserve of water; but her thirst was not quenched. Remembering that there was a little wine at the bottom of a vessel, Lydwine told her of it and she threw herself upon it, but it was like a drop of liquid on a hot shovel. More and more parched, this woman implored them to discover some kind of drink; but as it was quite impossible to satisfy her thirst, Lydwine gave her a piece of money with which she betook herself joyously to the inn, where she succeeded in extinguishing the fire with draughts of beer.

Some time later the Saint in her fever also wished to drink. Not remembering that the beggar-woman had swallowed her wine, she begged her father to pass the vessel that contained it, and it was immediately filled with an exquisite red wine so well prepared that she did not have to add any water to it. It lasted from the Feast of S. Rémy till the Conception of the Blessed Virgin, that is to say nearly two months; but at that time, widow Simon, who did not know of this miracle, kindly made her friend the present of a jug of wine, which she had chosen from the best to be bought in the village, and poured it into the pot still half full of the celestial wine, so that the flow of this precious cordial was thus dried up.

Some time later the Saint in her fever also wished of indispensable foods; she was always on the watch to see that her clients lacked nothing, and she found money to clothe them.

A priest was pointed out to her, who was in want of clothes, but unfortunately the necessary cloth could not be found in Schiedam. Seeing how troubled she was, a woman who was fond of her said:

"See, I have kept these six yards of black stuff which I have here, to make a dress for my daughter; with a little contriving it could be made to do for the purpose; would you like it?"

Lydwine accepted the present, appeared to measure the stuff, using her mouth and the arm which she was still able to move, and the piece held in her teeth stretched out so that there was more than enough cloth to cut the clothes for the priest and the dress for the girl.

Charity, as she understood it, should extend to all, anticipate want, be active and know no reserve.

One evening, when her confessor and some of his friends were feasting together, a voice was suddenly heard imploring alms. The priest, without hurrying himself, opened the door and saw nothing. He had hardly got back to the table when he heard the same voice again. He went out again and ran into the street, but it was deserted. As for the third time the voice continued to complain, he slipped out another way and ran round to surprise the person who was disturbing him; but it was useless, the street was empty.

Troubled by this episode and convinced that he was the victim of a joke, he went round after dinner with his guests to consult Lydwine.

"O men too slow to listen to the appeal of the poor," exclaimed she, "it was one of your brothers, the angels, crying to you. He came to prove you and to assure himself whether you forgot the Saviour in your merrymakings. I wish to GOD you had guessed who it was!"

This extraordinary charity also inflamed her passion

for suffering, which increased from year to year.   To release her neighbour from his ills and take them on herself seemed to her right and perfectly just; for resolute and pitiless towards herself, she could not see others suffer without wishing to relieve them.

She accomplished without faltering this mission of substitution which the Saviour had confided to her, for they tell us that she took the place of souls in Purgatory, to finish their punishment for them, and offered herself for Holland, for her native town, to expiate its misdeeds by her own chastisement.

At one time a civil war broke out in Schiedam.   As usual, instead of defending the town the peaceful folk fled and left it in great danger of being pillaged by the conquerors; but one of the exiles who had, at the beginning of hostilities, taken refuge in another village, returned, and said to his friends, who implored him not to stay:

"I know well the danger I run, but I know also that Lydwine's prayers will protect me and the town."

These words were repeated to the Saint, who murmured humbly: "I give thanks to GOD, who inspires in simple souls such confidence in the prayers of His little servant."

And she did indeed succeed—GOD alone knows in exchange for what new torments!—in disarming the factions and reconciling the foes.

Another time she had again to intervene with the Saviour to save the town from the destruction which threatened it.

An enemy's fleet, which had already ravaged the seaboard of other provinces, appeared off Schiedam. Lydwine offered herself as a hostage to Jesus, begging Him to turn His anger on her; and, whilst the inhabitants expected to be destroyed, the fleet, in spite of its efforts, and although the wind was in its favour, retreated instead of advancing, and at once disappeared, repulsed in some manner by the prayers of the Saint.

She was thus the lightning conductor for her country; but when she had been crucified for all the community, she wished also to suffer for each individual in it, as the following story shows:

Hearing one morning groanings in the street, she asked an ecclesiastic who was seated by her bed to see who was weeping thus without. "It is one of your friends who is tormented with frightful toothache," said he on returning. Lydwine sent the priest to fetch her, and in the most natural tone proposed to endure the toothache in her place.

"You have enough infirmities," replied the good woman, "without burdening yourself with mine; pray only to Our Lord that He will deliver me from this torture."

Lydwine prayed, and her friend was relieved immediately, but she herself suffered so terribly for twenty-four hours that she could not restrain her cries.

This transference of an ill from one person to another by means of prayer is accompanied by another phenomenon. From the bodily sufferings endured by the Saint emanated health and celestial powers of healing. Virtue went out of her, as is said of Christ in the Gospels; her decay engendered good health for others.

Thus one day a woman whose sick child uttered piercing cries, came and placed him on Lydwine's bed, and immediately his troubles ceased. She smiled at him and praised, in terms he could not yet grasp, the delights of chastity; and he thought over these words when he was older, understood them, and became a priest in memory of her.

In the same manner a merchant in England, who had never heard of the Saint and was afflicted with an incurable disease in his leg, dreamed one night that a voice said to him, "Send someone to Holland, to Schiedam: he will procure some water in which a virgin of the name of Lydwine will have washed her hands; thou wilt apply it to the trouble, and it will vanish away."

He hurried, on awakening, to send a messenger to the Saint; she gave him the water which had been used at her ablutions, and immediately the leg had been steeped in it it was healed.

In all these miracles, Lydwine only had recourse to prayer, and it is probable that, in giving a little water to the Englishman to carry back to his own country, she had prayed for the recovery of the person who was to use it as a lotion. She was indeed more a passive than an active agent; that is to say, she did not act by herself, as did many Saints who cured infirmities with the sign of the Cross or an imposition of hands. She laid their case before GOD, praying Him to hear her, and only played the part of intermediary between the suffering and Jesus.

One single exception to this rule which she appears to have laid down for herself is recorded in her biography, and this was when a woman who was dear to her—widow Simon perhaps—was attacked with a fistula.

Lydwine first begged her to visit the best physicians in the country. They all agreed in declaring that there was no hope of amelioration. Then the Saint had recourse to the Great Physician. She betook herself to prayer, touched the fistula gently with her finger and it disappeared.

Her tireless charity did not confine itself to material acts, to cures, to alms, or even to the substitution of herself to bear the ills of others; she exerted it also in the spiritual domain, and there she once practised mystical substitution of a kind till then unknown, and, I think, unparalleled in the annals of later Saints.

Is not the following fact indeed unique? I content myself with giving it as it occurs in the collected lives of the Bollandists.

A man who was a true rascal was assailed by remorse but did not dare to address himself to a

priest and reveal his life to him.   One day he sought
out Lydwine and, in spite of her resistance, made her
a complete and detailed avowal of his crimes, praying
her to take them on herself and confess them in his
stead.

She accepted this substitution of soul; called a
priest, to whom she confessed the wickednesses of
this man, as if she had herself committed them, and
fulfilled the penance he inflicted.

Some time after the ne'er-do-well returned.

"Now," said he, "that you have confessed my
sins, point out to me what penitence I should practice;
I swear I will execute it."

"I myself have undergone your penance," replied
Lydwine.   "I only ask you for your mortification to
pass one entire night without stirring on your back."

The sinner smiled, thinking the punishment light
and easy.   In the evening he stretched himself in the
position ordered, and resolved, as he had agreed with
the Saint that he would not turn himself either to the
right hand or to the left; but he could not sleep, and
this immobility soon appeared to him insupportable.
Then he reflected and thought: "I complain, and yet
my bed is soft and I have not, like poor Lydwine, my
shoulders resting on straw, and all sore as well.
Moreover, she is innocent, whilst I—!"

Remorse, which had so tormented him, wrung him
anew.   He looked back on his life, bewailed his
misdeeds, reproached himself for cowardice, and when
the day began to break ran to confess himself to a
priest; and this rogue was in future honest, this
impious fellow became pious.

Lydwine's task was at other times less disagree-
able; instead of listening to the avowals of debauched
scoundrels, she received the confidences of good and
simple souls.   Thus an ecclesiastic, with admirable
candour, approached her to be enlightened on the state
of his soul, and of those which his ministry obliged
him to direct.

Lydwine received him pleasantly, but refused to reply to certain questions, which she judged indiscreet. Persuaded that he had displeased her, he went and knelt weeping in the church, before the Altar of Our Lady.

There he fell in a trance—a thing which had never happened to him before—and saw a young girl advancing towards him, accompanied by two angels, who sang the "Salve Regina" and filled him with such joy that his soul would have burst if the ecstasy had not then ended.

As soon as he came to himself, he ran to the house of the Saint.

"Well," she said, when he entered, "fine weather has succeeded rain, father."

Surprised, he cried, "It was you then who walked past me, escorted by two angels, when I was prostrated in the chapel of the Madonna."

She smiled, but was silent.

On another occasion an excellent woman who was tempted by the devil, and after struggling vainly began to depair, was led by her friends to the Saint, who said to her gently, "Be at peace and wait."

Some days after, this woman walked with Lydwine, in the spirit, in a gorgeous palace, and was there so saturated with the most exquisite perfumes that, after her return to earth, even the most delicate odours appeared nauseous to her. But her troubles had evaporated in the celestial waves of those perfumes, and when the Evil Spirit tried again to enter her, she met his assaults without a tremor.

Another such case was that of a woman married to a cruel brute, whose incessant ill-temper found vent in storms of blows. "Patience," repeated Lydwine, when begged to pray that his violence should abate; but the weeks went by, and the wretched woman continued to be beaten at the least word. Tired of this existence, she resolved to hang herself, but some friends discovered this in time and prevented her.

Then she thought of drowning herself in the Meuse and took advantage of a moment when her husband was absent and her intimates were not watching, to run to the river; but on the way she reflected: "Lydwine has always been so kind to me that I do not wish to die without bidding her good-bye," and she turned towards Lydwine's house.

At this instant Lydwine, surrounded by her nurses, exclaimed: "Go quickly and open the door to her who is knocking there, for her heart is breaking!"

And no sooner had the wretched woman entered the Saint's room than she sank on her knees and sobbed.

"Do not think any more of suicide, my dearest," said Lydwine, "but go back home, for the tyrant whom you fear is changed into the most loving of husbands."

Relying on this promise, the woman, after having begged and received the sick woman's blessing, went home.

Her husband was in bed and asleep; she undressed noiselessly, so as not to disturb him, and also went to sleep; and the next morning she found a smiling man, who no longer abused her or knocked her about. "If it only lasts!" thought she; but it did last. This violent fellow became, by a miracle, gentle and pleasing from that time forward.

CHAPTER X.

ALTHOUGH so comprehensive, Lydwine's charity was not of the kind that can be easily duped. The Saint formed her estimate of souls in the twinkling of an eye and did not hesitate, if it seemed necessary, to censure them. It was thus that she treated a woman of Schiedam, who under a devotional exterior hid malicious cunning, imploring alms from charitable families of the town and spending them in gaieties.

Widow Catherine Simon met her one morning in the street and, moved by her petitions but knowing there was no money in the Saint's house, took her to Jan Walter, who was also deceived by her pious jeremiads and helped her. On the next day Lydwine, to whom nobody had mentioned this adventure, said to Catherine:

"This woman has deceived you and my confessor also; be more prudent in future; remember what the Scriptures say: there are people who, under an aspect of humility, conceal hearts full of malice and wickedness. Beware, above all, of believing anyone without enquiry."

She shewed no pity in exposing hypocrites who had the audacity to boast of their virtues before her.

She gave a good rating one day to an intriguing woman, who pretended to be a virgin and affected the manners of an extravagant bigot, although she had relations with a demon.

"You, a virgin, you!" exclaimed the Saint.

"Certainly I am."

"Well, my girl, let me tell you that twenty-five virgins of your sort could easily dance on a pepper

pot," replied Lydwine, thus revealing the duplicity of
this hypocrite, who did not press the matter and left
furious at being exposed.

A young girl who was present was shocked at this
severity, and asked Lydwine why she treated this
virgin so harshly.

"Do not repeat that devil's lie," cried the Saint;
"this woman is as GOD knows her. As to her
pretended piety, you are at liberty to prove it. Go to
this shameless woman and mention to her some one
of her imperfections; if she listens patiently to you
and owns it, it is I who am wrong; if, on the contrary,
at your first words she fumes with rage, you will know
what to think."

This young girl tried the experiment, but was met
by a virago, who loaded her with abuse directly she
spoke to her of her faults.

The unhappy woman died some months after she
had drawn on herself these remonstrances; and when
Lydwine prayed for her, her angel said: "You waste
your time; she is in the abyss from which there is no
escape."

The following misadventure befell a priest, who said
to her one morning: "I must leave you, for I have to
celebrate Mass."

"I forbid you," said Lydwine.

"You forbid me! I am curious indeed to know
why?"

"Have you forgotten the sin against the sixth
commandment which you committed yesterday?"

He was silent and confused.

The Saint added: "Put your affairs in order, for
you will die in three days."

He groaned in fear, imploring her to intercede that
his existence might be prolonged.

"That is impossible," she replied, "for your sin
has been going on too long and the measure is full;
all that I can promise you is to pray fervently for your
salvation."

On the third day this ecclesiastic got up feeling well, and betook himself, triumphant and a little sarcastic, to the Saint's house.

"Well," he said, "do I look like a man who is going to die to-day?"

"Do not trust to an appearance of health," answered Lydwine, "by such an hour you will be no more."

And his death took place indeed as she had predicted.

At another time, she advised a young girl in love with the beauty of her body to change her mode of life as quickly as possible. The girl agreed to do so, but did not keep her word. Soon after she swelled up, and everyone thought her pregnant.

"It is a tumour due to her corruption," sighed Lydwine; and the miserable woman died of tumour, after long sufferings.

If she rebuked men and women of the lower or middle classes, she reprimanded the great with equal frankness. Nobility and riches left her perfectly indifferent, and she spared princes no more than she spared burghers and priests.

One of these, whose name has not been preserved, came from a distant country to consult her on a case of conscience. He lost himself in digressions, and did not dare fully to disclose his shame. Very simply she applied her finger to the wound, and, tortured by remorse, he wept.

"Ah!" she cried, "you weep, Monseigneur, for a sin much less grave than some of which you have been equally guilty: to those you do not even give a thought, so blunted is your conscience!"

And firmly she laid bare his soul to him and there revealed some frightful misdeeds which she begged him to confess without delay. He listened to her advice, and it is as well he did so, for hardly had he returned to his State when he died.

Amongst the visitors, who succeeded each other from morning till night around her bed, figured a large number of ecclesiastics.   Several of the answers which Lydwine gave to the questions put to her have been preserved.

A monk of Citeaux, having been promoted to the episcopate, trembled with fear and did not wish to accept the charge; but before resisting his superiors, he went to consult the Saint.   He was not open with her, but said:

"My dear sister, one of my brothers, thinking he has not sufficient ability, refuses a prelacy which they urge him to accept.   Do you approve?"

Lydwine, who knew very well it was himself who was in question, replied:

"I am very much afraid that the reasons alleged by this brother are only subterfuges; anyhow, he is a monk, and therefore subject to the rule of obedience; if he does not decide to follow that, he may be sure of one thing, that in seeking to avoid a small danger he will run into one much greater."

The Cistercian, only half convinced, went away and finally declined the honours of the episcopate; but this refusal was not of much use to him, for, as he had to confess later GOD made him pass through much worse tribulations than those from which he had resolved to fly.

Other priests and monks who came to see her, belonged to that discontented class of people who are always dissatisfied with their lot in life and sure that some other place would suit them better.   Lydwine had great pity for these restless souls; she tried to cheer them by persuading them that things are not improved by change of one's place, that one's soul is always with one, that there is only one means of subduing it, namely, by subjecting it to obedience, by taking from it all self-assertion, and by confiding it humbly to the keeping of one's abbot and director.   Sometimes she succeeded in bringing them peace, in making them love that cell, which, as the "Imitation" tells us, is truly sweet when rarely quitted, but engenders a mortal weariness in those who often stay away from it.

Others implored her to preserve them from temptations or take away those of others, and among these was a canon of a monastery situated at Schonhovie, about seven leagues from Schiedam. This man doubted his vocation, which, in the opinion of his masters, was certain. The prior, Fr. Nicholas Wit, tried vainly to console him, but neither his advice, nor his objurgations pacified him; and at last the canon determined to unfrock himself. The prior, in despair at this resolution and distressed at the scandal which would result, brought the unfortunate man to the Saint.

She was suffering a martyrdom of pain at the time, and the least noise maddened her, but she consented to see Nicholas Wit on condition that he should come alone.

" Dearly beloved father," she said to him, " I beg you to excuse me if I speak the first word, but I am constrained by my tortures, which prevent my hearing the voices of others, and force me to speak very little myself. The good ecclesiastic whom you have brought with you is sorely pressed by Our Saviour, but assure him his trial will be short; let him not lose courage, and do you, father, continue to sustain him by your prayers."

The prior's astonishment was inexpressible. He did not know what to reply.

Then the Saint said to him: " Farewell, exhort your brother to be very patient and do not forget him before GOD."

And the canon was, indeed, released from his obsessions, as she had predicted.

She excelled in sweeping away scruples and comforting those who were unhappy enough to be led away by the ingenious wiles of the devil.

At Schiedam a woman was the victim of such scruples, and was so disturbed by them that she always lived in a state of confusion, and was ready to fall into despair at any moment. The devil completely deranged her by showing her, during her sleep, a written word of a certain sin, which she had, nevertheless, confessed.

" Thou mayest indeed have received absolution and accomplished the penance imposed, but this sin cannot be forgiven in this world or the next," he cried; " to whichever side thou turnest thyself, thou art damned."

The woman was dying of terror, when an inner voice said to her: " Run to Lydwine." She rushed, like a hunted animal, to the Saint's house and there melted into tears, crying out that she was a lost soul.

"This writ with which the spirit of darkness threatens you is a lie," Lydwine assured her. " I will pray to the Lord to suppress it; be re-assured and do not think of it again."

Directly the woman had gone out, Lydwine begged Heaven to free her from the infernal snare; and at the same moment she was thrown into an ecstasy and saw the Blessed Virgin take the writing from the hands of Satan and destroy it.

When she came to herself, the torn pieces of parchment littered her bed; her confessor, Jan Walter, whom she called in, examined them, and the woman was exonerated.

Another strange history is that of one of the burgomasters of Schiedam. He had for a director a chaplain, who often celebrated Mass before him; Jan Pot, according to Gerlac's account; a curate of the parish, according to Brugman, who omits his name.

I see no serious reasons to prevent our believing that this curate and Jan Pot were identical.

Now the said burgomaster was haunted with the desire to hang himself, and Jan Pot, having exhausted all the means at his disposal to prevent this suicide, had recourse to the Saint.

" It is a question of diabolical temptation," she assured him; " and here is the expedient you should employ.   After having confessed the man, you should impose on him just this penance, that he should hang himself.''

"And if he should do so?"

"He will be careful not to do so; for the Evil One, who incites him to hang himself at the command of an evil inspiration, will never let him kill himself in obedience to GOD; he hates the Sacrament too much for that!"

Although he had great confidence in Lydwine's clear-sightedness, Jan Pot left her in a very doubtful mood.

He preferred to temporise with the monomaniac; but the hour came when he had to make a decision. The man's family constantly had to snatch away the cord which he kept knotting round his neck.   As a last resort, Jan Pot followed Lydwine's instructions. "You will hang yourself in expiation of your sins," he ordered, and the burgomaster returned home delighted.   He hurriedly attached a cord, which he had knotted round his neck, to a beam of the ceiling, climbed on a stool, and was going to cast himself down, when the demons cried, gnashing their teeth, "Do not kill yourself, wretched man, do not kill yourself!"

At the same time one of them broke the rope, whilst another struck him so that he fell between an enormous trunk and the wall; and the blow was so violent that he remained unconscious and crushed for three hours, without being able to lift the trunk and get up.   Finally his relations, who had searched for him everywhere, discovered him half flattened in this narrow place, and when they had drawn him out, he blessed the Lord and swore that he was for ever cured of this madness.

And Brugman, a little disturbed by the manner in which Lydwine handled the situation, adds that comment so dear to Catholics whom a mere nothing will upset: "This is one of those actions which one must admire but on no account imitate."

K

If she was audacious in advice and bold in counsel, she was also singularly humble when constrained to resolve problems which she could not know. GOD then instilled knowledge into her, enlightening her so that she surprised the theologians who would have been glad to confuse her.

One of them, a Dominican professor of theology at Utrecht, tried to do so. He came to Schiedam and, after several feints, said clearly to Lydwine:

" I wish you would explain to me the manner in which the three Persons accomplished the Incarnation of the Word of GOD in the womb of the Blessed Virgin."

Surprised, she did not answer; but the Dominican was firm and said in a commanding tone: " I adjure you, by the judgment of the Living GOD, to reply at once to my demand!"

Lydwine was frightened by this brutal injunction and wept; but as the Dominican, in spite of her tears, insisted with a more and more menacing voice, she wiped her eyes and replied:

" Father, that you may be able to understand my thought, I must have recourse to a comparison. I imagine a solar body from which three rays emanate and re-unite into one only; they are broad at the point of their departure, but the farther they stretch the narrower they become and the closer they draw together, till they end by becoming a fine point. You see already by this picture what my thought is, do you not? Nevertheless, for clearness sake, I will develop it if you wish. By the solar body I mean the Divinity itself; by the three distinct rays which emanate from it, the three Persons; by their stretching out to the same end, the unity of the operation in which the three Hypostases concur; by the extremity of the point, the Word. This point, which penetrates into an interior, signifies then the entry of Jesus into the womb of the blessed Virgin Mary, where he took a part of her blood, so that there were in Him, when clothed upon with flesh, two natures and one only person, the Person of the Son.''

The Dominican was struck with the lucidity of this explanation and left her, convinced that she had been indeed animated by the spirit of GOD.

After this preaching brother, who seems to have been very coarse, it was the turn of a tax gatherer, a vain and grasping man, who came with the intention of submitting captious questions and contradicting her.

He addressed her in a familiar manner:

'' Suppose, Lydwine, you have Our Lord present before you on the altar in the Host placed in the monstrance, and that at the same time you see the same Saviour appear to you in the visible form He wore on earth; to which of the two would you render homage? ''

She was silent and wept; then, whilst this miscreant flattered himself that he had reduced her to silence, she said, in a singularly imposing tone:

'' Learned and venerable persons have sometimes wearied me with specious questions, with the intention of proving me, but I do not remember that they have ever addressed a more shocking proposition to me than that of this tax collector, whose soul only venerates bags of money? ''

Witnesses seated in the room, who were aware the Saint did not know this individual, nor his profession, nor his vice, blushed for him and left, whilst he himself, annoyed at having been thus exposed, went his own way alone.

They also abused her patience, more or less politely. Under the pretext that she was of a benignant character and that her opinion was useful, they came to her for mere nothings, preventing her from suffering at her ease, and constantly disturbing her meditations and her intercourse with angels. This was mere curiosity, to know for example, when the coming of Anti-Christ would take place; or again to consult her on the case of some idle woman who had insinuated herself into the house, as to whether it were better she should work or do nothing.

Lydwine was kind-hearted enough to restrain herself and repeat simply what all the world knows: that idleness is the source of vice, and that since this woman was without fortune but clever at spinning wool, she ought to practice this trade and live honestly by it. She added, however:

"Instead of undertaking this trade in the hope of gaining money, it would be better to undertake it to help the poor; then each time she acquired a bale of fleeces she would reserve one for the Lord's poor, or, if she preferred it, she could reserve for them five pieces of money on the produce of the sale of each piece of her stuff, in memory of the five wounds of Christ. Also she would avoid exploiting the poverty of the work-women whom she employed; she would pay them their earnings exactly, without abusing their work, and I guarantee that GOD would bless her efforts."

The woman followed this advice to the letter, and at first, whilst she remained honest, made considerable profits; but there came a year when she had to sell her goods at a loss, and to recover herself, she defrauded the supplier of fleeces and wools of a gold piece. This merchant, who died soon afterwards, appeared to Lydwine, revealed his client's fraud, and insisted that the sum should be spent in buying candles and ordering Masses for the repose of his soul.

The Saint sent at once for the thief, who, stupefied at finding herself reproached for a theft of which the world knew nothing, satisfied the desires of the deceased and amended her ways.

Sometimes these tiresome folk, who importuned her with their requests, met with amusing disillusions.

"I should be obliged if you asked the Lord to take away from me what most displeases Him."

The Saint undertook to pray with this intention, and

a little while afterwards this canon, who was endowed with a beautiful voice, became voiceless.

He consulted doctors, employed all the gargles and electuaries known in the pharmacopœia of his time; but it was useless. One day when he was present at a new consultation of doctors, one of his companions cried: "Leave it alone; your sedatives and emollients are useless, the magnificent voice of the reverend canon is lost for ever!"

"And why so?"

"Because I was with him when he begged Lydwine to have his most harmful defect taken away from him. Now our friend was not a little vain of the superb resonance of his voice; he is now delivered from this imperfection; the intercession of the Saint has been heard; so much the better."

"And it is probable that this loss aided his spiritual advance," concludes the good Brugman gravely.

One might suppose that after days passed in receiving visitors, days which exhausted her, for, her biographers tell us, that after them her face was all red and bathed with sweat, Lydwine would take breath and rest herself. Not at all; she made use of every free moment, between two audiences, to attend to those who, as her insight showed her, were threatened with danger.

She sent them a messenger or wrote to them to warn them. She acted thus towards a trader whom she loved and prevented from embarking with his comrades on one of the ships leaving for the Baltic.

"But," said the merchant, much upset by this advice, "if I do not set out at the same time as my companions I shall have to undertake this long and perilous voyage alone!" And as, without explaining herself further, Lydwine insisted that he should do as she said, he obeyed sadly, for all his friends rallied him for his credulity. However, the boat had hardly reached the open sea when she was boarded by pirates and sunk, and those of the passengers who were not

drowned were led into captivity.   The Saint's protégé
set out afterwards alone, and returned from his
expedition without having, either on the outward or
return voyage, suffered the least discomfort.

Another time, this gift of double sight which GOD
had accorded her, allowed her to be present, away
from her own home, at the following scene.

One evening, one of the most inveterate drunkards
of Schiedam, a man named Otger, sat down with other
boon companions to drink at one of the taverns of the
town, and his comrades, after having swallowed
copious draughts, were pleased before subsiding under
the table to rail against Lydwine.   According to them,
she feasted in secret and was both a hypocrite and
possessed.   Although he had, like his companions, a
head fuddled with drink, Otger felt indignant and
exclaimed :

" Look here, it would be better to be silent, than to
calumniate a poor sick girl in this way, whom all the
world knows to be pious and charitable ; our habitual
stupidity incites us to commit enough faults without
adding this one."

It irritated them to be called to account like this,
and one of the most violent of the drunkards struck
Otger, crying : " How hast thou, born and nourished
in sin, the audacity to meddle with us ?   Go, scoundrel,
get out of this ! "

" I receive this box on the ear without retaliating,"
said Otger, suddenly sobered.   " I receive it because
it has been given me for having defended the honour
of a Saint " ; and he went out.

Lydwine watched this scene from her bed, and
sending for Jan Walter, told him of it, and said :

" To-morrow morning, father, you will go, as early
as possible, to this good man and speak to him as
follows : " Lydwine thanks you, on behalf of GOD, for
having been struck for her ; and she charges me also
to assure you that you shall be rewarded."

" But," asked Otger of the priest, " how has

Lydwine been able to learn a fact that occurred very late last night and has not yet had time to be spread abroad?"

"Let it suffice for you to be sure that she has learnt it," replied Walter; "have confidence, and you will see that her prophecy will be fulfilled."

This mystery occupied his mind. Otger thought often of the Saint's existence and compared it with his own. Ashamed of his life, which was passed sitting at tables in smoky rooms, amongst bottles and beakers, drinking in the company of fuddlers, whose stupid conversation grew more and more foolish as the wine and beer diminished in the pots, he resolved to break with his old friends and to cease frequenting taverns. This alteration of habit was at first very wearisome to him. He wandered about quite lost; but he had the courage to persevere and to call heaven to his aid; and, helped by the prayers of his friend Lydwine, he died, after many wholesome trials, at peace with GOD.

This faculty, which Lydwine possessed, of seeing at a distance, was at last admitted almost without question at Schiedam, and it was the means of attracting a crowd of intruders, who came in search of her as people now resort to a somnambulist.

We can cite three other instances of this gift of second sight.

The first is connected with a duel. The mother of one of the adversaries bemoaned the event to Lydwine, begging her to pray that her son might not be killed. "Fear nothing," replied the Saint; "the two enemies will embrace; no combat will take place." And truly the reconciliation was effected at the moment she announced it.

The two others concern ecclesiastics.

One morning an Augustinian, a native of Dordrecht, who had some days previously made profession in a convent of canons regular of Eemstein, entered her house on his journey through Schiedam. She saluted him at once by name, and talked to him of his profession, as if she had been present; and when he cried in astonishment:

" How extraordinary!   How do you know me ? " she replied, simply : " By the Lord, my brother! "

Another time a burgher called Wilhelm de Haga wished to have news of his son who had disappeared for several months without leaving any trace.   He had hardly crossed her threshold when she accosted him also by name, and, without waiting for him to question her, said:

" Learn that, by a signal favour of Christ, your son Henri has been received and is going to take the vows at the Chartreuse of Diest."

The good man was astounded and would have liked to know more, so he begged her to tell him the origin of her second sight.

" Pray," said she, " cease your questionings.   I am often forced by charity to distribute the leaves of my tree to my neighbours, but the root does not belong to them and should remain hidden in the ground; be content then with that leaf which I have given you of my own accord and do not ask for more."

These two last facts were confided to Thomas à Kempis by Father Hugo, sub-prior of the monastery of S. Elisabeth near Brielle, who had learnt them himself from persons interested.

One asks how, living among such a crowd of people, the poor girl could withdraw her mind and follow this way of the Cross which she had so strictly laid down for herself.   The truth is, perhaps, that the Holy Spirit spoke by her mouth whilst she was herself absorbed in GOD, far from her assailants ; and that Our Saviour, less severe than his angels, whom these visitors irritated, remained at her side.

Perhaps, also, she did as S. Gertrude did in a like case—feigned sleep or stupor in order to snatch a moment's respite; but her real hours of tranquillity were certainly those of the night.   As she did not sleep and her room was then clear of clients, she was free to escape from herself and seek her divine Spouse, taking from contact with Him a store of patience and courage to support her in the trials of the morrow.

CHAPTER XI.

HER room was a hospital of souls, always full. They flocked there from all corners of Brabant, Flanders, Germany, and even England; but if curious and impertinent persons often persecuted her by their presence, how many sad and sick pressed round her couch, how many, worsted in the battle of life, knelt at her feet!

This was no doubt the most painful part of her task; the necessity of consoling these poor people, of rousing and sustaining the souls of all these sick, who had come to ask one more sick than themselves to console them.

Around this martyr, who suppressed her own complaints, there arose a chorus of groans varied by exclamations of impatience and cries of anger. Exasperated by their sufferings, the impotent rose against what they called the injustice of their lot, wishing to know why the hand of GOD was heavy on them and not on others, clamouring that Lydwine should explain to them the horrible mystery of pain, and should bring them ease.

These people tortured her, for they were in despair, and hung on to her and would not let her go. Others expected that she would heal them, and when she replied that it did not depend on her but on the Saviour, they did not believe her and accused her of want of pity.

The number of maladies to which she subjected herself in place of persons of whom she often knew next to nothing was extraordinary.

" You will kill yourself for people who do not deserve it at all," said her friends; but she replied:

" Do you call it little to preserve for the Saviour so

152

many souls, for whom the Demon is lying in wait? Besides, who should be rebuffed, when there is not a single one for whom the Son of the Virgin did not shed His blood!"

And she received all, without distinction, only uttering a sigh if they left her dissatisfied. Men of the world could not understand how virtue may be perfected in weakness, how much it depends for its very existence upon it.

Gerlac and Thomas à Kempis tell us very little, indeed practically nothing at all, of these conversations. Brugman seizes the occasion, as he does many others, to point a moral and attribute to the Saint a series of platitudes manifestly invented by himself.

His faulty rhetoric and the obscure poverty of his Latin cannot be overlooked. Under pretext of being energetic, he constantly makes use of such expressions as "the bitter cucumbers and absinthes of the Passion"; under pretext of being pathetic, he apostrophizes Lydwine on every occasion; under pretext of expressing his tenderness, he makes use of all the diminutives he can imagine. She becomes, under his pen, the little servant of Christ, the little woman, the poor little thing, the little plant, the little rose, the little lambkin, Lydwinula, the little Lydwine! The smallest exact document would be of much more use to us than all this affectation of sentiment; but we have to be content with what we can get. Besides, in the absence of conversations noted down at the time, it is quite possible, knowing the mentality of the Saint, to guess what she would reply to so many recriminations and complaints.

To those women, who, accusing heaven of cruelty, wept hot tears over their infirmities or the difficulties of their households, she would naturally reply: "When you are in good health, or when your husband and your children do not worry you, you no longer fulfil your religious duties. How many priests, assailed for months in their confessional by troops of frightened penitents, find themselves deserted by them one fine morning! There is little need to ask the cause of these desertions. The women stay away from the Sacrament simply because their lot is changed, they are no longer miserable; and such is the astonishing ingratitude of human nature that in happiness GOD does not count. If all the sheep were both fortunate and well, the sheepfold would be empty. It is to their own interest then that the Shepherd should bring them back, and there is no other way than to despatch after them His terrible watch-dogs, sickness and misfortune.''

To those men, who, sorrowful over the loss of their health or distressed by calamities of all kinds, became irritated and reproached their Creator with their misfortunes, she would reply: '' You only come back to Jesus because you can no longer pillage and rob your neighbour under cover of trade. You only bring Him the ruins of your bodies, the remains of your souls, the residue which no one wants. Thank Him, then, that He does not reject them. You are afraid to suffer, but it were better to thank GOD for it, since the more you undergo down here, the less you will endure above. Grief is a portion of one's heritage taken in advance from Purgatory. Understand that the mercy of the Saviour is so measureless that it accepts the least ill, the smallest trouble, in payment for the most disquieting of your debts. Nothing, not even a headache, is lost. If GOD did not afflict you, you would persist in being insolvent till the hour of your death; acquit yourself then whilst you are able, and do not grudge that pain which alone is able to restrain your instincts of self-indulgence, to break your pride, to soften the hardness of your hearts. The proverb, ' happiness leads to egoism,' is only too true; you do not begin to experience compassion for others till you have been yourself in want; well-being and strength sterilize you, and you only perform acts which are vaguely correct, till you are lamed or reduced to poverty.''

And she could have added, with one of her future heirs, Sister Emmerich: " I see in each malady a particular design of GOD, the sign of a personal fault, or of the fault of a stranger, which the sick man, whether he knows it or not, is obliged to expiate. Or, again, it is capital which Christ assigns to him, and he ought to increase its value by patience and resignation to His holy will."

How many of these visitors had to be convinced that the Saviour only acted as a surgeon who amputates the gangrened part and tortures him on whom He operates in order to save him! How many rebelled and broke out into drunken oaths, promising to be good if they were healed! How many returned to their idle question, to their ceaseless enquiry: " Why me and not so many others who are more guilty? "

Then she had to explain to them that, in the first place, it was not their duty to judge others, and moreover, that those others would perhaps suffer in their turn later on. Besides, if GOD always loaded the good with rewards and the evil with ills, there would no longer be either merit or profit in faith, for, from the moment Providence became visible, virtue would become nothing but an affair of commerce, and the conversion which resulted in it, nothing but a servile fear. This would be the very negation of virtue, since it would make it neither generous, nor disinterested, nor gratuitous, but a sort of whitened cowardice, a chapel of ease for vice.

To other visitors who were not touched in their bodies or in their means of subsistence, but came to her, mad with grief, because they had seen the death of a husband, child, or other being whom they had adored; to those men who, after the obsequies of their wives, confessed to her their temptation to throw themselves into the Meuse, she would, after some consoling words, put this question:

" Will you affirm that she for whom you weep is with the elect in Paradise? Your answer is ' No,' is it not?

For, without denying her virtues, you must believe that, according to the ordinary rule, she has to pass through a probationary state of waiting, that she must sojourn for a space, the duration of which is known to GOD alone, in Purgatory.

" Do you not understand that your prayers and your grief can draw souls from thence? What they have not had the chance to suffer themselves, so as to purge themselves here below, you will suffer in their stead; you will substitute yourself for them and finish what they could not end. You will pay your grief in ransom, and the more sharp your pain, the sooner will the debt of her you loved be paid.

" Who knows, indeed, if the Lord, touched by the goodwill and supplications of a husband, will not give credit to the wife on the capital of his mourning and yield her deliverance at once?

" You will then be paid in return for your pain; your wife will make herself the accomplice of time; she will soothe the acuteness of your wounds; she will deaden the regret of her loss, and will only leave you a gentle memory, distant and sweet. Do not talk then of suicide, for, besides the loss of your soul, it would be the negation, entire and absolute, of your love; it would be abandoning her whom you pretend to love at the moment when she finds herself in peril, plunging her back into the abyss of Purgatory, when she had already mounted to the top; and depriving yourself of the hope of ever seeing her again."

Then she would conclude simply: " Admire the goodness of the Creator, who causes the one to suffer in order to free the other. Think that human love, which is only a parody of a true love, very often excludes GOD; that it is a form of egoism, since for people who truly love each other the rest of the world does not exist; and that it is fair that this forgetfulness of GOD and this indifference towards your neighbour should be expiated."

To others, to the sick, and, above all, to the

incurable, who cried to her : ''You have cured such and such a one; oh my good Lydwine, cure me!'' she would reply: '' But I am nothing ; it is not I who cure; I cannot!'' And she would weep to see them so cast down and sad. She would implore them to be resigned, and murmur: '' Retire into yourself and reflect ; do not curse that pain which makes you so despondent, for it is the plough which the diligent husbandman employs to work the ground of your souls before sowing the seeds. Say to yourselves that, later on, the angels will lay by for you in the granaries of heaven the harvest they would never have reaped, if the ploughshare of suffering had not torn your poor soil! The supplications of the sick are the most agreeable to GOD.''

To priests, to men more conversant in the ways of the Lord, who were nevertheless overcome by the storm, she would say: '' Pain and Love are almost synonymous words.'' The cause of the mystery of the Incarnation and of the mystery of the Cross is not only the love of Jesus for us and His desire to buy us back, but also the inexpressible love which He bears, in His quality of Son, to the Father.

Not being able to glorify Him as His superior and master, since He is in all things His equal, He resolved to abase Himself by becoming so truly incarnate that, whilst still remaining His equal by His divine nature, He is no longer so by His human nature, and is able from henceforth to render infinite homage, to witness to Him His love and His respect, by the way of weariness, suffering and death.

If pain is not the exact synonym of love, it is in all cases the means and the sign of it. The sole proof of affection one can give to anyone is to suffer, when possible, in his place, for caresses are easy and prove nothing ; so that he who loves his GOD should wish to suffer for Him.

Such would be the language of the Saint. She would certainly also repeat to the souls most specially

designed for the work of sacrificial reparation the
lessons she herself had learned from Jan Pot. She
would assure them that, at this degree of altitude,
suffering vanishes in the flames of love; that one covets
it and calls aloud for the permanent means of sacrifice;
that GOD moderates and softens the torture to keep the
soul alive, alternating joys and griefs; that His graces
are the forerunners of trials, and that tribulations only
precede ecstasies by a very short interval.   She would
certify, without doubt, that, for the lovers of the
Saviour, suffering properly so-called does not exist
at all; and that truth, of which she was the living
example, has been and will be the truth for all time.
There are no Saints, since the death of Lydwine, who
have not confirmed it.

Listen to them formulating their vows:

" Always to suffer and to die," cries Saint Theresa.
" Always to suffer and not to die," corrects Madeleine
de Pazzi.   " Still more, O Lord, still more! " exclaims
S. Francis Xavier, dying of pain on the shores of
China.   " I wish to be broken by suffering, so as to
prove my love to GOD," declares a Carmelite of the
seventeenth century, venerable Marie de la Trinité.
" The desire to suffer is a veritable martyrdom," adds
in our days, a great servant of GOD, Mother Marie du
Bourg, and she confides to her daughters in the convent
that if " they sold pain in the market, she would go
quickly and fetch some."

Lydwine then could assure them that the certain
antidote to suffering is love.   " But," would reply
the poor people, " I do not love! "   " How do you
know that? " the Saint would reply; " is not this state
of torpor, this disgust even at prayer, more often than
not the result of lassitude due to your ills? Is not
this the work of the Lord, and sent to try you? It is
not your own fault if you feel like this; do not get
discouraged; pray even when you cannot understand
a single word of the prayers you are repeating;
importune Jesus, repeat to Him without ceasing,

' Help me to love you! '   You are miserable when you
do not feel love already flowing in you, but indeed, to
weep because you do not love is to love already! ''

But she who spoke in this way could not always
succeed in consoling herself.

Saintly as she was, she had not yet arrived at that
maturity which GOD desired for her.   He exacted from
her more than He would have exacted from any other,
for her task, of which she could not measure the
enormity, required exceptional virtues and extraordinary pains.   She was in the hands of Christ a
weight which He used to counterbalance the crimes of
Europe and the disorders of the Church.   She was a
victim of reparation for the living and also for the
dead ; and the divine Spouse tried her to the uttermost.
It was necessary that He should smite her without
compunction, and human sentiments, which He
tolerated in others, irritated Him in her.

He allowed her to deplore the death of old Pierre,
her father, when he passed away on the vigil of the
Feast of the Conception of the Blessed Virgin.   He
softened the weight of this blow by warning her in
advance, and Lydwine informed Jan Walter, begging
him not to go to Ouderschie to say Mass that day, as
he had intended, so that he could be present at the
old man's last moments.

He also consented that she should not be the victim
of a diabolical illusion which possessed her ; for she saw
her father after his decease tormented by demons, and
He sent an angel to assure her that the good man was,
as he had deserved, in Paradise with the Just.   But
He was less patient when, some years later, in 1423,
her brother William died, whom she loved tenderly.

He began by rewarding her for her probity and
disinterestedness.   William left no fortune but his
debts to his two children Petronille and Baudouin,
and it would have been difficult for him to have done
otherwise.   He had succeeded his father as night
watchman, and he had with his modest salary to

educate his children and provide for Lydwine and his father. It is also possible that the scold whom he had married—and who died no doubt before him, for the historians do not mention her again—had been extravagant, and had reserved for her own follies the greater part of his wages. Anyhow, Lydwine sold some little family heirlooms, which her brother had preserved as souvenirs, and gave the money in a purse to a sieur Nicolas, her cousin, who lived with her, begging him to pay the creditors.

Who, in parenthesis, was this Nicolas, whose name we have mentioned before, when telling how the Saint's confessor hid in her house to surprise her angel? We do not know. We only know that Nicolas acquitted himself of the commission, and restored the empty purse to Lydwine on his return, when she emptied it on her bed and drew out eight pounds in coin of the realm, the exact amount which she had scraped together to clear the debts.

She recommended her relation not to noise this miracle abroad, and decided that this purse should be called the purse of Jesus; and the Saint could always in future draw upon it for the wants of the poor. It did not become exhausted, for even on the day of her death it was still half full.

But if GOD let her feel on this occasion that He was pleased with her, and relieved her for the future of the care of seeking means wherewith to feed her poor, He was angry and punished her by depriving her of her habitual ecstasies when, losing all control after the death of her brother, she fell into a state of prostration and did not cease to weep.

He judged that this excess of grief would drown the divine charm in her, and would prevent her from climbing the last heights on the mystic way which separated her from Him.

In this connexion all the historians narrate the following curious episode :—

A long time after William had disappeared, Gérard,

a young man of the diocese of Cologne who was burning with the desire to live like the ancient hermits, visited her to make quite sure that this craving, which he could not succeed in mastering, was not a madness or a tempting of Providence, since it required that he should be miraculously fed in a desert solitude.

Lydwine removed his doubts regarding his vocation as an anchorite, and said to him prophetically:

"The first three days after your arrival in the desert you will suffer hunger; but do not be downcast, for the third day, before sunset, the Lord will provide you with food."

Confident in this promise, he set out with two companions; but as soon as they reached the plains of Egypt, these friends, frightened by the sea of sand which stretched before them to the horizon, turned tail and went back to their own homes.

Gérard, more intrepid, plunged into the desolate regions of the Nile and discovered in the centre of the desert a great tree, in the branches of which was perched a cell, like a nest, made of palms and mats, so high above the ground that wolves and other wild beasts could not reach it. He installed himself in this cell, and, after lacking food for two days, he was, according to the prediction of the Saint, provided for by the Creator, who sent him flakes of manna as formerly to the Hebrews.

In this airy cell he lived lost in GOD, and he had reached the topmost heights of contemplation, when an English bishop, who was returning from a pilgrimage to Mount Sinai, where he had been to venerate the relics of S. Catherine of Alexandria, virgin and martyr, ventured to cross these deserts with his followers.

Surprised to see a tree in a country denuded of all vegetation, he approached it, and discerning the hut lodged in the branches, he cried:

"If a servant of Christ is living here, I pray him, for the love of Jesus, to answer me."

At this appeal to the name of Jesus, an enormously

fat being dressed in rags and horribly dirty emerged from the network of matting.

The bishop was disconcerted when he saw this mass, which, rather than the body and face of a man, resembled a colossal demi-john, whose neck was surmounted with a bladder of lard instead of a cork. He began to be frightened when this round face was irradiated by the luminous smile of an angel.

"Tell me, father abbot," said the Prelate, reassured by this smile, " how long have you lived in this tree?"

" For seventeen years," replied the hermit.

" How old were you when you fled from the world?"

" Nineteen years."

" And what do you live on? " continued the Englishman. " I can discover no trace of roots or vegetation round your lair, and yet your obesity is unrivalled."

" He who fed the children of Israel in the wilderness sees to it that I want nothing," replied Gérard.

The bishop thought he was speaking of spiritual food and asked him if he knew any other human creature who lived without eating.

" Yes, in Holland, in a little town called Schiedam, a virgin has lived fasting for years, and has raised herself to such a high state of perfection that she is far in advance of me. We converse, however, and have done so for a long time, in the uncreated light; but one thing does astonish me at this moment: for some days now she has not left the earth and I do not perceive her spirit in ecstasy; and yet she is not dead!"

"I think I can divine, nevertheless," pursued Gérard, after a pause, " that she has afflicted herself more than is justified over the loss of one near and dear to her, and that GOD has allowed her to do this in order to humiliate her. I think it is because of the intemperance of her tears that the Saviour deprives her for the moment of His grace. When you return to Europe, if you go by the Low Countries, go and see her and put these three questions to her from me.

" How long has your friend Gérard been withdrawn in the desert?

" What age was he when he adopted his present mode of life?

" Why does he no longer meet you as he used to do? "

That was enough to determine the bishop to go to Holland before he went back to England.   The instant he arrived, he hurried to Schiedam and was taken by his hotel-keeper to Lydwine's house.

He related his conversation with Gérard, and begged her to answer the three questions.

She hesitated at first, saying humbly: " How can I know?   It is GOD who knows."

But the prelate insisted, and was almost angry, so she at length avowed that Gérard had lived seventeen years in his tree; that when he had first conceived the idea of living the life of the fathers of the desert he was seventeen, but that he had not been able to realise his design till two years after, that is to say, at the age of nineteen.

Then she was silent.

" You do not reply to the third question? " insisted the bishop.

Then she sighed:

" Alas! Monseigneur, I am obliged to live amongst secular people, and cannot avoid being mixed up in the affairs of the world.   I am polluted by that dust which springs up round the people of the age, and I advance very slowly in the ways of GOD.   My brother Gérard is not, happily for him, in the same case.   He exists alone with the angels, no earthly being disturbs him, and he can abandon himself in all liberty to the thoughts of Heaven.   It is very natural then that he should pass me in the sublime ways of contemplation, and that I cannot always follow him in them.

" I would add also that if I have dropped behind and am slow in rejoining him, it is my own fault.   I have wept too much over the death of my brother William, and GOD has put me back many paces."

After he had thus verified the exactitude of the details with which the hermit had furnished him, the bishop blessed Lydwine and recommended himself to her prayers.

When he had gone she talked to her intimates of Gérard. She told them that his stoutness, which was due to the nutritive qualities of the manna, was such that rolls of flesh dropped from his neck and ran in cascades down his back, so that he could neither sit nor lie down, but was forced to remain constantly kneeling or standing in his tree. When he died, in the year of the Incarnation 1426, on the 2nd October, she was warned of his decease by her angel, who took her to render the last duties to the dead.

She then saw his soul separated from his body and carried by the celestial spirits into Paradise, where they bathed it in a fountain whose water was so pure that one could see the bottom to a depth of at least a mile.

CHAPTER XII.

THE anger of Jesus with His poor servant did not last long, and He testified His reconciliation by miracles.

Lydwine's angel frequented her again, and there were more journeyings to Paradise and into the churches. Whilst her soul journeyed, her body remained insensible, for ecstasy rendered her so unconscious that she was one day horribly burnt without perceiving it.

On three occasions we hear of fires occurring in the life of the Saint. On the first, as we have noted above, through the fault of her brother, the fire one morning burnt the straw of her bed; and her bed was again burnt on another occasion.

One winter afternoon the women who served her, not knowing how to warm her, since, for the sake of her eyes, there could be no fire on the hearth, conceived the idea of slipping a vessel full of hot cinders under her blankets.

Lydwine was at the moment in ecstasy far from the world, and the women went out to look after their own affairs. When they returned they smelt a smell of burnt flesh and rushed to the bed, where they found that the cover of the vessel had come unfastened and the coal was burning one of the Saint's ribs.

At this instant her trance ceased.

" O Lydwine," cried her friends, " what a frightful wound! Do you not feel it? "

" Yes," she said, " I feel it now, but I did not suffer at all whilst I was with the Saviour."

The good women wept, reproaching themselves for their imprudence.

"Do not grieve," she murmured, "but bless the Lord, who has so absorbed me into Himself that I did not even know the hot cinders were burning my side."

In the year 1428 a fire threatened to be even more disastrous to her. A few week before it broke out Lydwine had exclaimed several times: "The wrath of God is on Schiedam!" and in tears she owned to her intimates that she had offered herself as a victim to Christ, who had refused to accept her sacrifice.

"What is going to happen?" they asked her.

"A fire will destroy Schiedam, for the iniquity of this town is ripe and the hour of the harvest is here. I cannot, alas! disarm the resentment of the Just One."

Then, addressing Catherine Simon, she added:

"I know, my dear sister, that you have in reserve a certain number of planks which were left over in the construction of the house they built for you. Give the order for them to be transferred without delay to the garden here. We will use them to build a shed wherein the homeless may deposit the things they have saved from destruction."

Catherine obeyed and Lydwine thanked her. Then, on the eve of the day whereon the fire broke out, she said to her:

"You remember you have vowed to go in pilgrimage to Notre Dame de Bois le Duc. Fulfil that promise to-morrow; go, and come back as soon as you can."

"But," cried Catherine, "you have told me that a fire will take place in Schiedam to-morrow. It is really not the moment to absent myself, for if I go away I am certain to lose all that I possess."

"Listen to what I say to you," replied Lydwine; "the Lord must know better than you what will be profitable to you."

And the widow Simon, who never rebelled against the Saint's injunctions, went off to Bois le Duc.

The next day was a Saturday in July, the feast of S. Frederick, bishop and martyr, and of S. Arnulphe,

confessor. It was the eve of the day on which the
sailors of Schiedam went to sea at the beginning of
the herring fishing, and, following an ancient custom,
they assembled to celebrate their departure by a
banquet. When the repast, which was long and
accompanied by much drinking of beer and cervoise,
was ended, the cooks left an oven, which they thought
no longer burning, near a bundle of reeds. Towards
eleven at night sparks ignited the reeds, and the fire
leapt from one building to another till the whole town
was involved. It spread from house to house, and,
as most of them were of wood, they flared up like laths
without a chance of being saved. Fanned by the wind,
the flames crossed empty spaces, licked up the gardens
in passing, and burnt the trees, darting through the
clouds of smoke great tongues of fire which, once they
had seized on a building, did not let it go. The flames
beat upon the windows, which burst before them, and
forced the doors. Nothing was seen in the quaking
framework but red beams, which stood erect for a
moment, flared like a torch, and then fell back broken
in a rain of charcoal; and, as each house fell in, a great
tongue of fire illumined the night. It rained cinders
and hailed fire; and one heard nothing but crackling
furnaces, the noise of the beams breaking up, the
explosions of barrels when their hoops burst, the cries
of terror of the crowd which fled before these fiery
serpents and these wings of flame writhing in all
directions.

Thus it continued from the beginning to the end of
the night, and next morning the parish church, a
convent of nuns next to it, and the greater part of the
streets of Schiedam were nothing but a heap of ruins,
while the fire still raged.

In vain the inhabitants, encouraged by the light of
day, tried to limit the area of the fire; it continued to
rage unchecked.

At one moment flames broke out in the direction of
Lydwine's house. Some good people ran and wished

to carry the Saint away, but she refused, affirming that she had nothing to fear. They left her on her couch, but demolished, as a precaution, the wooden beams and ceiling of the house, and left only the stone walls standing. But as it was the month of July and the sun scorched cruelly, they had to throw an old covering over the remains of the walls to procure a little shade, seeing how she suffered and how her eye bled at the light.

This precaution would have been quite useless, for the fire could just as easily burn the stuff as the wood of the ceiling, and it would have spread immediately to the straw of the bed. Moreover, they had not succeeded in mitigating the patient's pain, so, being at a loss what to do, they replaced the planks which they had moved, and left her alone.

Lydwine remained alone the whole of that Sunday. She had the fever and was grilled under the leaden sun; but though she armed herself with patience, prayed, and invoked her angel, she met with no response. When evening fell she thought herself dying, for the heat collected under the planks, and the smoke of the ruins, drenched with water, suffocated her. At her last gasp, she groped for a stick which usually served her to draw open the curtains of her bed and also to knock when she wanted to call assistance; but though she felt in all directions with the only arm serviceable to her, she could not find it.

She was sure that the scourge would not reach her and that she would not perish; but fear and suffocation were stronger than reason; nature gained the upper hand, the silence of her angel overwhelmed her, and she gave way and wept, thinking she was going to die alone in her corner without the aid of the Sacraments.

Weakness, the outcome of the fever which raged within her, heightened her panic; and thus we can see how, when the Saviour wishes it, souls vacillate and err, even when most advanced in the vocation of sacrifice. In reality nothing is more difficult than to kill what S. Paul calls "the old man." He may be stupefied, but in most cases he does not die. A trifle may rouse him from his lethargy and he awakes. It is as if the Demon watered the old roots in secret to prevent their ever drying up; and the first shoots which they produce in the shadows of the soul are those of vain glory, that special tare of privileged beings! Lydwine was far from indulging in this sentiment, but nevertheless GOD wished to humiliate her once more by permitting that she should doubt the efficacy of her prayers, that she should fly from peril and fear purely human dangers!

Yet He was merciful to her weakness, as He had not been in the case of the grief she felt at her brother's death, because these trances were His work, because it was He Himself who had imposed them on His poor servant; and the proof of His mercy is that He intervened at once to help her.

The angel, till then invisible, appeared and gently placed on Lydwine's chest a piece of wood about a yard long. She seized it and raising it with difficulty, parted the curtains and drew long breaths of air. Next morning, when she looked closely at this stick, she perceived that it was not only heavy and rough, but still untrimmed and freshly cut from the trunk; and she could not avoid thinking that her angel would have done better to find her old wand, than to bring her this ill-suited stake. When therefore Jan Walter arrived to know how she had passed the night, she gave it to him and begged him to have it trimmed.

Walter visited the carpenters of the town, but their tools had been burned and they could not undertake the work. Tired of his search he made a bargain with a barrel maker who still possessed an adze and worked energetically at the stake. Sweet-smelling chips flew from it, and under the bark appeared the colour of fresh wax.

"It would be a kind of cyprus," replied the man to Walter, who wanted to know what kind of tree produced this wood. "But," he added, "I have never seen any so scented and so hard."

Then, whilst the persons who were looking on in the workshop stole the shavings on account of their perfume, he said to the priest:

"Look here, I cannot properly shape your stick with an adze; it would be better to keep it as it is."

Walter was annoyed at this delay, and set out in quest of another workman. At last he found one whose tools had not all been destroyed in the fire, and this man set to work; but he had no sooner smelt the stick than he wanted to appropriate the chips, which Walter wished to keep, and to have more of them he would have whittled away the wood with his plane to such an extent that none would have been left, had not the priest wrenched it out of his hands and fled with it.

He asked Lydwine, when he took her back her stick, if she knew the name of the tree which had produced it.

"God knows," she said, "and I do not; my brother the angel did not tell me."

Later, on the feast of S. Cyriaque the martyr, that is to say at the beginning of the month of August, the angel took Lydwine to the regions of Eden. There he reproached her for having valued his present so little—which distressed her very much—and he showed her the tree, a cyprus of a particular species, and the place whence he had cut the bough, telling her that this twig would chastise the Devil and would be an object of terror to him.

And indeed Brugman declares that he was present on such occasions, and that to approach a possessed person with this wand was enough to draw from him plaintive cries and to make him shudder from head to foot.

A century later, Michel d'Esne, bishop of Tournai, adds: "That is very true, as I have not only heard but have seen with my own eyes; for I have seen demoniacs cry, grind their teeth, and tremble before a little piece of this wood."

When the history of this stick was noised abroad, the town came in procession to the Saint's house to look at it and to present flowers.   It smelt deliciously, but a shameless person touched it out of curiosity, and thenceforward it ceased to exhale its resinous perfume.

Widow Catherine, who had performed her pilgrimage, came back to the town at this juncture to find in place of a dwelling a heap of burnt sticks and cinders.

This loss afflicted her and she came weeping to Lydwine's house.

" You see," she cried, " that I ought never to have absented myself.   If I had not listened to you I should perhaps have saved at least some of my poor things."

But the Saint smiled:

" You have long wanted to take up your abode with me," she exclaimed, " only the sacrifice which cost you most was to separate from that house to which you were too attached.   Now that it no longer exists what should stop you?   Come and settle here, and, instead of groaning, thank GOD who has so precipitated events that He dispenses you from disputing with yourself."

And Catherine hastened to come and live with the Saint, and did not leave her till the hour of her death.

Another question which it would be interesting to decide is how the people of Schiedam, who were, for the most part, drunken sailors, but no worse than at other seaboard towns, had managed to draw down the wrath of GOD so heavily upon themselves. If we consider their attitude at the time when their late curé, André, was charged with having thrown the Eucharist into a heap of mud, we should say that these people had faith and venerated the body of the Lord, for they waxed indignant and wanted to chastise this recreant priest.   If then they were neither miscreants nor haters of GOD, how can we justify the resentment of Christ?

Thomas à Kempis tells us that they had jeered at the miraculous statue of the Virgin, and he cites amongst the offenders a priest and a woman whose open attachment to each other was a scandal to the people. By some details which he gives, it is easy to recognise in this ecclesiastic and this lewd woman, Joannés de Berst and Hasa Goswin, of whom we have already spoken. But besides this sin, we may, I think, admit that because of the favour which she had obtained in possessing within her walls a Saint, whose miracles rendered the grace of GOD visible, Schiedam ought to have been a more religious, more mystic town than others; a model city, which she was not. GOD spared her once, at the instance of His servant, when a fleet was advancing to destroy her; but she did not amend, and the Judge therefore grew weary and struck her. Such is the sole plausible explanation.

In spite of everything, Lydwine could not prevent herself from thinking that if she had been more pure her prayers might perhaps have been better heard; and yet she knew that her merits had been carefully taken account of.

Had she not some years previously, when she was in ecstasy, contemplated that spectacle, which was vouchsafed to many Saints besides, of the Spouse holding a crown set with gems? She had examined it and noticed that certain settings were empty.

"The stones which are missing will be set in time," said Jesus; "this crown is that which I prepare for thee."

When she came to herself, she thought truly that the unfilled settings symbolised the griefs which still remained for her to undergo, and she prepared herself to endure them.

She examined herself closely and humbly, reconsidered past events, concluding that she had never offered to the Well-beloved a heart truly free and a spirit entirely unoccupied. She reproached herself that she had never entirely freed herself from her own will, never entirely banished self from herself, never sufficiently sifted the dregs of this world; and she implored Jesus to put her in the way of expiating this self-indulgence by loading her with abuse and ill-treatment, such as He Himself had to bear.

He satisfied her immediately.

At this moment Philip, Duke of Burgundy, who claimed the possession of the united provinces by right of inheritance, to the detriment of his niece, the Countess Jacqueline, invaded the Low Country at the head of an army and installed garrisons in various places. On the 10th October, the day when the feast of the martyrs, S. Géréon and S. Victor was celebrated, he entered Schiedam, where he was received with great ceremony and invited to a banquet, to which all the authorities of the town were admitted, and also the curé, Jan Angeli, who was still living at this time.

After the banquet, four men of Picardy, who were of the Duke's following, asked the Curé to take them to see Lydwine, of whom they had heard marvels on all sides.

He consented to accompany them there; but hardly were they introduced into the room when they began to make a noise, and when Jan Angeli begged them to leave, they pretended that he was the Saint's lover and pushed him behind a little altar, which had been put up to receive the body of Christ when he came to communicate the sick woman.

There he crouched in helpless misery.

" There is not a drop to be seen in this tavern ! " cried one of these brutes, who then lit a candle, tore the curtains and coverings of the bed away, and exposed the dropsical stomach of the wretched woman, like a great bag of water. They were convulsed with laughter, and said she was pregnant through her confessor !

Lydwine's niece, little Petronille, was present with the Curé at this scene, and when they exposed her aunt's body she could no longer contain herself, but ran to cover her up. They wished to prevent her, but she opposed them with such determination that they finally struck her and threw her with such violence against the steps of the altar that she was badly hurt and fainted.

This encounter exasperated the scoundrels. They called Lydwine a loose woman, accused her of being the mother of fourteen children and of getting drunk at night! Then, whilst one held a torch to light the couch and abused the martyr, yelling: "They are going to take down the swelling you dirty creature!" the others dug their fingers into the stretched skin of the stomach and burst it.

Water and blood flowed out in abundance from three wounds, and the bed was inundated.

After they had accomplished this martyrdom, they went to wash their hands and then returned to abuse her.

Lydwine, who had only replied by groans during these tortures, then looked at them and said:

"How is it you do not fear to touch the work of GOD; do you not fear the chastisement His justice prepares for you?"

They shrugged their shoulders and, after a parting broadside of jokes and outrages, left her and went away.

The Curé rushed out at once for help. Lydwine's friends arrived, restored Petronille with a cordial and put her to bed, dressed her aunt's wounds, and changed the straw of her couch, which was drenched with blood like the litter of a slaughter-house.

The next day, the Duke of Burgundy, who did not know of this assault, set out for Rotterdam; but hardly had his army left Schiedam when the news of the crime ran throughout the town. There was one universal cry of indignation against the bandits. The burgomasters presented themselves at Lydwine's house to console her and to announce that they were going to embark for Rotterdam and demand that the Duke should punish these men.

"Do not worry the Prince on my account," replied Lydwine; "GOD reserves to Himself vengeance for this crime; the arrest of these unfortunate men is already decreed."

And indeed the fate that awaited them did not tarry. The man who carried the torch and had so grossly insulted the Saint, was seized with vertigo at the very moment of entering the port of Rotterdam. He strayed like a madman on to the bridge of the vessel and falling, broke his skull. The second was struck down near Zieriksee in an access of delirium, and was abandoned in a sloop where he died; the third, who belonged to the navy, was killed during a battle with the English; the fourth, who called himself a doctor, was seized with apoplexy near Sluis and became speechless. His servant then recalled his crime to him and asked him if he was sorry, and making a sign that he was, he died.

After his burial, this servant, who was a good and pious man, came to Schiedam to beg in his master's name, that Lydwine should pardon him; and we may be sure that this favour was willingly granted.

This dreadful adventure distressed the Saint for years.

She wept, not so much over the wounds she had received, as over the perversity of those miscreants whom her prayers did not succeed in rescuing; and she would not let anyone pity her in her sufferings.

"Weep, rather," she said one day, "for the magistrates and bailiffs of Schiedam who chatter amongst themselves over this affair; weep for yourselves, for I see you menaced with a danger you know nothing of."

And indeed, a short time afterwards, they were convicted of treason by the Duke of Burgundy, and threatened with execution.

After these events the angel of the Lord came to

M

Lydwine and said: " The divine Spouse admits you, according to your desire, to the tortures of the Passion. You have suffered abuse, you have been stripped and covered with shame, you have poured out blood and water by your wounds.   Be joyful, my sister, for the brutality of these men of Picardy has helped to complete the number of precious stones which were still lacking in your crown."

CHAPTER XIII.

GOD generally gives to each of his Saints a special devotion in accord with the task which each of them is more particularly charged to accomplish. Lydwine's devotion, as a missionary of Pain, would naturally be the way of the Cross; and she practised it, as we have said, in a canonical manner, dividing the way of agony into seven stages, according to the number of liturgical hours. But this daily meditation on the Passion, this ardour to follow the steps of Christ on the road to Calvary, did not cause her to forget that other joy which she had had when quite little, the joy of the Blessed Virgin.

Did she not meet her each day when she climbed the hill of Golgotha? Our Lady of Tears had always a look for her, when she saw her amongst the crowd of women Saints; but often in thinking over the days of her past life and going back even to the hours of infancy, Lydwine thought of that Notre Dame de Liesse, whose statue had smiled so sweetly at her in her chapel, and was seized by the desire of seeing her again under the form of sculptured wood, which recalled many memories.

She had indeed visited it since in ecstasy, when her angel had laid her before it, but this was not quite the same thing, and she would have loved to contemplate it with what remained of her sight, if it were but for a second.

This wish seemed to her quite incapable of fulfilment, for how could she presume to think that they would take this image from the church and bring it to her house? She dared not express the wish, neither was she the woman to solicit a miracle in order to humour a caprice.

But this desire continued to haunt her nevertheless; and she was trying to put it from her as a temptation, when she was warned that the Virgin was going to content her.

It was some days after the fire of Schiedam, and blessed Mary arranged things in the most simple manner.

The church had been much damaged by fire, but the statue was safe; and whilst waiting for her chapel to be repaired, the image had to be placed in some suitable spot. The thought came to them to transfer it to the Saint's room, where it was installed on the little altar put up to receive the sacred species on the day of Refection; and so long as it stayed there it seemed to all those who approached it more beautiful than it was in reality. There was a sweetness and gaiety of expression about it which was lost when it was separated from Lydwine.

She could hardly contain her joy; but we can imagine the crowd which invaded the little dwelling to pray to the Madonna!

How could Lydwine endure the coming and going and the incessant clattering of feet, even though she was closed in by the curtains of her bed, for the door, constantly open, admitted rays of light which would have pierced her eye like arrows if she had not been sheltered by the hangings. The truth is that the murmurings of prayers which she heard around her, recompensed her for the discomfort and gave her pleasure, for she thought how the blessed Mother loved them; and it was heartbreaking to her when they carried off the statue to its newly-decorated chapel.

The Blessed Virgin was gone, but she charged Lydwine's guardian angel to take her more often to Paradise.

She treated her like a spoilt child, questioning her

and amusing herself at the ingenuity of Lydwine's answers.

One night she said to her in a serious tone:

"How is it, my dear, that you have arrived here so carelessly dressed? You have not even a veil on your brow!"

"My dear Lady Mary," stammered Lydwine, horrified, "my angel brought me just as I was; and besides, I have neither robe nor veil in the house, as I am always in bed."

"Well," said the Virgin, smiling, "would you like me to give you this veil?"

Lydwine looked longingly at the veil the blessed Mother held out to her; she was dying to accept it, but she feared to displease Jesus by gratifying her own desires, and she looked at her angel who turned away his eyes.

More and more fearful, she murmured: "But it seems to me, good Virgin, that I have not the right to express a wish"; and again she cast an imploring look towards her angel. He replied this time by these words, which increased her embarrassment:

"If you wish to possess the veil, take it."

She was more and more puzzled how to decide, when the Madonna finished by laughing at her distress.

"Come," she said, "I am going myself to place it on your head; but listen well. On returning to earth, you will keep it in your house for seven hours, after which you will entrust it to your confessor, praying him to fasten it on the head of my statue in the parish church of Schiedam."

And after this exhortation Our Lady disappeared.

On emerging from her trance, Lydwine felt her forehead to be sure she was not the plaything of an illusion, but the veil was there, she took it off and examined it. It appeared truly woven with the thread of the blessed Virgin, the web was so fine; it was of a water green colour, very pale, and it exhaled a very exquisite perfume, at once penetrating and fugitive.

Contemplating it, Lydwine was so absorbed in thanksgiving that she had lost all sense of time, and suddenly she realized that the limit of hours given by the blessed Mary for her to keep the present was just an end.

Immediately she sent for Jan Walter and told him of her vision.

He felt the veil, in a state of stupefaction.

" But," he cried, " you forget that the night is very dark, the church is shut, and I have not the keys. Even if I could get in, that would be of little use, for I could not in the darkness reach to the top of the statue, which is high above the altar; let us wait till dawn, and then I will go."

" No, no," rejoined the Saint, " the order which I received is precise; do not disquiet yourself with all these details, for the church will be open and the lantern which you lit to come here will furnish sufficient light for you to see a ladder leaning against the side wall, on the north side of the sanctuary. Once mounted on that, nothing will be easier than to veil the statue; therefore, I beg you, father, to go without delay."

Walter went off and woke the sacristan, who opened the church door for him, and he at once found the ladder in the place his penitent had described.

" What do you want to do?" asked the sacristan, astonished to see him move the ladder.

"You would not understand now," replied the priest, " but GOD will explain it to you by the result."

The man, in a hurry to get back to bed, did not pay much attention to this reply and went off.

After discharging his commission, Walter knelt before the statue and prayed; but when he was on the point of leaving and wished to admire the delicate beauty of the veil, it was no longer there. As Lydwine told widow Simon later, when she asked her what had become of it, the angel had already taken it away.

These relations of the Saint with the Madonna were

continual. In the horrible nights of insomnia and fever, when the sick woman had to restrain herself from waking her nephew and niece by her cries, she would suddenly perceive the Virgin leaning over her bed, who raised her pillow and tucked her in, so that she was quieted and happy.

Did she also sometimes hear the sweet pity of the Son's Mother? It is impossible not to picture Mary's compassion before this accumulation of woes! Certainly she, whose heart was riven by sharp swords, knew the necessity of these acute sufferings; but she was too tender not to pity the martyrdom of her poor daughter, and we can see her imploring the mercy of Christ, who smiles and says to her:

" O Mother, recall on Calvary that Cross which, in their satanic pride, men wished to make greater than their GOD; recall how it was higher and wider than my body, which did not fill it. In this frame of wood, with which they surrounded me, the executioners left me spaces which only a multitude of tortures can fill; and it is precisely because there remains a space for suffering that I have given to my Saints the supreme privilege of occupying it and of completing with their own pain the torments of the Passion. Remember then that if Lydwine does not expiate the faults of which she is innocent, a multitude of your other children will be damned! But that does not prevent your child from having suffered enough for this night; take her into your arms and make her oblivious of earthly sorrow!"

And the blessed Virgin hushed Lydwine, and gave her, radiant with joy, to her angel, that she might walk in the gardens of heaven.

On another occasion, during Christmas night, she was suddenly transported to Paradise, and there, like the venerable Gertrude d'Oosten, that Dutch beguine who had preceeded her on her way of sacrifice, was made the object of a singular grace, which had been announced to her beforehand, though she had not revealed it to her intimates.   Widow Catherine Simon, who now lived with her, had a dream, wherein an angel revealed to her that her friend would receive, on the night of the Nativity, a mysterious milk, which she would permit her to taste.

She spoke of this to Lydwine, who, from humility, gave an evasive answer; but she returned to the charge, and at last, wearied by the vagueness of Lydwine's replies, she exclaimed: " Do you know, my dear, that it is a little odd to dare to deny what an angel has told me! "

Then the Saint owned that she had also been warned of this miracle, and advised Catherine to prepare herself by confession and prayer to receive this favour.

During the night of the Epiphany, Lydwine was seized with divine ecstasy, lost the use of her senses, and in spirit flew to Eden.

There she was admitted to the company of virgins, clothed in white and crowned with miraculous flowers or circles of gold set with gems.   All held palms and were grouped in a semi-circle, in the centre of which Mary was seated on a sparkling throne, which one would have thought to be carved in solid lightning, in tangible thunder; and multitudes of angels crowded behind them.

All these pure spirits Lydwine beheld in a human form, but the contours alone existed under the pleated snow of their robes.   These glorious bodies were filled only with a pale light which shone from the eyes, mouth, and forehead, and rose behind the head in nimbi of gold; and from this kneeling company, with folded hands, arose endless adorations to the Maternity of the Virgin; adorations whereof the liturgy melted into a tongue of fire, a flashing light of perfume and song.

Great seraphim flamed, unloosing from harps of fire the gorgeous pearl of sound; others offered those vessels of gold full of sweet essence, which are the prayers of the Just; others chanted messianic psalms and sang in alternate choirs transporting hymns; others again, near a standing archangel at the right of the altar of perfumes, saw to the lighting of the incense and wove with threads of blue smoke the warm linen with which they should envelop the Holy Child.

In haste they prepared the robes of cloudy perfume, the scented clothes of the new-born, for the delivery was near.

Lydwine found again in heaven the formulas of adoration, the ceremonial practices of the office which she had known below when she was well and strong; for the Church militant had been initiated by the inspiration of apostles, popes, and saints, in the liturgical joys of Paradise. In humble imitation she repeated the language of praise; but how differently from the chords of those harps, the power and subtilty of those fragrances, the thundering zeal of those voices.

Lydwine listened and looked in ravishment. As the hour of the Nativity approached, the accents of the choirs of angels, the vibrations of the chords, became more imploring and sweet; and when the hour rang in the divine belfries, when Jesus appeared, radiant, cn the knees of His Mother, when a cry of joy mingled with the holy vapours of the thuribles and the ecstatic vibrations of the harps, the chaste robe of the blessed Virgin opened, and the milk flowed in an inexhaustible stream.

Then some of it was given to the Saint and her companions; the Holy Child letting us thus understand, says à Kempis, that He associated them in the honour of the celestial Maternity; or showing, as Gerlac says, that all the virgins were ready to nourish the Saviour.

Poor Lydwine was beside herself now with joy: she was so far removed from her mortal gehenna! But the vision was already fading, and socn there remained nothing on the midnight sky but the immense trajectory of that milk, lit up by the millions of stars behind it.

One would have said it was a new milky way; an arch of snow powdered with stars.

The entrance of Catherine Simon into the room, impatient to see the promise of her dream realised, recalled Lydwine to herself; and when her friend begged for the milk, she touched the flower of her breast with her left hand, and the milk, which had disappeared, returned. The widow drank of it three times and could not for several days take any other nourishment. All other food seemed to her, in comparison with this, dull and flat in savour; and the same scene was renewed in after years, at that season of Christmas.

Brugman assures us that the confessor, Jan Walter, obtained the same favour as Catherine, and that he also drank of this milk; but Gerlac, on the contrary, says that he was not with his penitent at an opportune moment, and that he did not experience this grace.

If we consider the astonishing miracles by which this life was accompanied—this two-fold life, burdened with sufferings while it was lived upon the earth, but overflowing with joys when it escaped to Eden; if we remember the exceptional privileges which the Saviour bestowed upon Lydwine and reckon the sum of His favours to her, we can almost believe that, by prayer and suffering and devotion to others, this blessed Saint had indeed reached the height of the perfect way.

Unhappily for herself, she had not yet quite attained it, and there were ladders still to be climbed. The terrible truth, on which S. John of the Cross continually insists in the " Climbing of Carmel," that any attachment, even when it only constitutes the smallest imperfection, clouds the soul and makes an obstacle to its perfect union with GOD, is applicable to Lydwine in spite of everything. She was still too much attached to herself, she possessed the defect of her qualities, and was too much bound up with those about her.

It is right to state in her defence that, although so

far advanced on the path of the Saviour, it was still very difficult for her to determine unaided the limits which she was forbidden to overpass.

GOD did not indeed forbid her to love her neighbour; on the contrary, what He does forbid to those who desire to disengage themselves that they may live in Him alone, is that abandonment to human affection which upsets His loving designs by running counter to them. But the poor soul which, without defiance, abandons itself to these excesses, brings them, or believes itself able to bring them, to its Creator, to whom it speaks constantly of those it loves. It prays for them, and would think it had not fulfilled its duty towards Him and was wanting in charity towards them, if it did not do so. The soul imagines, in short, that it loves its neighbours in Him, whilst in truth it loves them more than Him; and in this there is an error which excites the Spirit of Malice, for, as is expressed in clear terms in the " Treaty on the spiritual life and of prayer " of Madame the Abbess of S. Cécile de Solesmes, " the Demon loves violence, and all, even good, is pushed to a degree of absurdity."

It is the last refinement of his art to destroy a virtue by exaggerating it!

Now this is what happened to Lydwine; she had not been able to rid herself of that excessive tenderness, which had already drawn reproof upon her at the time of her brother's death. Since that death, her delight in her two sick-nurses, her nephew and her niece, had increased, and the Saviour struck her to the heart when He took from her Petronille. This young girl was then seventeen years old, and since she had been wounded by the Picardians in attempting to save her aunt, she had pined and languished, and had never, in spite of treatment by the best doctors, been able to regain her strength.

One night Lydwine was rapt away in the spirit and saw a procession coming out of the church of Schiedam. Advancing in double line in a slow march, preceded by the candles and the Cross, the patriarchs, prophets, apostles, martyrs, confessors, virgins, holy women, all the personages of the communion of saints, proceeded from the sanctuary towards her house, took up a body exposed at the door, and accompanied it to the church.

And she beheld herself behind the convoy with three crowns, one on her head and one in each hand.

When she came to herself, Lydwine thought at first that this vision concerned herself, and foretold her end; but she was undeceived by Jesus, who revealed to her that this apparition referred to her niece, and indicated to her, at the same time, the day and the hour at which Petronille would be born into Heaven.

Lydwine at first began to weep, but, in thinking of the agony of her whom she loved as a daughter, she ceased and cried: " Ah! Lord, grant me at least one mercy in my distress. This hour which you have appointed is one wherein I am consumed with that fever which returns as Thou knowest at fixed hours; and then I am no longer good for anything, but incapable of all attention and of all effort. I beg you to alter the course of my fever, so that I might be fit to help my poor Petronille when the moment of my separation from her comes."

Jesus granted this prayer, and to the great astonishment of those who tended the Saint, the access, so regular in its return, occurred six hours earlier and lasted for a shorter time than usual.

Hardly was she free from it, when Petronille's agony began, and Lydwine, who saw her trembling, could sustain and pray with her until she died and went to receive the three crowns which her aunt had carried in her trance; one for the virginity of her body, the second for her spiritual chastity, the third for that wound which the bandits of Picardy had given her.

Lydwine had, till this moment, braced herself to bear her troubles; she had listened in distress to the Saviour's sentence, but she was not weak when the time came to comfort her niece; she had suppressed her tears and had softened the last moments of the child by her apparent firmness.   But when Petronille was buried, her courage failed; she gave way to grief and did not cease to weep; and instead of improving with time, her grief was aggravated, for she cultivated it, fed it with constant regrets, and was so overcome by it that Jesus was angry.

He did not reproach her, but He left her.

Then was repeated what she went through when she first entered on the purgative life—the anguish of the soul of a prisoner in darkness.   She heard nothing, not even the furtive step of the gaoler, but an absolute silence, and black darkness prevailed.

It was the burial of the soul chained to a motionless body. She was constrained, in this solitude, to examine and question herself; but she only found in her heart the ruins of happiness, for a tempest had laid all low, and all she could do when faced with the ruins of her being was to revive the bitter memory of the time when the divine Spouse deigned to visit her, and to remember how happy she had then been to serve her guest, and how He had repaid her poor cares a thousandfold! Ah! this resting-place which the angels helped to prepare for the reception of the Well-beloved; what was it now?   An instant's inadvertance, a moment of forgetfulness, and it had all crumbled away!

She comforted herself with despair, and under the force of her grief her soul seemed to be breaking; but this distress, if we consider it, could not be the same as that which she had endured when she first entered the mystic way.   It was like it certainly, but it differed in certain points; for on the first occasion, which is evidently that "obscure night" so marvellously described by S. John of the Cross, there was also the grief caused by inward lassitude, a form of the torment of the damned. We might imagine indeed that this state would endure for ever, that the Saviour had abandoned us for ever; and that thought would be fearful: but a being must have been the victim of this anguish, of which nothing else can give any idea, to realize what the damned in Hell suffer.

Now Lydwine had seen the Lord too closely to fear such a misfortune. She knew herself loved enough to be certain that her repentance would disarm the anger of the divine Spouse; and besides, she did not, as at the beginning, find it impossible to collect herself and pray. She prayed without feeling any sensible softening, but all the same, she could force herself to pray; it was a feeble light which penetrated into the darkness of her prison, but it proved that she was not completely repudiated. She was, indeed, in the situation of a soul in Purgatory, which suffers, but awaits its deliverance with resignation.

And yet what a miserable existence hers was! There was nothing now to counterbalance her bodily tortures; no relaxation to moderate them, no pause to soften them. They were really enough to kill her, for nature, deprived of her supernatural support, broke out into wild cries, and Lydwine vomited mouthfuls of blood.

In vain Jan Walter, who was devoted to her, attempted to console her; she felt distaste for counsel, a disgust for everything.

Alarmed to see her thus depressed, her faithful Catherine cried in despair one day: "What, in Heaven's name, is it all about?"

Lydwine was more calm at the moment and answered:

"It is because of my sins that you see me so unhappy; I have lost, by my own fault, all spiritual interest, even when I make communion. I have nothing now, neither ecstasies, nor prophetic light, nor comfort. All the Saviour has left to solace me is the power to meditate on His life, as heretofore, without distraction; but I find no comfort in it. It is as if I were deported to a world of ice, to an unknown region where there is no light, and where I am only nourished on vinegar and myrrh.''

This trial lasted five months; then on one 2nd July, the feast of the Visitation of the blessed Virgin, the wings of night, which had shadowed the soul of the Saint, lifted, daylight flooded it, and Jesus appeared.

There was but one leap and one cry; the soul threw itself abandoned at His feet, and He raised her and pressed her tenderly to Him. She swooned with joy and for nearly ten days lived in ecstasy above place and time, immersed, as it were, in the ocean of the divine Essence. If she had not breathed, her friends would have thought her dead.

But what caused them to marvel most of all, was a new perfume which escaped from her stigmata and wounds. That scent, so essentially hers, so unique in the lives of the Saints; that aroma which she alone had so long exhaled and which seemed a quintessence of the aromatic scents of the Indies and the spices of the Levant, faded away and was replaced by another which, though refined and sublimated, recalled the perfume of certain flowers newly plucked. Brugman says indeed that, even in the depths of winter, she gave out the scent of the rose, the violet, or the lily.

We hear of these emanations, though more rarely perhaps, in the lives of Saints both before and after Lydwine.   Rose de Viterbe, who lived in the thirteenth century, is said to have exhaled the perfume of the rose; and S. Catherine de Ricci and Saint Theresa, who lived in the sixteenth century, were scented, the first by the violet and the second by the lily and violet, symbols of humility and chastity.

This change took place when she was entirely dispossessed of the body and when the end of her days was near; it seemed as if the spring breath of flowers succeeded the winter smoke of spices, and announced the end of her earthly winter and the arrival of that eternal spring on which she would enter after her death.

Her room was perfumed to such a degree that all the town came to breathe the scent.

"What is that? We have never smelt the like," cried the silly folk; and Lydwine replied:

"GOD alone knows, for I am but a poor being and it has cost me many chastisements to make me understand how much I am still subject to the infirmities of human nature. Praise GOD, and pray to Him for me!"

This seems to be the right place in which to draw attention to the fact that the hagiologies do not contain any biographies which are more perfumed than Lydwine's. I know of none where the benevolence of GOD is thus shewn on each page. Besides the fact that the Saint was a living vessel of perfumes, every time that Our Saviour, His Mother, or His angels came to visit her, they left fragrant traces of their passage; and even the persons whom Lydwine led with her to Paradise were saturated there with celestial effluences, which inebriated their soul and healed their ills.

CHAPTER XIV.

OF all Lydwine's numerous family there only remained to watch over her a nephew, twelve years of age. Of her eight brothers, two were dead, William, the father of Petronille and Baudouin, and that other Baudouin, whose name has been revealed to us by a vision of the Saint's. Were the six others dead, or did they live at a distance? We do not know; but, in any case, none of them is ever described as doing anything for his sister.

Baudouin, her nephew, was a good and pious little boy. We can easily picture him to ourselves as, like so many Dutch children, a fair child with a round and rather heavy face, rendered pleasing by good eyes. He led a sad life, for, instead of playing with the other children of his age in the streets, he had to stay quietly in a room, attentive to the wants of a sick woman. His aunt wished to show her gratitude for his devotion and care, and she did this in a singular manner. Fearing that when she should be no longer there he might perhaps be tempted by doubts against the faith, she was anxious that he should never forget the surprising marvels of which he had been a witness in that house, frequented by Our Saviour, by His Mother, and by the angels, and, as a great endurer of suffering herself, she thought that suffering alone would be strong enough to strike the imagination of the child and to confirm in it for ever the remembrance of so many favours.

She therefore prayed the Lord to send him an access of fever, which should not endanger his life, but recall to him, in after years, the time when he lived with her.

This request was granted.

One evening, towards the feast of the Nativity of
the blessed Virgin, Lydwine asked her nephew, who
was holding a jug of small beer in his hand, to put it
on a table at the head of her bed.   Baudouin obeyed,
and the jug was there all night.   The next day this beer
had changed into an aromatic elixir, with the feathery
bark of cinnamon and the fresh peel of wonderful
citrons in it.   Several persons tasted this and it
stimulated them like a cordial, but the child, having
drunk a few drops, was immediately seized with a fever
which did not leave him before Martinmas.

After he recovered, it was Jan Walter's turn to be
ill.   He was the victim of an intermittent fever, whose
attacks coincided with those of Lydwine, and one of
his sisters, named Cécile, asked the Saint how many
days this sickness would last.

"Till the Sunday of Lent," she replied.

And Walter indeed did recover at that date.   Later
he was again attacked with illness, but this was so
serious that all his friends thought him lost except
Lydwine, who, after having besieged heaven with her
supplications, obtained his recovery.

She lessened the tortures of others by her prayers,
but her own were proportionately augmented.   She
was drawing near her end.   In telling us the story of
her nephew's fever, Gerlac gives us to understand that
it took place in the year of her death; but Thomas
à Kempis antedates it by one year and places it in
1432.

What is certain is that her years were now numbered,
and GOD perfected her in her mission as victim of
reparation by crushing her beneath a last avalanche
of woes.   There was no part of her body free from
ills, and yet He found portions almost void of pain and
filled them with it.   He struck her with fits of epilepsy,
and she had as many as three in a night.   Before the
first, she warned her intimates so that they might hold
her and prevent her from breaking her skull against the
wall.

" That is all very well," they replied, " but it would be better to avoid these seizures you say you are going to have, by asking the Lord to preserve you from them. You have enough maladies without adding another." But she blamed them for judging the will of the Lord.

Soon, to the furies of epilepsy were added fits of madness, but they were very short and only endured just long enough for us to be able to say that, except leprosy, no illness had been spared her. She was also struck down by a fit of apoplexy, from which she recovered; but neuralgia and violent toothache never left her; a new ulcer declared itself in the breast, and then, from the feast of the Purification until Easter, the stone renewed her terrible torments. Finally she suffered such contractions of the nerves that her limbs were contorted and she became grotesque to look at, a thing without form, from which dropped blood and tears.

She endured the most pitiless martyrdom, but she embraced in its entirety the task she was charged to accomplish.

Jesus laid before her, in a frightful vision, the panorama of her times.

Europe appeared to her convulsed—as she herself was—on its earthen bed, and she sought with a trembling hand to cover the decomposing body. An internal rottenness was bursting its sides; a frenzy of sacrilege and crime made it groan like a beast at the slaughter; it was infested with the vermin of its vices, devoured alive by the canker of simony and the cancer of uncleanness; and Lydwine in terror beheld the rejection of the tiara-crowned head now by Avignon and now by Rome.

" See," said the Christ; and on a background of conflagration she saw, under the leadership of crowned maniacs, the abandoned riot of the peoples. They robbed and murdered each other without pity; and farther off, in regions which seemed peaceful, she saw the cloisters overset by wicked monks, clergy who trafficked in the Flesh of Christ and sold at a profit the gifts of the Holy Spirit, heresies, sabbaths in the forests, black masses.

She would have died of despair if, to console her, GOD had not also shown her the counterpart of all this, the army of Saints on the march. They overran the world unceasingly, reforming the abbeys, destroying the cult of Satan, subduing the peoples and restraining the kings, passing, in spite of all obstacles, through a storm of obloquy and opposition. All, whether active or contemplative, suffered and helped to pay, by their prayers and their tortures, the ransom of so much evil!

Before the immensity of the debt she felt herself most poor. What were her infirmities and her afflictions in the face of that quagmire of filth? A drop of water, and hardly even that; and she implored the Saviour not to spare her, but to avenge on her the multitude of offences!

She knew that the term of her existence was near, and she feared now that she would not have accomplished her vocation through having been too happy. She felt herself an unproductive worker, who only brought a feeble and insignificant store of treasure to the hive of pain; and yet, poor sufferer, she was often wearied when, emerging from her ecstasy, she returned to her own room! But the apparitions comforted her.

One day, when she was in a trance, she met her grandfather at the gate of Paradise.

"My sweetest child," he said to her, "I cannot let you enter this place of rest, for it would be a calamity for those who have need of your services; you have still the sins of others to amend and souls in Purgatory to free; but console yourself, my dear child, it will not be long now."

Another time her angel showed her a rose-bush, which was as tall as a forest tree and covered with buds and flowers, and he explained to her that she would not be liberated from the pain of life till all the roses had blown.

" But tell us," asked Jan Walter and the widow Catherine, " are there still many buds to open? "

" All the roses are actually open, except one or two," said she, " so that I shall not be long in leaving you."

She said also to a prior of canons regular, whom she seems to have held in special esteem :

" I should be very grateful, my dear father, if you would return to see me after Easter, but if GOD should take me from this world before your visit, I recommend my soul to your charity."

The prior concluded from this that she would not sing Alleluia upon earth at that festival, and at last she admitted to her intimates that she would die during Eastertide ; but she did not say the day or the hour, because she wished to go away alone, having no one present with her but Jesus.

" And your house ; what will become of that after your death? "

" Do you remember," said she to her friends who put this question to her, " do you remember what I replied to a good Fleming when, touched by my poverty, he offered to build me another house? As long as I live I shall have no other dwelling but this ; but if, after my death, someone wishes to convert this sad place into a hospital for the destitute, I pray beforehand that GOD may reward him."

This was, as she knew, a prophetic utterance, for a pious doctor, Wilhelm, son of that good Godfried de Haga called Sonder Danck, who had cared for her in her youth, fulfilled it after her death.

To some who, hearing that her death was near, asked her if GOD would work miracles at her tomb, she replied :

" I am quite aware that simple souls imagine my departure will be accompanied by extraordinary phenomena, but they are absolutely mistaken. As to what will happen after my burial, GOD alone knows and I have no wish to enquire. I only desire that my friends should not exhume my remains until thirty years have gone by, and that my body which has not touched the earth for thirty-three years should not touch it on my bier. I hope that my obsequies will be performed as rapidly as possible."

Such were her last wishes, and she communicated them to her intimates, who did not doubt, on hearing her express herself in this way, that her end was imminent. They were the more certain of it when, having gathered them round her bed, she said:

"I implore you to pardon me the trouble I may have caused you; do not refuse me this mercy which I beg for the love of GOD; on my part I pray and will pray heartily for you."

All burst into tears, protesting that far from having troubled them she had, on the contrary, greatly edified them by her goodness and patience.

At last Palm Sunday came, and Lydwine threw aside all reserve with the divine Spouse.

He flooded her with such delights that she threw herself on His heart and murmured: "Oh, how tired I am of life; take me hence, my Saviour, take me!"

Jesus smiled, and the Blessed Virgin and the twelve Apostles and a multitude of angels and saints appeared behind Him. Jesus put Himself at the right hand of Lydwine and Mary at the left; close to the Christ a table appeared, on which was a cross, a lighted candle, and a little vessel; the angels approached the bed and uncovered the patient. Then the Saviour took the little vessel, which contained the oil of the sick, and made the accustomed unctions without uttering a word; the angels covered her again; Jesus placed the candle in her hand and the crucifix before her eyes, and remained there, visible to her alone, until her death.

Lydwine said to Him humbly:

"My sweet Master, since you have deigned to abase

yourself to the most miserable of your servants; since you have not shrunk from anointing my unhappy body with your most holy hands, be merciful to the end. Grant me this last grace to suffer as much as I deserve, so that, at last exonerated from living, I may be admitted without passing through Purgatory to the contemplation of your most adorable face."

And Jesus replied:

" Thy requests are heard, my child; in two days thou wilt sing the alleluia with thy sisters, the virgins, in Paradise."

When the sun was risen towards four o'clock in the morning, her confessor, Walter, visited her. He had been entranced in contemplation during the night, and he had seen Lydwine, radiant with joy, amongst the angels. The room was perfumed when he entered.

" Oh!" cried he, " I know that your divine Spouse has just left; if I had not guessed it, I should have known by breathing the scent of the flowers of Eden! Has He announced to you your deliverance? Hide nothing from me, if it is possible, dear sister."

Transported with joy, she exclaimed: "My sufferings are going to be redoubled; but it will soon be over."

And indeed the stone tortured her without relief, and she lived through Easter Monday in horrible torments. On the Tuesday she prepared to die, and, as her room was full of people, she said gently:

" Leave me alone to-day with the child,"—she pointed to her nephew, Baudouïn, seated near the bed—" if you are my friends grant me that favour. Do not be uneasy; if I want you I will send the child to fetch you."

All believed that she wished to withdraw her mind and pray in peace, and, not thinking that death was close at hand, they left her; Jan Walter, too, went away and repaired to the church to recite the vigils of the dead for the superior of the convent of the sisters tertiary, who had just died. Hardly had he left her than her agony began; it lasted from seven in the morning till four in the evening; she was torn with vomiting and threw herself exhausted on the tiles.

" O my child," she said to the little one who wept, " if the good Walter could see how I suffer!"

Baudouin exclaimed, " Aunt, do you wish me to fetch him?"

She did not reply, she had lost consciousness.

Then the terrified child rushed to the church, which was so near the cottage that one could hardly recite the psalm "Miserere" three times in passing from one to the other. Walter hastened and found the Saint inanimate. He hoped she was only rendered insensible through ecstasy; but he went to fetch Lydwine's friends all the same, and they, not wishing to believe her dead, and ignorant that the Lord Himself had given her Extreme Unction with His own hands, as He did to S. Anthony of Padua, asked her to make known to them by a sign if she desired to receive the last Sacraments; but Lydwine did not stir. Then Walter lit a candle and placed it behind the head of the Saint, for fear the light should hurt her eyes, to see if she still breathed, and examined her closely, but doubt was no longer possible, she had ceased to live.

The women burst into sobs, but Catherine, who suppressed her tears, enjoined them to be quiet.

"Let us see," said she, "if, as Lydwine has so often predicted to me, her hands will be clasped after her death; let us see if it is so."

Her right arm had been consumed by the plague, and although a surgeon had succeeded, with a nostrum of his own composition, in keeping it attached to the body, he had not cured it or made it useful, and it was therefore humanly impossible that the two hands should be brought near to one another.

Catherine raised the covering and found that the fingers of both hands were interlaced on the chest; and she was amazed to discover that the rough belt of horse-hair no longer encircled the body, but had been folded, without the strings which fastened it having been undone, and placed near the shoulders at the head of the bed, doubtless by Lydwine's angel.

"I have felt this cincture," says Brugman, "I have scented the perfume which it exhales, and I affirm, having made use of it in exorcism, that it revealed an irresistible power against demons." "As for me," attests Michel d'Esne, "I have taken it in my own hands and know by experience that devils have a great horror and fear of it."

The night after Lydwine's death, Walter, who could not sleep for grief, saw the soul of his penitent under the form of a white dove, whose beak and breast were gold-coloured, the wings silver, and the feet of a vivid red. Brugman explains the symbolism of these colours as follows: the gold of the breast and beak signifies the excellence of her teaching and counsels; the silver of the wings represents the flight of her contemplations; the scarlet of the feet indicates the placing of her steps in the blood-stained footprints of Christ; the whiteness of the body shows the striking purity of the blessed one.

One of Walter's three sisters, who had also watched by the body, saw the soul of Lydwine carried to heaven by angels; and Catherine Simon saw her enter her room, accompanied by a great number of the heavenly host, and participate in the celestial wedding feast.

Frequently, in that same night, she showed herself to holy virgins who loved her without knowing her. She was dressed in white, crowned with roses by the Saviour, and leading a chant of the sequence "Jesu Corona Virginum," which the angels sang before the blessed Virgin, who placed round her neck a circlet of gems, and pressed her tenderly in her arms.

The next day, at dawn, Walter went to the house of mourning, knelt before the bed, and wept; but at length he rose and said to his sisters and to Catherine Simon: "Take off the veil which covers the face of our friend." They obeyed, and a cry of amazement followed.

Lydwine had become again as she had been before her illnesses, fresh and fair, young and dimpled; one would have thought it was a girl of seventeen, who smiled there in her sleep. Of the cleft in the forehead, which had so disfigured her, there was not the least trace; the ulcers and wounds had disappeared, except the three scars of the wounds made by the Picardians, which ran like three threads of purple across the snow of her flesh.

All were astounded at this spectacle and eagerly inhaled a scent which they could not analyse, so sustaining, so fortifying, that for two days and three nights they felt no need of sleep or nourishment.

But soon there was a concourse of visitors, for directly the news was confirmed that the Saint was dead, not only the inhabitants of Schiedam, but also those of Delft, Rotterdam, Leyden, and Brielle, passed in procession through the poor room.

À Kempis puts the number of pilgrims at several millions, as do also Gerlac and Brugman. He tells that a woman of evil life touched the neck of the deceased with her rosary, and that after her departure the beads of the rosary were marked like drops of tar on the skin. The same effect had been produced during life, for when her fingers had touched an impure hand they were immediately covered with blemishes. Walter then forbade the visitors to touch the corpse with objects of piety or with cloths.

They hastened to satisfy Lydwine's wishes that her body might be quickly buried; but the magistrates of Schiedam would not allow this. "They did not dare to bury the body," says Michel d'Esne, "because the Count of Holland had said he was coming to see it."

It is a fact that all the little potentates of Holland used to come and see the Saint. We have noted her relations with Wilhelm VI., the Countess Marguerite, and Duke John of Bavaria. Philip, Duke of Burgundy and Count of Holland evidently knew her too, for he proposed to be present at her funeral. The name of

Jacqueline, the legitimate sovereign, is alone absent from the list. Owing to the perfidy of her uncles, she lived exiled from her dominions and wandered from one province to another, sometimes in prison, sometimes besieged in some stronghold. She must have known of Lydwine's existence, but though she could have gone to see her when she was at liberty and her enemies were not occupying Schiedam, she may not have cared to ask her advice or receive her counsel concerning her various marriages—counsel which would have very certainly displeased her. Anyhow, her name is not once mentioned by the three historians.

To return to Lydwine : when Walter learnt the refusal of the burgomasters to authorize the interment, he was indignant and wished to disregard it, but he was forbidden, under pain of imprisonment and the confiscation of his goods, to move the corpse. He was therefore forced to submit. Although, in spite of her attachment to the sisters tertiary, Lydwine was not admitted to the third order of S. Francis—for Brugman, who was a Franciscan, would certainly have told us if she had been—they clothed her in a woollen robe and a girdle, like those of this order, and placed on her head a cap of parchment, on which were written in ink the names of Jesus and of Mary. Then Walter slipped a pillow of straw under the head and, as she had desired, a little case containing what she called her " roses," which were nothing else but the tears of coagulated blood she had so often shed. Walter detached them from her face when he went to her in the morning, and placed them carefully in a little box.

She remained thus exposed for three days, and at last, as the Duke of Burgundy had advised the magistrates that they must not count on his presence, the order for burial was given.

On the Friday morning, after a solemn service conducted under the presidency of P. Josse, prior of the canons regular of Brielle, whom she may have begged to visit her after Easter, she was interred precisely at mid-day, in the southern part of the graveyard near the church.

According to her wishes that her body might not touch the earth, they placed beams of wood on the floor and walls of the grave; then they covered the tomb with bricks, in the form of a vault, and sealed it above with a red stone two feet high, whereon were traced crosses in vermillion. A year later, the clergy had a chapel of stone constructed over her tomb, which communicated by an opening into the church.

Lydwine was fifty-three years and some days old when she died, on the 18th of the calends of May (otherwise the 14th April), the day of the feast of S. Tiburce and S. Valerian, in the year of the Lord 1433, on the Tuesday in the octave of Easter, after vespers, at about four o'clock.

Miracles occurred without delay, and amongst those that are attested we will quote three.

The first took place at Delft. A young girl, who had kept her bed for eight years, had been given up by the doctors, when one day Wilhelm, son of Sonder Danck, who, like his father, practiced medicine, said to her, after owning that her sickness was incurable:

" What are your sufferings in comparison with those which blessed Lydwine endured; she whom my father treated? GOD now works, by her merits, numerous miracles in our country. Invoke her aid!"

The sick girl, thus instructed, implored the Saint, who appeared to her and healed her.

The second miracle took place at Gouda. There was in a convent there a nun who had one leg shorter than the other, and it was so contracted that she could not walk. She begged that they would take her to Delft to be examined by this Wilhelm Sonder Danck, who had treated a friend of hers; but her superiors refused. She was in despair, when Lydwine appeared in her cell during the night and invited her to beg the nuns each to recite five paternosters and and five aves in honour of GOD and also for her, after which they were to take her down on the following Sunday into the chapel of the cloister, where she would recover her health.   It happened as predicted; the lame woman left the church full of joy and completely cured.

The third miracle was accomplished at Leyden to the benefit of another nun, who, for eight years, had suffered from a tumour on the neck as big as an apple. She was told to make a pilgrimage to Lydwine's tomb barefoot and dressed in a simple woollen robe, without linen beneath.   She went there, but on coming back she was distressed, for the tumour had not disappeared. She went to bed, imploring the Saint not to despise her thus, and fell asleep; but when she awoke the tumour had gone and her neck was restored to health.

These miracles, which have been duly attested and have been made the subject of strict enquiries, took place in 1448 under the pontificate of his holiness Pope Nicolas V.

CHAPTER XV.

SUCH was the life of Saint Lydwine of Schiedam, which will no doubt rejoice the pious and distress the numerous Catholics who, in weakness of faith or in ignorance, would relegate the mystic to the lunatic asylum, and the miracles to the region of superstition and legend. For these the expurgated biographies of the Jansenites would suffice, if they had not at the present time a whole school of hagiographers ready to satisfy their hatred of the supernatural by fabricating histories of Saints confined to this earth and forbidden to escape from it; of Saints who are not Saints. Was it not one of those rationalists who, when consulted some years ago on the subject of a revelation by the incomparable Sister Emmerich, who had just confirmed a discovery near Ephesus, replied : " I have already told you that it is impossible to introduce into a serious debate a book such as those visions of Catherine Emmerich ; archæology is founded on witness and not on ' hallucinations '."

What a good sentiment for a priest to utter, and how he despises Mysticism !

In spite of oracles of this nature it is possible to affirm that, strange as it may seem, Lydwine's life was marked by nothing abnormal and by nothing new.

If without speaking of the spiritual graces, the apparitions of Our Lord and of the blessed Virgin, and the intercourse with angels, which abound in all the lives of the Saints, we confine ourselves simply to physical phenomena, most of those we have quoted in the course of this book can be found in the biographies of numberless elect who lived before and after Lydwine.

If we seek, for instance, for other Saints and servants of GOD who lived, like Lydwine, without other nourishment than the Eucharist, we discover amongst many so privileged, the venerable Marie d'Oignies, Saint Angèle de Foligno, S. Catharine of Sienna, blessed Elizabeth the good of Waldsee, S. Colombe de Riétie, Dominic de Paradis, blessed Marie Bagnesi, Francis of Jerrone, Louise of the Resurrection, Mother Agnes, blessed Nicolas of Flue, and S. Peter of Alcantura.

Amongst the large number who also lived without the blessing of sleep we note Saint Christine the admirable, S. Colette, S. Catherine de Ricci, blessed Agatha de la Croix, S. Elphide, and S. Flore or Fluer, hospitalier of the order of S. John.

Of wounds which became thuribles of perfume, acting not only on the sense of smell but also on souls, to sanctify them, we find instances in the story of S. Humiliane, S. Ida of Louvain, Dominic de Paradis, Salomani de Venise, the Clarisse, Jeanne Marie de la Croix, Venturini de Bergame, blessed Didée, and the leper Bartholomew.

The blessed odour of sanctity was present after death with Pope Marcel, S. Aldegonde, S. Menard, S. Dominic, S. Catherine of Boulogne, blessed Lucy of Narni, blessed Catherine de Racconigi, S. Claire de Rimini, S. Fine of Tuscany, S. Elizabeth of Portugal, S. Theresa, S. Rose of Lima, S. Louis Bertrand, S. Joseph de Cupertino, S. Thomas of Villeneuve, S. Raymond de Pennafort, and many others.

Amongst the Saints whose bodies were, like Lydwine's, re-established in youth and beauty after death, we find S. Francis of Assisi, S. Anthony of Padua, S. Laurence Justinian, S. Lutgarde, also a victim of reparation, S. Catharine of Sienna, S. Didace, S. Colomb de Riéti, S. Catherine de Ricci, S. Madeleine de Pazzi, the venerable Dorothea Frances, Marie Villani of Naples, S. Rose of Lima, and I could prolong the list still further.

On the other hand, Lydwine was not of the group
of Myroblites, that is to say, of the godly whose bodies
distilled essences and balms after death.   Such were
S. Nicolas de Myre, S. Willibrod, apostle of Holland,
S. Vitalien, S. Lutgarde, S. Walburge, S. Rose de
Viterbo, blessed Mathie de Mazzarei, S. Hedwige,
S. Eustochie, S. Agnes de Montepulciano, S. Theresa,
S. Madeleine de Pazzi, and Marguerite Van Valkenissen.

To return to the life of this Saint, who was never
seen standing alone, it may be said that though she
was the greatest sufferer of whom we know, she was
also the least, and she never murmured.   This
Saint, so sick in body, had to give counsel and advice
to the sick in soul; her chamber was a hospital for
the maladies of the conscience; she received them
indiscriminately, priests and monks, burgomasters and
burghers, patricians and women of the people, men
of the lowest extraction and princes; and she operated
on them and dressed their wounds.

It was a spiritual hospital, open to all comers; and
GOD wished it to be thus, that the gifts He dispensed
might be known to the public, that the miracles which
she effected in His name might be seen.

Her vocation as healer of bodily ills was, if we reflect
upon it, an important one.   She had the power in a
less pronounced degree than many other Saints; but
she presents this peculiarity, that the maladies which
she removed were not, in most cases, destroyed, but
simply transplanted to herself.

In the matter of asceticism, we must note that the
Saviour exacted from her more than He exacted from
other elect; she had already attained to the height of
union with Him, when He plunged her back into the
night, or rather the twilight, of the purgative life.

That division of the three stages of mystic ascension,
so distinct in the theologians, is confused in her case.
It is not a question of a halt between the stages of
enlightenment, but of two extremes, the first and last
stages only, in which she seems at one epoch to be

living simultaneously. However much GOD humiliated her, He did not make her descend from the summits to which she had attained. He darkened the summits and He isolated her; but when the storm was over she found herself there uninjured, without having lost an inch of ground.

She was, in short, a fruit of suffering which GOD pressed until He had extracted the very last drop. The husk was empty when she died, and GOD was about to entrust to others of His daughters the terrible burden which she had left. She had herself succeeded other Saints, and other Saints in their turn would inherit from her. Her two co-adjutors, S. Colette and S. Frances of Romaine, had still some years to suffer; two other stigmatized Saints of her century, S. Rite de Cassie and Petronille Hergods, were nearing their end; but new bearers of suffering were springing up ready to replace them.

In a general sense, all Saints and all servants of Christ are victims of expiation. Apart from their special vocation, which is not always expiatory, for some are more particularly designed to effect conversions, or to purge the monasteries, or to preach to the masses, all nevertheless bring a victory over evil to the common treasure of the Church; all have been lovers of the Cross and have been granted by Jesus an opportunity of showing Him the authentic proof of love, which is suffering. We can therefore say with justice that all have contributed to the work of Lydwine; but she had some more direct legatees, souls more particularly set apart, as she herself was, to serve as propitiatory victims; and it is especially amongst the stigmatized that one must look for them.

Is it not significant that all these victims belonged to the feminine sex?

GOD appears to have reserved specially for them this vocation of sacrifice. The men who were Saints had a more expansive and more rousing part to play; they traversed the world, created or reformed orders, con-

o

verted idolators, were active in the eloquence of the
pulpit; whilst the woman, who is not endowed with the
sacerdotal character, suffers in silence on a bed.   The
truth is that her soul and her temperament are more
loving, more devout, less egotistical than those of a
man.   She is more impressionable, more easy to move;
and Jesus meets with a warmer welcome from her, for
she has delicate thought and care for others, which a
man, if he is not a S. Francis of Assisi, ignores.
Moreover, in the case of virgins, suppressed maternal
love mingles with the delights of the divine Spouse,
which are thereby doubled for them, and He becomes,
when they so desire it, the divine Child.   The joys of
Bethlehem are more accessible to them than to a man,
and one can easily understand that they offer less
resistance to divine absorption.   In spite of their
changeable nature and their tendency to illusions, it
is from the women by preference that the divine Spouse
recruits His victims; and it is this, without doubt, that
explains why, of the 321 stigmatized who are known
to history, 274 are women and only 47 are men.

The list of these victims of reparation, Lydwine's
heirs, is given at length in a wonderfully authenticated
work, "La Stigmatisation," by Dr. Imbert-Gourbeyre.

We will only extract from it the history of those
whose vocation of expiatory sickness is undoubted;
and we will add to them some victims who, if they did
not bear on their body the bleeding signs of Christ,
were great ecstatics and notable sufferers, whose life
presents the most complete analogy with that of
Lydwine.

Amongst these women who, after the death of
the Saint of Holland, paid by their sufferings the
ransom of the sins of their time, we find a record of the
following:—

IN THE FIFTEENTH CENTURY.

S. Colombe de Riéti, an Italian of the third order of
S. Dominic, was not stigmatized, but was charged by
the Lord to summon the Pope to correct his morals and

purify his court.   She was submitted to the most
drastic examination and the worst tortures at Rome;
atoned by sicknesses unknown to the doctors, for the
evils of her age, and died at her work in 1501.

Blessed Osanne, patroness of the town of Mantua
in Italy, tertiary of the order of S. Dominic, was born
six years after Lydwine's death, and when she was
seven years of age Jesus placed His cross on her
shoulder and predicted for her a life of tortures.
Her room was like that of the Saint of Schiedam, a
consulting room for spiritual troubles.   Princes,
ecclesiastics, laics, streamed through it, and she
lanced the wounds of vice and dressed them.   She
died, after a life of terrible pain, in 1505.

S. Catherine of Genoa, an Italian, was married and
lived at first a mundane life.   Then Jesus threw His
imprint upon her, and her conversion took place in an
instant, like that of S. Paul.   She was, to use her own
expression, " torn from head to foot " by supernatural
diseases ; she endured in her lifetime the fires of
Purgatory to save souls, and she has left on this life
of martyrdom a persuasive and elevating tract.   She
also knew the torments of the Passion, and died in
1510, after a series of tortures and sufferings, whose
details are harrowing.   Her body still exists in a state
of incorruption at Genoa, where all may see it.

IN THE SIXTEENTH CENTURY.

Blessed Marie Bagnesi, an Italian of the third order
of S. Dominic, was not stigmatised, but her life seems
a copy of Lydwine's.   She suffered, to make reparation
for the iniquities of man, all that it is possible to suffer.
For forty-five years she was prostrated by headache,
burnt with fever, stricken with dumbness and deafness ;
and the Bollandists say that she had not a single one
of her members intact.   She died of the stone, as did
Lydwine, in 1577.

S. Theresa, a Spaniard, reformed the Carmelites,
and became the unequalled historian of the struggles

of the soul.   Her history is too well known for us to
speak of here; let us only note that she was constantly
ill and made expiation, as did the Saint of the Low
Countries, for the souls in Purgatory, for sinners and
for wicked priests.   Her heavenly birthday was in
1582.

S. Catherine de Ricci, an Italian, daughter of an
illustrious family in Florence, belonged to a convent
of the third order of the Dominicans, of which she was
elected abbess.   Her desire to submit her body and
soul to the chastisements merited by the spread of
heresies and moral disorder was granted, and her
existence became a very hell of suffering.   She died
in 1590, and the bull which canonizes her affirms that
the Saviour had printed the signs of the Passion in her
flesh.

Archangèle Tardera, an Italian tertiary of the order
of S. Francis, was ill for thirty-six years, and passed
the twenty-two last years of her life on her bed.   Her
mission was to redeem the offences of the impious,
and she died in 1599.

IN THE SEVENTEENTH CENTURY.

S. Madeleine de Pazzi, an Italian Carmelite, had
besought the Saviour to burden her with the sins of the
world, and she was taken at her word.   She was
always ill and in an almost permanent state of ecstasy.
She was endowed with the spirit of prophecy and
dictated spiritual works which take the form of
dialogues between the soul and GOD.   She died in
1607.

Pudentienne Zagnoni, an Italian, daughter of a
tailor in Bologna, was a tertiary of S. Francis.   She
was weighted with infirmities whose supernatural
origin was recognized by the doctors; and she was
also dragged by the hair and tormented with blows by
the demons.   In this way she made satisfaction for
sins which she had not committed.   For nine weeks
before she died, in 1608, the nine choirs of angels
communicated her, each in their turn.

Blessed Passidée of Sienna, an Italian of the order of Capucines, sacrificed herself to disarm the Saviour's anger at the impurities of her time. Judging her maladies, which no remedies touched, inefficacious, she inflicted overwhelming additional penances on herself; she lashed herself, till the blood flowed, with branches of juniper and thorny twigs; she dressed the wounds with hot salt and vinegar; she walked barefoot in the snow, and put bullets of lead in her shoes; she plunged into barrels of icy water in winter, and in summer hung head downwards over the fire; she was communicated by Jesus, by His Mother, and by the angels, and her trances were so frequent that Fr. Venturi, her historian, wrote, " They caused her to live much more in Paradise than on the earth." She died in 1615.

Venerable Stephanie of the Apostles, a Spanish Carmelite, was not stigmatized, but implored and received from the Lord permission to expiate for sinners. She increased the troubles of her already feeble health by prolonged fasts, hair shirts, iron circlets, and chains. She completed her vocation of suffering in 1617.

Ursula Bénincasa, an Italian, foundress of the congregation of the Theatins, averted by her tortures the dangers which threatened the Church. She burnt with the flames of Purgatory to exonerate souls, and divine love fired her in such a way that a column of smoke proceeded from her mouth. Besides her propitiatory maladies, she was subjected, at Rome, to the harshest treatment, and died in 1618.

Agatha de la Croix, a Spanish tertiary of the order of S. Dominic, became, by her desire for self-sacrifice, both lame and blind. Her flesh, like that of Lydwine, fell into corruption, and she was also consumed by the fires of Purgatory. She died in 1621.

Marine Escobar, a Spaniard, reformer of the rule of S. Bridget, was ill for fifty years, and passed thirty of them stretched on a couch. She exhaled, like the Dutch Saint, the most delicate perfumes. When they changed her linen, says her biographer, it seemed to those who took it from her body a flower-bed of sweet-scented flowers. She died in 1633.

Agnès de Langeac, a French tertiary of the order of S. Dominic, endured all the torments of Purgatory to liberate souls. She lived infirm, dragging herself about on crutches, atoning by her sufferings for misdeeds of her neighbours, and she died in 1634.

Jacqueline of the Holy Spirit, a French Dominican, was bedridden and always obliged to live in one room. She died, after terrible sufferings of reparation, in 1638.

Marguerite of the Sacred Sacrament, a French Carmelite, endured extraordinary torments, and suffered from such pains in the head that, after having vainly pierced it with red-hot nails, the surgeons trepanned her. But she was not relieved by these tortures, and relics were the only means of alleviation. She expiated more especially the offences done to the Lord by want of charity among the rich, and she offered herself to the Lord as a victim to deliver France from the invasion of German armies. She ended her sacrifice in 1648.

Lucie Gonzales, an Italian, was shaken by fevers and had no whole part in her body. She expiated more especially the abominations which the revolutionaries of Naples committed in 1647. Her life was a record of pain, which closed in 1648.

Pauline of S. Theresa, an Italian of the third order of S. Dominic, took on her the sins of the seculars and priests. She lived bedridden, as Lydwine did; was communicated by the hand of Christ, and liberated by her sufferings the souls in Purgatory, who surrounded her on all sides. Her death took place in 1657.

Mary of the Most Holy Trinity, a Spanish tertiary of S. Dominic, was weighed down with infirmities and compelled, when not stretched out on a sheet, to drag herself along on her knees. Her pious vocation ended in 1660.

Pudentienne Zagnoni, an Italian Clarisse, must not be confused with her sister, the stigmatized mentioned above, who bore the same Christian and surname. She was ill for thirty-two years. Like Lydwine, she travelled with her angel into Paradise and made amends on her sick bed for the sins of others. She died in 1662.

Marie Ock, a Belgian tertiary Carmelite, suffered the pains incurred by those persons for whom she did penance; relieved the souls in Purgatory; was beaten, thrown down staircases, and plunged into wells by demons. When she was not prostrate on her bed, she ran to evil haunts to spoil them of their guests. She was one of the bravest and most fruitful victims of reparation, whose curious biography is well worth reading. She died at her work in 1684.

Jeanne Marie de la Croix, an Italian tertiary Franciscan, was constantly ill and tortured by atrocious bodily pains. She had to submit to the most barbarous treatment from the doctors, who, however, at last recognized the preternatural origin of her ills and permitted her to groan in peace. She received the mystic ring, exhaled from her person inexplicable perfumes, healed the sick by her blessing, and multiplied loaves. She sacrificed herself more especially to combat heresy, and was born into heaven in 1673.

Marie Angélique de la Providence, a French Carmelite tertiary, interceded for debased communities and for the priests. The Lord Himself showed her the sinners whose offences He wished her to neutralize by her sufferings. She was extremely devoted to the Holy Sacrament, and one of the most frequently molested victims of demons, who beat her like a carpet, knocked her against walls, and trod her underfoot. She died in 1685.

IN THE EIGHTEENTH CENTURY.

Marcelline Pauper, a Frenchwoman, sister of charity at Nevers, was an expiatory victim for the profanations of the Holy Sacrament and the thefts of the Sacred Host.   She it was who said: "My life is a delicious Purgatory, where the body suffers and the soul rejoices."   She died in 1708.

Fialletta-Rosa Fialletti, an Italian tertiary of S. Dominic, lived through a series of expiatory diseases and died in 1717.

S. Veronica Giulani, an Italian Clarisse, was a living image of Christ on the Cross.   Whilst her maladies devoured her she cried: "Long live the sacred cross; long live suffering!"   Like Lydwine, she offered herself to the Lord to atone for the sins committed by debauches on fast days.   Like S. Theresa, she had transverberation of heart; and like S. Claire de Montefalco, she bore the mark of the instruments of Calvary.   She died in 1727.

S. Marie Frances of the five wounds of Jesus, an Italian of the third order of S. Francis, lived in continual sickness and suffered from frightful pain, fevers and gangrene.   Like Lydwine, she took upon herself the maladies of her neighbour, was persecuted by her family and by her confessor, and was communicated by the angels.   Endowed with the spirit of prophesy, she announced the French Revolution and the death of Louis XVI. beforehand; but at the ight of the sufferings of the Church which were shown to her, her heart broke and she implored the Saviour to deliver her from life.   Her request was granted in 1791.

IN THE NINETEENTH CENTURY.

Mary-Josepha Kümi, a Swiss Dominican, was an expiatory victim for the Church, for sinners, and for souls in Purgatory, whose torments she shared.   She died in 1817.

Anne Catherine Emmerich, a German Augustine, was the greatest mystic of modern times, and, although illiterate, a magnificent artist.   Her history is too well known to need recalling, for her books are read everywhere.   We will only state that this stigmatized Saint was always confined to her bed, and that amongst the victims of reparation it is she who, with Marie Bagnèsi, is most like Lydwine. She was her direct inheritor down the ages, and died, after a life of indescribable suffering, in 1824.

Elizabeth Canori Mora, an Italian of the third order of the barefoot Trinitarians, paid more than any others the debt of the persecutors of the Church and died in 1825.

Anna-Maria Taïgi, an Italian of the third order of the barefoot Trinitarians, was prostrated by a series of tortures; troubles of the head, fevers, gout, and asthma. She had not an instant's repose, and her eyes, like Lydwine's, shed blood when they were exposed to the least light. She sacrificed herself more especially for the persecutors of the Church, and her sacrifice was ended in 1837.

Sister Bernard of the Cross, a French woman of the congregation of Mary Theresa at Lyons, accepted the temptations of persons too weak to bear them, and suffered death and passion for them. She died in 1847.

Marie Domenica Lazzari, one of the stigmatized of the Tyrol, was a mediator for miscreants. Her life was a continual agony; tortured by convulsions, by a perpetual cough, and by pains of the stomach. For fourteen years she lived solely on the Holy Species, taking no other food. Her death took place in 1848.

Marie-Rosa Andriani, an Italian of the third order of S. Francis, was a martyr from her fifth year, and the Lord aggravated her torments, giving her no consolation. She tore live bones from her chest and was sustained for twenty-five years by the Eucharist. She died in 1848.

Marie of S. Peter of the Holy Family, a French Carmelite, was not stigmatized, but interposed between GOD and France, which was on the point of being chastised. She obtained her desire, but suffered martyrdom. She herself sums up her life in this phrase, " It is for reparation that I was put into the world, and that is the object of my death." She died in 1848.

Marie Agnes Steiner, a German Clarisse of a convent in Ombrie, underwent, for the good of the Church, the most cruel maladies. She exhaled, like Lydwine, celestial perfumes, and died in 1862.

Marie du Bourg (in religion Marie de Jésus), a French woman, founder of the congregation of the sisters of S. Saviour and of the blessed Virgin, suffered terribly for the impious, for the possessed, and for the waiting souls. " She is entirely occupied in peopling Heaven and emptying Purgatory," said one of her daughters. She suffered furious attacks of demons, and died in 1862.

Marie de Moerl, the best known of the Tyrolese stigmatized, was a tertiary of the order of S. Francis. She suffered chiefly for the Church, was endowed with the spirit of prophesy, and could read souls. The Abbé Curicque, one of her historians, narrates this incident, which might have figured in the life of Lydwine. An ecclesiastic, whose name even was unknown to her, came, accompanied by many persons, to recommend himself to her prayers. She agreed to invoke GOD on his behalf, but she judged it necessary to tell him of one fault, which he alone could know, and of which he must at all costs rid himself. Not willing to humiliate him before others, she took from under her bolster a psalter, opened it, and showed him with her finger the passage which expressly dealt with this failing; then she smiled sweetly and fell back into the ecstasy his visit had interrupted. She died in 1868.

Barbara of Saint Dominic, a Spanish Dominican, assumed the sins of her fellow creatures, was a butt for the assaults of the Evil One, and died the victim of mystic substitution. She offered her life to Christ for the recovery of another nun who was dying; and while the other recovered her health, she took to her bed never to leave it again. She was hardly thirty years old when they buried her in 1872.

The case of the Belgian, Louise Lateau, is celebrated. She was bedridden, atoning by her sufferings for the sins of others, and for twelve years the communion was her only food. Too many books have been written on this holy virgin for it to be necessary to speak more of her here. She died in 1883.

Marie-Catherine Putigny, a French woman of the Visitation, offered herself as a victim of reparation to the Lord, and suffered the most acute agonies for the souls in Purgatory. She saw, like Lydwine and Sister Emmerich, visions of the Passion, and died in her convent at Metz in 1885.

The suit for the beatification of most of these women has been instituted at Rome; but without forestalling the judgment in any particular case, we may hope that the celestial origin of their vocations and of their sufferings will be recognized.

It is noticeable that, amongst these heirs of Lydwine, there are none from the Low Countries. There are Italians, Spaniards, French, Belgians, Tyrolese, Germans, and Swiss, but no Dutch. Dr. Imbert-Gourbeyre quotes one, but without sufficiently precise details to permit us to affirm that she was a victim of reparation. She was named Dorothea Visser, and was born in 1820 at Gendringen; and towards 1843 she was stamped with the stigmata of the Passion. It would have been very desirable for some monk or Dutch priest to have investigated her case and told us whether the inheritance of Lydwine had indeed been taken up in her own country.

It is hardly necessary to say that these lists are very incomplete. They suffice, however, to prove that Lydwine's inheritance has not fallen into disuse, and that the designs of GOD do not change. His process of making appeals to the charity of certain souls to satisfy the requirements of His justice remains unaltered; the law of substitution remains vigorous; nothing has changed since the time of S. Lydwine.

It must be added that at the present hour (1901), the wants of the Church are immense, and a wind of wickedness is blowing over the regions unsheltered by believers.   There is a sort of slackness in devotion, a lack of energy, more particularly in those countries that are the spiritual fiefs of the Holy Seat.

Austria is eaten to the marrow by Jewish vermin; Italy has become a resort of the Freemasons, a resort of demoniacs, in the strict sense of the word; Spain and Portugal are also overrun with the Lodges of Freemasons; and little Belgium alone appears less enfeebled in faith and soul.   As to that nation so privileged by Christ—France—she has been attacked, half strangled, bruised with kicks, rolled in the dung-heap, by a mob financed by miscreants.   Freemasonry has unmuzzled for this infamous task a greedy crew of Jews and Protestants.

In such an upheaval, it were perhaps better to have had recourse to measures abolished long ago, to make use of shirts duly sulphured and some good dry faggots of wood; but the feeble souls of the Catholics would have been incapable of blowing on the fire to ignite it!   Besides, these healthy expedients have long since fallen into disuse, practices which some would qualify as indiscreet and are, anyhow, not in accord with the customs of the times.

It being granted then that the Church lies defence-less, we should be disquieted for the future if we did not know that she is rejuvenated each time she suffers persecution—the tears of her martyrs are to her the elixir of youth!   When Catholicism is rejected from one country, it filters into another and finally returns to its point of departure.   This is the history of the societies which, after having been chased from France, returned when they had founded new cloisters in foreign lands.   In spite of all obstacles, Catholicism, which appeared stagnant, is still in full flood; it has insinuated itself into England, into America, into the Low Countries, and has little by little gained a foothold in heretic lands, which it still retains.

If she were bound and her four veins cut she would revive again, for the Church holds a formal promise and cannot perish. She has seen others suffer, and she ought in suffering to wait patiently!

It is none the less true, that through sacrileges and blasphemies, the situation of France is lamentable. This century has opened, especially in France, with the country soaked, nay saturated like a sponge, with Satanism, and it does not appear to be even aware of its condition. Duped by the recantations of a foul regenade, the Catholics did not in the least suspect he lied on that day when he declared himself mocked by them, because for years he had overwhelmed them with documents, of which the greater part were correct but steeped in a medium of incredible lies!

One fact, at any rate, is undeniable; that, in spite of the denials of those interested, the cult of Lucifer does exist; it leads the Freemasons, and silently influences the sinister jokers who govern the country, although you would not imagine, when they direct the assault against Christ and His Church, that they were the servants of a master in whose existence they do not believe! Clever as he is to get himself denied, the Demon does lead them.

The twentieth century therefore has begun as the preceding one terminated in France, with an infernal eruption; an open struggle between Lucifer and GOD.

Truly one must hope that to counterbalance the weight of such an attack, the victims of expiation abound, and that in the cloisters and in the world, many monks, priests, and laymen accept the reparative work of sacrifice.

Certainly in the orders whose aim is mortification and penance, such as the Calvarians, Benedictines, Trappists, Clarisses, Carmelites, to name only five, women, whose maladies defy the doctors' diagnosis, suffer that they may neutralize the demoniacal abominations of our day, but we have to ask ourselves whether the convents are numerous enough, for when we come to know the details of certain terrible calamities like that of the charity bazaar, for example, it is very difficult to believe that there was nothing more in it than the material causes enumerated in the magistrates' report.

On this day there were, indeed, truly pious women present. Women who came not merely to show off their clothes and exhibit themselves, but to help in ministering to the unfortunate and to do good; women who had all, or nearly all, heard Mass that morning and made their Communion, were burnt alive. The others managed to get away. It seems then that it was the will of Heaven to choose in this crowd the best, the most saintly of the visitors, and oblige them to expiate in the flames the number of our unrepented sins.

And finally one puts the question to oneself: Would such a disaster have been avoided if there had been more monasteries of strict observance, more souls determined to inflict voluntary suffering on themselves and endure the chastisement which sin had made inevitable?

We cannot reply directly to such a question; but it is possible to affirm that never till now has there been such need of a Lydwine; for such as she alone will be fit to appease the certain anger of the Judge, and to serve as a shelter against the cataclysms which are preparing!

I do not blind myself to the fact that in speaking thus in a century where each pursues but one aim, to rob his neighbour and to enjoy in peace either adultery or divorce, I have little chance of being understood. I know very well, too, that in face of this catholicism, whose foundation is self-forgetfulness and suffering, the faithful who are in love with small works of devotion and hardened by reading pious nothings, will repeat once more the pleasing theory that " GOD does not ask so much as that, because He is so good."

Unfortunately, He does demand so much of us, although He is nevertheless infinitely good. But we must repeat once more that those who pray are compensated for these afflictions, even here below, by inward joy, and that in those privileged beings whom He tortures, the exuberance of joy exceeds the pain. All have souls which rejoice in their broken bodies; all cry like Lydwine, that they do not wish to be healed, that they would not exchange the consolations they receive for all the enjoyments of the world.

Moreover, the sheep who are alarmed by the sufferings of these protectors are wrong in feeling fear, for GOD will have pity on their ignorance and weakness and will doubtless spare them more than He spared His own Son. It is only amongst those whom he has endowed with very robust souls that He seeks a weight to counterbalance sin. Just as no person is tempted above his strength, so no person is loaded with pain which he cannot somehow endure. GOD administers suffering to each man according to his powers of endurance, but those who suffer only moderately would be wrong to rejoice too much, for that absence of torments is neither a sign of spiritual health nor of loving preference.

Besides, this book is not written for them. It is difficult for persons who enjoy good health to understand it, though they will apprehend it better later on, when evil days come. It is addressed more especially to those poor things who are attacked by lengthy and incurable maladies. These are, for the most part, the victims of choice; but how many amongst them know that they accomplish the admirable work of reparation both for themselves and others? That this work may be truly satisfactory, it must be accepted with resignation and presented humbly to the Saviour. It is not a question of saying to oneself : I could never do it willingly, I am not a Saint like Lydwine; for

neither did she penetrate the designs of Providence
when she first entered the way of mystic pain.   She
also pitied herself, like her father, Job, and cursed her
destiny; she also asked herself what sins she could
have committed to be treated in this way, and did not
feel at all anxious to offer her torments to GOD of her
own free will.   She very nearly fell into despair, for
she did not become a Saint all at once; and yet, after
many efforts to meditate on the Passion of the Saviour,
whose sufferings interested her much less than her
own, she succeeded in loving them at last, and they
raised her in a whirlwind of joy to the summits of the
perfect life!   The truth is that Jesus begins by making
His followers suffer, and explains Himself afterwards.
The great thing then is to submit first, and claim the
reward afterwards.   He is the greatest beggar that
heaven and earth have ever produced; the terrible
Beggar of Love!   The wounds of His hands are purses
always open, and He stretches them out that each may
fill them with the small change of His sufferings and
His tears.

There is nothing to be done then but to give to
Him.   Consolation, peace of soul, the means of
utilizing oneself and transmuting at last one's sorrows
into joy can only be obtained at this price.   After the
necessary period of preparation, the great work is
accomplished; the gold, that is to say the love, which
consumes distress and tears, arises from the brasier
of suffering; and this alone is the true philosopher's
stone.

To return to Lydwine, we must narrate in a few lines
the fate which was reserved for her relics.

As was said above, the rectors of the church of S.
John the Baptist, at Schiedam, built a little chapel in
1434 above her tomb; and Molanus adds this detail,
that the chapel was decorated with pictures represent-
ing divers episodes of her life.

The relics were venerated there until the Protestants
became masters of Holland, which they have not since

left. They seized the remains of Lydwine at Schiedam, and the Catholics had to buy them back.

In 1615 the body was exhumed, by order of Prince Albert, Archduke of Austria and sovereign of the Low Countries, and of his wife Isabelle Claire Eugenie, daughter of Philip II. of Spain and grand-daughter of Henry II. of France.

This Princess, who loved the memory of Lydwine, had the bones enclosed in a silver reliquary and transferred to the oratory of her palace at Brussels.

A year later, in 1616, a part of these remains was brought back in a coffer of silver and ebony to the lady canonesses of Mons and confided to their care in the sanctuary of S. Waudru.

This ceremony was conducted with great pomp; a solemn procession of more than six hundred candles, in which were associated the magistrates of the city, the religious orders, the priests, and the people, assembled at the church of S. Elizabeth and accompanied the relics, carried by the Abbot of S. Denis, to the cathedral of Saint Waudru.

A second portion of the bones was given by the Princess, in 1626, to the convent of Carmelites which she had founded in 1607 in Brussels; and again a third presentation was made in 1650, after the death of Isabelle, to the church of S. Gudule in the same town.

A note of the Bollandists asserts that a fragment of the body and one of the pictures from the church at Schiedam were given, at the moment when the heretics were about to lay hands on these treasures, to the Superior of the Premontarians at Antwerp. They were deposited in the Chapel of the Holy Apostles, where they rested many years, until the picture deteriorated and was thrown away, and the relics disappeared, no one knows how.

At the present time, according to details we have been able to collect, no trace can be found at S. Waudru or at S. Gudule of Lydwine's remains, which must have been dispersed during the Revolution.   The

o

Carmelites alone at Brussels still keep their precious gift, but they abandoned part of it in 1871 that the town of Schiedam might possess at least some vestiges of its Saint. Most of what remains, namely, the entire bones of the two arms, is to be found now in the parish church of the Visitation, at Schiedam.

The Jansenites of that town also kept some fragments, but they concealed them and pretended they could not understand French if they were asked about them.

Perhaps their predecessors had robbed a reliquary, of which they could recognize the origin by deciphering the name or the arms engraved on the metal, and they did not care to have to explain how they came by it.

Let us add, whilst speaking of the honours accorded by the Church to Lydwine, that the Archbishop of Malines and Metropolitan of Belgium, Msr. Mathias Hovius, by a pastoral letter of Jan. 14, 1616, authorized the cult of blessed Lydwine in Flanders.

Years went by. Lydwine, whose cult was anterior to the decrees of Pope Urban VIII., was added to the number of the beatified; but it still remained for her to acquire the definitive title of Saint.

It was towards the end of last century that a priest of Holland devoted himself to the attainment of this end. The parish of the Visitation of Our Lady had just been instituted at Schiedam, and its first vicar was M. l'abbé Van Leeuwen, who admired and venerated Lydwine. He started a campaign to get Lydwine formally recognised as a Saint, and appealed to the Archbishop of Malines, the Bishop of Haarlem, and other prelates of the Low Countries, together with the Prior of the Carmelites in Brussels, to institute a suit in Rome for her canonization.

This was granted, and a decree of the 14th March, 1890, elevated Lydwine to the rank of Saint; but the true promoter of this result, Abbé Van Leeuwen, had not the joy of realising the success of his efforts, for he died before the promulgation of the decree.

CHAPTER XVI.

In the train which carried my friends and me to Schiedam, I thought of the first edition of "The Life of Lydwine," by Joannes Brugman, which I had consulted in the library at La Haye. This volume, which is as thin as a tract, was printed at Schiedam, at the expense of the builders of the Church of S. John the Baptist, in 1498, that is to say, sixty-five years after the death of the Saint; and it contains curious wood engravings, of which two may be specially mentioned. The one represents Lydwine standing, dressed as a great lady of the fifteenth century, with a long crucifix in her right hand, and in the left a branch of that rose bush whose buds signified the number of days she had still to live. In front of her, seated on a wooden chair, is the good brother minor, Brugman, in the act of writing his book; but he is so absorbed and in such a hurry that he only looks at his manuscript and does not see the Saint. The other picture shows Lydwine, older than she could have been at that time, stretched on her side and supported by two women, whilst a third stands transfixed with fright, and a man behind her draws the outlines of her limbs. To complete the little picture, some skaters appear on one side holding each other by the hand, and on the other side there is a tiny tower, indicated by a few strokes of the pencil.

The xylographs, which have been carefully studied from the point of view of the history of engraving in the Low Countries, appealed to me chiefly by their simplicity, but they were too small to suggest the aspect of the places in which the Saint lived.

P

Does her memory, so absolutely forgotten by the world in general, and almost forgotten in the Calvinist towns of Holland, still survive in Schiedam? Should I discover in this township, where she was born and died, any traces of her: the remains of the streets of her time, the site of her house, or any documents to bear out those which her first biographers gathered together so carelessly?

I was ruminating thus while turning over the pages of a Baedeker, which devoted a few unenthusiastic lines to the description of Schiedam, and did not even mention the name of the Saint.

To tell the truth, I found a Holland so unlike that which I had enjoyed in my childhood and since—a Holland rebuilt, with large towns full of avenues and new buildings, that I hoped for very little from this excursion. Would it not be the same at Schiedam, which I had never yet visited? Probably it would.

On the other hand, what marches and counter-marches we had to make to enable us to hear Mass in these Protestant agglomerations? Were we in Lydwine's country going to have the same difficulty in in these Protestant agglomerations! Were we in than possible; and yet my friends and I plucked up heart a little for we knew that a much frequented pilgrimage took place in this district, the pilgrimage of the martyrs of Gorkum, that is to say, of nineteen of the faithful, of whom eleven were Capucins, two Premontarians, one a Dominican, one an Augustinian, and four secular priests, who had been hanged after frightful tortures in 1572 by the reformed Church at Gorkum. They were beatified in 1675 and canonized in 1867.

Their memory was so fresh that pilgrims always came to venerate their relics, and therefore a current of Catholicism must exist in the country. Now Gorkum is not very far from Schiedam, and there was consequently a chance that either in going or coming back they might also do reverence to the remains of the Saint, and in that case there would certainly be at least a chapel.

The answer to these questions was not long in declaring itself, for we had hardly left the train at Schiedam that evening when we perceived a vast church. Glad of the chance, we entered, but it was so dark that we could distinguish nothing even at two paces' distance. Suddenly, as we groped our way along and asked ourselves if we were not in a heretic building, the light of a star shone at the end of the nave. The star moved and fixed itself in six different places in the air; and in the light that spread from the six candles above the altar, a coloured statue emerged from the darkness, the statue of a woman crowned with roses and accompanied by an angel. Doubt was no longer possible; as if to reassure us Lydwine showed herself immediately on our arrival, and whilst we were examining the apparition, the whole church became illuminated and a crowd silently filled it. Men, women, and children entered by all the doors and pressed into the benches; the altar was covered with light, and whilst the priests displayed the Blessed Sacrament, majestic waves of praise came from the great organ, and the " Tantum ergo," entoned in plain chant by hundreds of voices, mounted in clouds of incense along the pillars and under the arches. Then, after the Benediction, the " Laudate " was sung by the congregation, and in the darkening church fervent kneeling silhouettes were seen with clasped hands in the shadows.

The Benediction of the Blessed Sacrament! We are so accustomed to it in France that it no longer awakes any special sensations; we present ourselves happy to offer a proof of affectionate deference to Him whose humility was such that He was born into the most vile race in the world, the race of the Jews, and that He consented to heal the sickness of soul of His own people, to humble Himself for the part of spiritual healer, in the lowly aspect of a wafer of bread! But in a strange land, where for weeks we may be without a church into which we can enter at all hours, amongst people who do not understand our language, the sensation of joy and peace we felt in hearing the Latin tongue of the Church, and in finding ourselves suddenly again in the atmosphere of prayer, was truly exquisite.

What astonished me too, in this unknown sanctuary, was the number of men who were praying, and the ardent fervour of these Catholics whom we recognized as so deeply, so simply pious.

Returning to the hotel, where the excellent people who received us were also orthodox, we learnt that Schiedam possesses three churches, and that Saint Lydwine is the patroness and absolute mistress of the town.

In that dining room in the Hoogstraat, where we felt so much at home and at our ease in a warm and comfortable corner, memories of family and childhood came over me, called up by the smell of the room, that smell peculiar to the rooms in Holland, which is made up of ginger-bread and tea, ginger and cinnamon, salt meat and smoke; an emanation at the same time sweet and bitter, which recalls to me so many friendly dining rooms and light repasts.

All that is small and delicate in Holland rises up to greet us and to bid us, like Lydwine, whose celestial odours we recall, the most friendly of welcomes.

The next day we went to visit the churches, and our surprise of the evening before was increased; it was not Sunday and yet there were many at Mass, communicating either before or after the sacrifice, as is the custom here.

Of these three churches, which were always full, two belong to the Dominicans, who, in a Protestant country, cannot wear the dress of their order; and one of these churches, dedicated to S. John the Baptist, was the one we had entered by chance on the previous evening. In daylight its charm would be gone, if the

life of prayer which animates it did not compensate
for the vulgar ugliness of its nave. Adorned with
pillars with Tuscan capitals, it is of a melancholy,
unclassifiable style, and the image of the Saint which
we saw in the half light, is of common painted plaster.

The other church, that of the Rosary, is built half
of brick, half of stone, and lighted by green glass. It
is an awkward imitation of the Gothic style, but is
nevertheless lighter and more attractive than the other.
The chapel, dedicated to S. Lydwine, is ornamented
with glass, on which different episodes of her life are
depicted, and by a statue, bought ready-made, which
has no resemblance to a work of art, whether seen
close at hand or from a distance.

Much the best church is the third, the parish church,
which is served by a vicar and curates, and dedicated
in the name of the Visitation of Our Lady. Modern
like the other two, it is in imitation of the Norman
style, and though bare and inelegant, it contains an
incomparable chapel, full of the spirit of S. Lydwine,
whose relics, given by the Carmelites of Brussels, are
preserved in it.

This chapel, which is almost a miniature oratory, is
nothing when described; its charm lies in its atmosphere and not in its shell, which, with its beams and
its panels of white wood, looks like a temporary
building and is certainly unfinished. It seems as
though space had been lacking and a little yard had
been borrowed on which to build the shrine; but it is
the feeling of intimacy which this sanctuary gives,
unspoilt by the gimcrack ornaments of other churches,
that appeals to the pilgrim.

There rises a very simple altar of Gothic form,
ornamented by a cross and passion flowers and
surmounted by a statue of the Saint standing, to
whom the angel offers roses; a statue inspired by
the sculptors of the Primitives, and the only really
adequate one we have yet met in the country. On
the front of the altar, which is framed in woodwork, a

bas-relief, in marble, represents the Saint again, but this time in a recumbent posture, and the angel bringing her the symbolic branch.

In spite of its classic conception and its ordinary composition, this bas-relief, which is the work of M. Stracké, a sculptor of Haarlem, is interesting; and whilst I examine it narrowly I say to myself: Where have I already seen that figure, enveloped in bandages, regarding a crucifix held between its hands? Lydwine's heir, Sister Emmerich, appears before me, on her bed, as Clément Brentano drew her and Edouard Steinle engraved her; and I must say I think it a truly ingenious idea of the artist who, not being able to consult any authentic portrait of the Saint, drew his inspiration from the attitude and features of her more perfect image, her sister in GOD.

Pictures by the artist Jan Dunselman will complete the decoration of this chapel; five are already in place and three are still to come. Amongst these compositions, which tell the principal events in Lydwine's life, one depicts the fall on the ice in a manner which recalls the work of de Leys; and this picture, with the Saint's little house of brick and wood, the door with large hinges, the window with heavy leadwork, the groups of girls who surround the child prostrate in the snow, the men who are indifferent and walk about without realizing the gravity of the accident, and the old sweeper on the right, emerging at the cries of the girl distracted with fear, is a good piece of work, wonderfully drawn and cleverly painted. I cannot, however, believe that little Lydwine had a long nose, prominent eyes, and vulgar mouth. In point of fact, she ought to have looked frightful in these pictures, for she was already thin and ugly before she broke her rib; but while the artist was, in my opinion, quite right to neglect historical truth—for it would require genius to make spiritual splendour to appear through bodily squalor—yet I could have wished that he had imagined a Lydwine both more intellectual and more delicate.

She was pretty, well made, of an elegant figure, and her voice was sweet and soft. That is almost all we learn from her biographers, but, though little, it is enough to show that they intended to make her pleasanter and more refined than these artists have done.

Truly I believe, for my own part, that I saw her one Sunday amongst the orphans the Dominican sisters brought to Mass in that same church. She was kneeling, bending towards the altar, telling her beads; she had large blue, almost green eyes, and under the black hood her admirable hair was visible, that hair which, almost silver at the roots, becomes more golden at the tips and might be likened to a skein of silk lit by a winter sun. The child's pose was so modest, so pious, so truly absorbed in GOD, with her fair skin just tinted with rose colour in the cheeks, and her flower-like lips opened as if the frost had touched them, that I could not persuade myself Lydwine would have differed from her in any way.

As I have said, there is no authentic picture of Lydwine's features extant. Of the twenty pictures mentioned by Molanus, which formerly ornamented the walls of the chapel built in her honour by the rectors of Schiedam, twelve were reproduced in an insignificant form by the engraver Jérôme Wierik in the sixteenth century, and surround, in medallions, a larger portrait of the Saint receiving the famous branch from the hands of her angel. It is difficult to imagine anything more mean than this engraving; one does not know if Lydwine is a boy or a girl, for she grimaces like a hybrid being, whose prominent nose divides an absolutely chinless face.

On the other hand, I have examined in a private house at Schiedam a very beautiful engraving by Valdor, dating from the beginning of the seventeenth century, which portrays her more sensibly; but neither is this she. Other feeble portraits by Pietro de Jode and Sébastien Leclerc exhibit her, either alone or with her angel, brandishing a cross, a crown, or a twig of rose or palm. A last portrait, quite modern but interesting, in imitation of the Primitive style, is the work of a German painter, Ludwig Seitz; it is one of the best, but in that, as in all the others, the face is invented.

We are at liberty, therefore, since nothing certain exists, to picture her to ourselves according to our conceptions of art and our instincts of piety.

On that Sunday when I caught sight of the extraordinary little maiden, we could confirm the impressions which the town first made on us. The churches were too small to hold the crowd of worshippers; at the Visitation of Our Lady the people read their missals before the open doors on the pavement; the communions never ceased; after the men and women, the school children came forward. Nowhere have I ever observed such a placid warmth and, may I add, such an absolute respect for the liturgy; plain chant executed not by paid singers, but by volunteers who acquitted themselves conscientiously of their task and determined to sing well in honour of the Saviour.

This little chapel of S. Lydwine comes to me as a tender memory in hours of sorrow. How can I forget the cordial and delicate welcome of the good and learned vicar, M. l'abbé Poelhekke, who celebrated Mass for us one morning at her altar, on which he exposed the reliquary as on her fête day?

Apart from these few bones and her memory which shines in the town, nothing, alas! remains here of Lydwine, except her tombstone. It has been taken from the old church, which is disaffected and converted into a Protestant temple, and transferred to a little chapel of the Dominican sisters, who have an orphanage and a school for the children of the poor. This stone is carved with the figure of a woman, old and asleep, the hands folded on the breast, and enveloped from head to foot in a shroud. From above two little angels descend to surround her head with a crown, and, at the four corners, the evangelical emblems are engraved in circles.

This stone has been very well preserved; according to the Bollandists, the Calvinists turned it over, not to preserve it, but to prevent the Catholics from kneeling before it; while, according to another tradition, the Protestants, in deference to the Saint, made a détour in the church so as not to walk over the stone and destroy it. I do not know which of these versions is true, but I give them for what they are worth.

The building which it occupies is the subject of numerous controversies which I will sum up in a few lines.

According to some, Lydwine's house was situated in a little pathway called Bogarstraat; according to others, in a little street called Kortekerstraat. There was formerly in this street a well which healed fever cases and sick animals, and according to ancient documents, one can recognize the dwelling of the Saint by this sign; but although researches have been made, the well can no longer be discovered. A third opinion, which seems the most likely, would assign her residence to the Leliendaal, where there is a Protestant orphanage, a building of the eighteenth century, with the figure of a boy and girl carved and painted on each side above the door.

This at any rate is the history of Lydwine's dwelling.

After her death, the son of Doctor Godfried de Haga bought her house, which became what was called " a house of the Holy Spirit," that is to say, a refuge for poor women. Then in 1461, on the day of the fête of S. Gertrude, this house, which contained a chapel, was given by the college of the Holy Spirit, with the assent of the burgomasters and councillors of Schiedam, to a community of Clarisses, or grey sisters of S. Francis, who came from Haarlem. There was in this convent, says Molanus, an altar dedicated to S. Lydwine at the place her bed had occupied; and from here was distributed every year, on Lydwine's fête day, a loaf of white bread to all who presented themselves—rich and poor alike.

In 1572 the Gueux, after having devastated the church of S. John the Baptist, demolished the chapel of the Leliendaal, and pillaged the cloister. It became an orphanage in 1605 and was abandoned in 1779, for it then fell into ruin; but it was afterwards rebuilt, perhaps in the same place, that is to say, on the site of Lydwine's house.

This last point, however, is not universally admitted. I do not wish to take part in this discussion, which is only of interest to those of Schiedam. I ought, however, to add that a fourth opinion was expressed to me in Amsterdam, which has the advantage of putting all the others in the right; namely, that Lydwine might have occupied many habitations, and would, in any case, have been transferred to her brother's house on the death of her father.

I do not know how much this statement may be worth: I see no trace of it in the historians' narratives; but it suggests one comment.

Brugman tells us that the house of Lydwine's father was low and damp; more like a tomb than a cottage. Now, I ask, how could so many people exist in such a cockle-shell of a dwelling? After the death of her father, his son, wife, two children, a cousin called Nicolas, the Augustinian Gerlac, and finally, widow Catherine Simon, must all have lived there. It is very possible that they were not all there at the same time, but it is certain that this retreat must have been fairly large to shelter so many guests. It is therefore, perhaps, permissible to think that the house in which Lydwine died was not the same as that in which she was born and lived during the first years of her sufferings.

The location of the canal, on whose ice she broke her rib, is the subject of less discussion; the archæologists seem to agree in pointing out a street which still bears the name of lame man's lane, "Kreupelstraat." This street was a canal not so very long ago, for I obtained a photograph in Schiedam which shows it as such, but it is difficult to imagine the exact place where the scene related by the biographers took place.

In the days of Lydwine nothing existed but the old church of S. John the Baptist, now belonging to the reformed Church; but the Saint never prayed there, since this sanctuary was burnt in the fire of 1428, and rebuilt, in part, during her life, at a time when she was confined entirely to her bed.

This church, then the only one in Schiedam, is built of brick and surmounted by a high roofed tower, which has a little turret embellished by a very feeble carillon. The arches inside are supported by seven pillars with capitals of sculptured leaves; its ceiling has beams, and the nave is cut in two by an apron of wood. There are desks arranged as if for the distribution of prizes or to serve as a corn exchange, some benches, and a quantity of Bibles. The sadness of this polluted sanctuary, without altar and without masses, is indescribable.

More than in this basilica, more than in the streets of which I have spoken, the memory of Lydwine haunts you when you wander in the old quarters of Schiedam, which are less rebuilt and less repaired. How often, along the shady canals, whose bridges turn to allow strings of barges to pass, how often we have called up her image, whilst the great windmills bless the town with the crosses of their wings. They trace a circle of a Greek cross, and recall to my mind the memorial of that Passion which Lydwine so ardently adored. And whilst these silent crosses bless the skies, in the distance a policeman, pleasant looking in spite of his spiked hat and little sword, superintends the dock labourers who in red woollen clothes and short breeches disembark barrels on the quay, while sailors pump brown streams of hot grain into the barges drawn up in front of the breweries. I, for my part, think of

Lydwine's father, good old Pierre, who had been the watchman, the policeman, of his day at Schiedam.

Before us spread the water-ways, planted with mills of the eighteenth century, superb in their red brick bridges, their great collars of wood, their little window-frames painted apple green, their wings, sometimes without sails, like razor-blades ready to cut the air and looking like giants by the side of the little ones which are built now.

There are charming corners in this tiny city. In the old parts on the other side of the river Schie, to which the town owes its name, there is a network of little streets composed of smoke-blackened brick buildings, making quaint curves and designs in the water which reflects them; old, tumble-down buildings, like the drying sheds of tanyards, or high façades surmounted by great roofs, which the seagulls touch as they fly.

Suddenly, at the turn of one of these ways, immense spaces of country are revealed; plains intersected by canals, which seem to move with the clouds they reflect. Very far off, masts of ships, which we cannot see, seem to pierce the earth; a sail moves, and behind it appear the sweeps of a windmill, which it had concealed. Cows, sheep, and pigs can be seen as far as the eye can reach, under an infinite expanse of sky; and while we look at this vegetation, so fresh and green that in comparison the best watered meadows of France are yellow and dry, while we contemplate this almost polar sky of pale blue with its little silver clouds which slowly turn to gold, a very sweet melancholy comes over us.

These placid scenes, these quiet spaces, these solemn landscapes, have something personal about them, a nameless feeling of peace and love; and the charm of nature here offers a fellowship which smiles perhaps a little sadly and reflectively.

As a contrast to these plains and these little streets intermingled with narrow canals, there expands at the other end of the town a great stretch of water, the

Meuse, which here flows into the sea.   In the distance
Rotterdam emerges from the water, with her towers
rising against the limitless sky; the little steamboats,
which serve the shore towns, smoke on the horizon; the
whistle of a vast candle factory dominates all other
noises; the quay is bristling with steam-packets and
encumbered with barrels.   This recall to modern life
in Lydwine's country is disconcerting, and we begin
to regret the time when the clumsy fishermen set fire
to Schiedam, on the eve of the day when they embarked
from these shores, then empty and unoccupied, for the
herring fishing.

While speaking of fire we should note that the Saint,
who endured three in her lifetime, is here considered,
even by the Protestants, a saviour from its ravages;
and indeed there has not been a single case of a fire in
an alcohol distillery, where the adjacent houses have
suffered.   Lydwine is also, as is very natural, invoked
for the cure of illness.   From the Curé's house is lent
a little receptacle of silver containing a tiny relic, with
which to touch those who suffer; and every Monday,
at seven in the evening, they pray, before Benediction,
that Lydwine may avert epidemics from the town.

She still lives at Schiedam, where the Catholics
venerate her; and it must in justice be owned that the
dissenters are not hostile to her.   She possesses
friends, too, at Haarlem, but farther afield her memory
is effaced.

We have now spent nearly twelve days in the tiny
city, and besides its exterior aspect we begin to know
its antecedents and penetrate its inner life.

Schiedam was never a large town, but was formerly
a prosperous place.   Now she is declining; the old
rich families have gone; her particular industry,
the " Schiedam " gin, which takes its title from her,
has been on the decline since large towns such as
Antwerp have entered into competition with her.   She
used to possess three hundred distilleries, and now
there are hardly twenty.   Where are the boats which

used formerly to come from Norway with cargoes of blue berries? I have discovered none, and I am a little doubtful if the fruit of the juniper enters at all into the composition of the generous liquor. It seems to be concocted like Irish whisky and Scotch gin from wheat, maize and barley; and in all these streets, by all these canals, it is not the smell, like matches, of true juniper berries that we perceive, but the scent of hot linseed, of grain, of the dregs of hot barley. They throw out these things beside the factories in tanks along the quays, and there men pump them out and spread them in barges to serve as cattle food.

The population of the town consists of about 13,000 of the reformed church, 10,000 Catholics, 60 or 70 Jansenists, and 200 Jews.

The Catholics are therefore in a minority, as they are in most of the towns of the Low Countries; and this is doubtless why they keep together and form a little model colony of good and pious people. A Catholic who does not practise his religion and is Catholic only in name is rare here; there is nothing like having suffered for your religion to render it dear to you; and if Calvinism has decimated the Saviour's lambs, one must own that it has strangely strengthened those who stood firm. The Catholicism of the Netherlands, as I observed it here, has nothing of that effeminacy which one finds more and more among the Latin races. It adores a Christ on the Cross, inseparable from the body, whom it does not relegate, as so often with us, to a place after and below His Saints.

In a word it is a simple and a virile Catholicism; and it must also be owned that in Holland the clergy are excellent. Dispensed from the subordinate education of our seminaries, strengthened by arduous study, they are not filled with those prejudices which make of our ecclesiastics a class apart. The Dutch priest is a man like any other, mixing like any one else in everyday life; he is more independent than with us; his existence is passed in the open; and it is just because he has nothing obscure about him that he commands respect, even amongst dissenters, by the dignity of his life, by the fervour of his faith, by the recognized honesty of his priesthood.

His task is not always of the easiest. He must secure the safety of his flock, camped amidst infidels, and increase its numbers if he can; but in doing this he meets terrible obstacles, for it is but slowly that the Low Country returns to its original faith, because of the fervent defence of their religion by the Protestants and the isolation of the converted. He must be a very exceptional man therefore who returns to the sheepfold; he must be able to do without the help of his old co-religionists who, like the Jansenists, retain the money.

For riches lie with the sects, especially with the Jansenists. "Perette's box" has had some little ones, and these for their encouragement the prebends distribute to those who are married in their churches. It would not suit the Jansenists to foster a religion drawn from Port Royal, ascetic Christians sinning from excess of scruple. The disciples of Port Royal, who were certainly very interesting, no longer exist; their successors are shamefully heterodox, debased Protestants, and if they sin it is not by ultra rigorism, but rather by the other extreme, for Jansenius married and Quesnel also took a wife.

This Holland, which, with its Jansenist archbishopric at Utrecht, is the last refuge of the schism—for if I may believe the clergy year book, there are in a population of 4,800,000 inhabitants, 1,700,000 Catholics, or a little more than 35 per cent.—has been, nevertheless, a holy land, a greenhouse in which the monastic culture was intensive! Dominicans, Augustinians, Franciscans, Croziers, Alexians, Chartreux, and Antonites, built cloisters there and flourished in them. Frisia alone had ninety monasteries and abbeys, and in the single province of Utrecht, says Dom Pitra, they

P

have numbered 198 religious foundations.   All have disappeared in the storm.

In this country of S. Eloi, of S. Willibrod, of S. Wérenfride, of S. Willehed, of S. Boniface, of S. Odoulfe, of S. Lydwine, the Catholic cult is maintained in spite of terrible persecutions; instead of being submerged by the reformed religion following the confession of Calvin, it is actually extending.

In 1897 a Dutch paper, the "Katholicke Werkmen," enumerated the Catholic institutions in the Low Countries thus: 96 religious houses serving 66 parishes and giving instruction in the schools to 725 pupils; 44 brotherhoods tending the sick, aged, insane, orphans, deaf and dumb, and teaching 1,035 boarders and 12,120 day scholars; 22 houses of religion vowed to the contemplative life; 430 houses of nursing sisters caring for 12,000 orphans, incurables and blind. There are registered, at this moment, 592 convents in Holland.

According to other statistics appearing in 1900 in the "Residentiebode" of the Hague, the Netherlands numbered:

In 1784, 350 parishes and 400 priests; in 1815, 673 parishes and 975 priests; in 1860, 918 parishes and 1,800 priests; in 1877, 985 parishes and 2,093 priests; and in 1900, 1,014 parishes and 2,310 priests.

This progress is slow, but sure; the Church is re-occupying, little by little, the soil that once was hers; the old seed buried in the earth which the Reformation dried up, is rising.   One can hear, they say, certain reeds springing up in the tropics; it seems as though if we were to listen well in the Low Countries, we should hear the old bones and the dust of her ancient Saints stirring.

APPENDICES

IT appeared to me interesting to make some research into what was formerly, and what is now, the position of S. Lydwine from the liturgical point of view.

Here are some of the facts which I have been able to gather.

In the "Natales sanctorum Belgii" Joannes Molanus tells us under date of the fourteenth of April that they decorated the chapel and tomb of Lydwine, not on that day, but on the fourth day after Easter, and that they celebrated the office of the Trinity in her honour with solemn rites.

The Bollandists have preserved for us the sequence "De alma virgine Lydwina," which was formerly recited at Eastertide in Holland and in Flanders. We give this below with a translation, slightly incomplete, by Cardinal Dom Pitra.

Finally, from the year 1616, in which the veneration of Lydwine was authorised, until 1892, there was no special office for the Saint in the missal and in the breviary of the Catholics of the Low Countries; but, what is much more curious, a special office existed in the ancient Jansenist breviaries of Utrecht and of Haarlem.

I have succeeded in laying my hand on this book; and, as a matter of curiosity, I have extracted from the text the portion relating to the Saint and have subjoined it with a translation.

In conclusion, after Lydwine's canonization, a special office was appointed by the Congregation of Rites, and was first celebrated in 1892.

The appendix gives the text in Latin and in French. The Mass is the "Delexisti" of the Common Virgins, not martyrs, with the collect proper to the Office and the Gospel according to S. Matthew, "Videns Jesus turbas," which is the Gospel of All Saints.

SEQUENTIA DE ALMA VIRGINE LYDWINA

Alleluia festivale
Voce, votis, jubilo;
Tempus exigit Paschale.
Benedictione plenus
Jam refulsit sol serenus,
Pulso noctis nubilo.
Coronatur gloria
Christus pro victoria.
Victor victis inferis,
Deus surgens creditur,
Honor regni redditur,
Fitque pax cum Superis.
Expectatio Mariæ
Consolatur ipsam pie,
Tristem hanc inveniens,
Fit solatium beatis,
In extremo mundi natis
Omnes nos deliniens.
Gaudent Archangeli,
Fantur et Angeli
Virgini Lydiæ:
Hæccine Lydia
Vernat ut lilia
Santæ Cæciliæ?
Intra cujus cameram
Senserat Tiburtius
Rosam odoriferam,
Stupens vehementius.
Catharinæ virginis
Juxta natalitia
Fructum divi seminis
Metit hæc Cæcilia.
Lydegidis humilis,
Nata Christo Domino,
Sanctis extat similis,
Regnans sine termino.
Miræ patientiæ
Vixit in hoc tempore,

Nimiæ miseriæ
Particeps in corpore.
Non murmur resonat,
Non querimonia,
Sed laudem personat
Devota Lydia
De data gratia.
O vere humilem,
Quæ nunquam deficit,
Quam Christus debilem
Seipso reficit;
Hinc virgo proficit.
Per se Jesus hanc invisit,
Consolationem misit;
Circa lectum hujus sedens,
Et ab ea non recedens,
Donec ipsam pasceret:
Quæstione quadam facta
De nativitate nacta
Opus Verbi Incarnati,
Hæc adscripsit Trinitati.
Sic ut quærens quæreret
Radiosi luminis
Talis doctrix numinis
Impetret quod poscimus:
Solem sic inspicere
Ne contingat perdere
Lumen quod nos cupimus,
Trinitatem speculari,
Unitatemque mirari,
Quæ consistit in Divinis,
Quo dictaminis est finis.
Vale, felix Lydewidis,
Quam non ligat nexus Stygis;
Poscas nobis cum Maria,
Ut cantemus Alleluia.
                              Amen.

SÉQUENCE DE LA BIENHEUREUSE

VIERGE LYDWINE

C'est le joyeux alleluia
Qu'appelle le temps Pascal,
De voix et de cœur
    [réjouissons-nous.
Plein de bénédictions
A brillé un soleil pur,
Chassant l'ombre nocturne,
Et, couronné de gloire,
Le Christ a triomphé.
Vainqueur de l'Enfer vaincu,
Il se lève, il est Dieu,
    [croyons !
Il a repris l'honneur de son
    [trône,
Il fait régner la paix dans le
    [cœur,
Et cesser l'attente de sa Mère
Qu'il console avec amour.
Et les anges en chœur
    [réjouissent,
Disant à la vierge Lydie :
Est-ce donc là Lydie ?
Elle est blanche comme les lys
De Sainte Cécile !
Cécile en sa demeure
Fit sentir à Tiburce
Le parfum de la rose
Et le remplit de stupeur.
Cécile, au jour où naquit au
La Vierge Catherine,   [Ciel

Recueillit le fruit
Que sema la grâce de Dieu ;
L'humble Lydwine
Que le Christ fit naître pour
    [Lui
Est semblable à ses Saints
Et règne à jamais.
Exemple étonnant de patience,
Elle a vécu en nos jours,
Portant dans son corps
D'intolérables souffrances.
On n'entendit ni murmure
Ni plainte aucune ;
On n'entendit que les chants
De la pieuse Lydwine.
  . . . .
Adieu, Bienheureuse Lydwine,
Toi que la mort n'a pas
    [retenue captive ;
Veuille nous obtenir qu'avec
    [Marie
Nous chantions : Dieu soit
    [loué.
    Alleluia.—Amen.

(Dom Pitra, *Hollande
Catholique,* p. 136).

OFFICE PROPER TO BLESSED LYDWINE

Breviarium ecclesiasticum ad usum metropolitanæ ecclesiæ Ultrajectensis et cathedralis ecclesiæ Harlemensis accommodatum—pars Verna — jussu superiorum, MDCCXLIV.

Ecclesiastical breviary for the use of the metropolitan Church of Utrecht and of the Cathedral Church of Haarlem.—In the Spring of the year, printed by order of the superiors, 1744.

Festum subsequens in diœcæsi Ultrajectensi recitari poterit ad libitum.

The following fête ean be recited at will in the diocese of Utrecht.

DIE XIV. MAII.
In festo beatæ Liduinæ virginis.
Semi duplex ad libitum.

14 MAY.
In the festival of blessed Lydwine, virgin.

Omnia de communi Virginum non mart. præter sequentia
In I Vesperis et Laudibus.

All of the common of Virgins not martyrs, except as follows at first Vespers and Lauds.

HYMNUS.

Ut semper in suis Deus
Miranda præstat! infima
E fæce mundi seligens
Ut altiora deprimat!
Longis malis exercita
Liduina, tandem Numinis
Agnoscit occultam manum,
Tollit crucem, sese abnegat.
Dextræ o Dei mutatio!
Qui nauseam dabat calix
Jam corde toto sumitur,
Jesuque amore inebriat.
Qui virginis pœnas Deus
Pænis tuis iunxeras,
Fac nos dolores quoslibet
Amore pro tuo pati.
Qui traditum Cruci Pater
Nobis redonas Filium,
Da carnis angores sacro
Commitigari Spiritu.
            Amen.

HYMN.

GOD as always works marvels in his own!
From the world's deepest mire He chooses instruments to humble pride.
Long tried by sickness, Lydwine recognizes at last the secret hand of GOD; she accepts her cross and makes her renunciation.
O conversion wrought by the hand of GOD.
This cup, once so repugnant, she now accepts with all her heart and inebriates herself with the love of Jesus.
Saviour, who hast united the sufferings of this virgin to thine own, enable us to bear our pain for love of Thee.
Father who hast given Thy Son to suffer for us on the Cross, grant that the Holy Spirit may soothe the sufferings of our flesh. Amen.

Oratio ut infra ad Laudes.

The prayer as below at Lauds.

AD NOCTURNUM.

Invit. Agnum quem sequuntur Virgines, *Venite, adoremus, Alleluia.—Apoc. XIV.

Ps. 94. — VENITE
Hymnus ex laudibus de Communi.
Ant. v. RRR.
Lectio de Scriptura occurrente.
tribus in unam redactis.

LECTIO II.

Liduina, virgo Schiedamensis, insignis futura Dominicæ Passionis imitatrix, sæculo decimo quarto in lucem edita fuit, die Dominica Palmarum, ipso sacrificii Missæ tempore, dum Passio Dominici nostri Jesu Christi in ecclesia recitabatur, parentibus pietate magis quam seculari nobilitate conspicuis. Ab infantia singulari devotione erga Deiparem Virginem ferebatur; eamque perpetuæ virginitatis proposito imitari studebat. Cumque pater tenellam filiam ad conjugium adhortaretur, ipsa ferventi prece a Deo obtinuit ut in sancto proposito firmaretur, carnis mortificatione id agens, ut species sua, qua placere hominibus posset, periret. Piis conatibus atque gemitibus, opitulatus est Dominus, qui castitatem virginis variis ægritudinibus, tanquam lilium inter spinas, custodivit. Anno siquidem ætatis decimo quinto, cum forte per hiemalem glaciem puella incederet, costulam dextri lateris cadendo fregit, quam læsionem continua series morborum et cruciatum per annos triginta octo secuta est. Febris æstuens, in-

AT NOCTURNS.

Invit. "And the Virgins follow the Lamb."—Come let us adore Him, Alleluia.—Apoc. XIV.

Ps. 94. — Hymn of Lauds as of the Common.
Anthems, versicles, responses.
1st Lesson from the same Scriptures.

2ND LESSON.

Lydwine, virgin of Schiedam, who was to be a signal follower of the Passion, was born in the fourteenth century on Palm Sunday, at the moment when, at Mass, they were reciting the Passion of the Saviour. Her parents were more renowned for their piety than their birth. From her infancy she showed a singular devotion to the Virgin Mother of GOD, and was eager to imitate her by devoting herself to perpetual virginity. When her father exhorted her to marriage, she strengthened herself in her pious resolution by the fervour of her prayers and by practising mortification of the flesh in order that she might be delivered from that beauty which was a pleasure to men. The Saviour was moved by the piety of her efforts and by her petitions to protect her virgin chastity with various diseases, like a lily among thorns. She had attained her fifteenth year, when, walking by chance on the ice, she fell and broke a rib of her right side. This lesion induced a series of diseases and tortures, which

tensus capitis dolor, hydrops, calculus, vernium scaturigo, pulmonum et hepatis per particulas ejectio et quod tandem morbi genus eam non afflixit, omni interim remedio ac requie, sed et ad fundandam humilitatem, animi etiam consolatione destitutam?

LECTIO III.

Post annos probationis quatuor, famulæ suæ misertus Dominus animum ejus sic erexit ministerio Joannis Pot, magnæ pietatis viri, ut omni deinceps in Deo solo fiducia collocata, ex contemplatione Christi patientis tota in amorem Sponsi crucifixi inardesceret, parata jam, si Sponso liberet, immissos cruciatus ad indefinitam annorum longitudinem ferre. Triginta ergo annis continuis lecto tanquam Cruci eam affixit infirmitas, quorum ferme viginti solius capitis ac brachii sinistri mobilitate peregit ; cor ejus interim sacrosancta Eucharistia ad patientiam stabiliente, debili vero stomacho, ut fertur, omnem alium cibum recusante. Donec, cursu peracto, feria tertia post Pascha, absque arbitrio, quod quadrienni prece a Deo postularat, et appropinquante morte, ut ita contingeret, ipsa procurarat, obdormivit in Domino, decima quarta aprilis, anno millesimo quadringentesimo trigesimo tertio, annos nata quinquaginta tres. Variis post mortem miraculis clara, quorum aliqua refert oculatus testis Thomas A Kempis, illico

lasted thirty-eight years. Burning fever, violent headache, dropsy, gravel, worms, ejection of fragments of the lungs and of the liver, from what form of illness was she indeed free?—and, during this time, she was without remedy, without sleep, and even, to strengthen her humility, without consolation !

3RD LESSON.

After four years of this novitiate of pain, the Saviour had pity on His servant, and to raise her fainting soul, made use of a priest of great piety, Jan Pot. Thereafter, putting her trust in GOD alone, absorbed in the contemplation of the sufferings of Christ, and fired with love for her Spouse crucified, she was fortified to bear, as long as it should please Him, the most cruel sufferings. For thirty years she was nailed to her bed as to a cross by her infirmities ; and for almost twenty of these years she could move only her left arm and her head. She drew from the most Blessed Sacrament the strength necessary to sustain her, for her enfeebled stomach refused, we are told, all other nourishment. At last, having finished her course, on the third day after Easter, without witnesses—for this had been her prayer to GOD for four years, and when death drew near, she arranged that it should happen so—she fell asleep in the Saviour, on the fourteenth of April, fourteen hundred and

cives suos habuit cultores, erecto in ecclesia sancti Joannis Baptisti speciali sacello ad annuam ejus memoriam celebrandam, quam nec jussit, nec impedivit Sancta Sedes. Beatæ Liduinæ ædes quam desideravit pauperibus ad refugium deservire, conversa fuit in xenodochium. Ejus reliquiæ, anno millesimo sexcentesimo decimo quinto subductæ fuere Bruxellas sub Mathia Hovio, archiepiscopo Mechliniensi, qui ad vota Archiducum Alberti et Isabellæ, edito Pastorali decreto, publicum eis cultum impendi permisit.

thirty-three, being fifty-three years of age. After her death numerous miracles added to her fame, some of which are recounted by Thomas à Kempis, who saw them with his own eyes. Soon her fellow-citizens honoured her by erecting a special chapel in the Church of S. John the Baptist, in which to celebrate her memory yearly—and this without either the approval or the disapproval of the Holy See. Blessed Lydwine's dwelling, which she had desired should be made a refuge for the poor, was converted into a hospital. Her remains were transferred to Brussels in 1615, Mathias Hovius being then Archbishop of Malines. He also, at the request of the Archduke Albert and his wife Isabella, published a pastoral decree authorising public veneration to be paid to them.

AD LAUDES.

Hymnus "ut semper in suis" supra ad 1 Vesperas.

ORATIO.

Domine Deus noster, qui beatam Liduinam virginem ab illecebris sæculi præservatam ad tuæ Crucis amplexum toto corde transire docuisti; concede ut ejus meritis atque exemplo discamus et perituras mundi calcare delicias et Crucis tuæ amore omnia nobis adversantia superare, qui vivis et regnas, etc.

Reliqua omnia de Communi.

AT LAUDS.

Hymn "GOD always works"—see first Vespers.

PRAYER.

O Lord our GOD, who hast preserved Blessed Lydwine from the vanities of the world, and has taught her to prefer with all her heart the embrace of Thy Cross, grant us by her example and her merits, to learn to tread under foot the perishable delights of this world, and to surmount, by the love of Thy Cross, all our adversities. Who livest and reignest, etc.

All the rest as of the Common.

OFFICE OF SAINT LYDWINE

In festo
B. Liduinæ virginis
Schiedamensis.
Pro civitate Schiedamensi.
Duplex ii classis.
Pro diocœsi Harlemensi
et pro monasterio
Carmelitarum Bruxellensium.
Duplex majus.
Omnia de communi Virginum
non Martyrum, præter se-
quentia:

On the Festival of the
B. Lydwine, virgin of
Schiedam.
For the town of Schiedam—
Double of 2nd class.
For the Diocese of Harlem,
and for the monastery of
the Carmelites of
Brussels—Double Major.
All as of the Common of
virgins, not martyrs, except
as follows:

ORATIO.

Deus, qui B. Liduinam virginem admirabilis patientiæ et charitatis victimam effecisti, tribue, quæsumus, ut ejus exemplo et intercessione, hujus vitæ ærumnas pro tua voluntate perferentes et proximis nostris propter Te succurrentes, æterna gaudia consequi mereamur.   Per Dominum, etc.

COLLECT.

O Lord, who madest the blessed virgin Lydwine a sufferer of wondrous patience and charity, grant, we pray Thee, by her example and intercession, that after having borne according to Thy will the miseries of this life and succoured our neighbour in Thy name, we may be found worthy of attaining to the joys eternal.   Through our Lord and Saviour, etc.

In I Nocturno.
Lectiones de Virginibus ut
in Communi.
In II Nocturno.

At 1st Nocturn.
Lessons of Virgins as of the
Common.
At 2nd Nocturn.

LECTIO IV.

Liduina virgo Schiedami, in Hollandia nata est, die Palmarum, ipso tempore quo in oppidi ecclesia inter Missæ sacrifiicium Passio Domini decantabatur, re quasi jam præsagiente, quam insignis illa Christi pro humano genere patientis futura esset imitatrix. A prima ætate variis virtutibus conspicua, virginitatem perpetuo custodiendam sibi etiam statuit. Quum itaque duodennis, utpote egregiis animi corporisque dotibus instructa, a pluribus honestate ac divitiis præstantibus, in conjugem peteretur, cœlesti tamen quem elegerat Sponso fidelis permansit, Deumque exoravit ut, ne quispiam deinceps conjugium sibi offerret, deformitate potius morbisque afficeretur Voti compos facta est, eique quintodecimo ætatis anno, infausto casu, dexteri lateris costa confracta est. Mox, per reliquum vitæ tempus, octo nempe et triginta annos tam incredibili morborum et dolorum multitudine atque vi exagitata fuit, eosque tam invicto imo lubenti animo toleravit, ut humanæ miseriæ simul et heroicæ patientiæ prodigium æstimaretur. Tota enim mente cœlestia mysteria,

LESSON IV.

The virgin Lydwine was born at Schiedam, in Holland, on Palm Sunday, at the moment when in the Church of the Town, at Mass, they were singing the Passion of the Lord; which seems to foreshow in what marvellous manner she should follow the steps of Christ suffering for men. From her childhood she was adorned with many virtues and vowed herself to perpetual virginity; but since, at the age of twelve, she was endowed both in mind and body with the most enviable gifts, many rich persons of good repute in the town asked her in marriage. She remained constant, however, to the divine Spouse whom she had chosen, and prayed to GOD to afflict her with disease and deformity in order that no one thereafter might offer her marriage. Her prayer was heard; she was fifteen when an accidental fall broke one of the ribs on her right side. During the rest of her life, that is to say during thirty-eight years, she endured an incredible number of sufferings and ills, with so much courage and even joy, that she was considered a

Dominicam præsertim Passionem assidue contemplans, quum vel acerbissime cruciaretur, quandoque etiam interna consolatione careret, Deo placide gratias agens, tribulationes augeri sibi magis quam minui optabat.

prodigy of human misery and heroic patience. Her whole spirit was absorbed in the rapt contemplation of celestial mysteries, especially of the Passion of Our Lord. When her sufferings became most acute, or when internal consolation was withdrawn, she gave thanks to GOD without flinching, and implored the increase of her torments rather than their diminution.

LECTIO V.

Animi demissione, obedientia ac mansuetudine in exemplum prædita atque Dei amore flagrans, eximia etiam proximorum inimicorum, licet et persequentium, dilectione refulsit. Pauperes, ipsa pauper, de sibi erogatis eleemosynis sustentabat; spirituali qualicumque ope indigentes, omni quo poterat modo adjuvabat, maxime si de homine a vitæ pravitate convertendo, vel anima e Purgatorio exsolvenda ageretur. Variis insuper prodigiis insolitisque gratiis, diu jam ante obitum late innotuit. Altissimæ, inter alia, contemplationis dono gaudens, multoties in extasim rapta, cœlestibus sæpe apparitionibus familiari imprimis Angeli sui societate honorata, cordium abscondita perspiciens, prophetico spiritu absentia et futura revelavit. Plures mirabili ejus interventu corporis animæve sanitatem obtinuerunt. Tandem Dei famula, passioni-

LESSON V.

A model of humility, patience and obedience, burning with the love of GOD, she showed a noble affection for the enemies, and even the persecutors who came about her. Poor herself, she relieved the poor with the alms she received.

Any who were in need of spiritual help could rest assured of finding it with her, especially if it were a question of the conversion of a man from a life of sin, or of the deliverance of a soul from Purgatory. A long time indeed before her death, her exceptional gifts and the graces vouchsafed her were known afar. Endowed with the power of the most high contemplation, frequently carried away into ecstasy, often favoured by divine visions, and living always in close and familiar converse with her guardian angel, she penetrated the secrets of many

bus et meritis cumulata, piissime in cœlum migravit, decimo octavo calendas Majas, anno Domini millesimo quadringentesimo tricesimo tertio. Corpus integrum et decorum repertum ingenti hominum concursu tumulatum; sepulchrum, sacello desuper erecto atque majori loco ecclesiæ conjuncto, multis miraculis claruit.

hearts, and prophetically revealed the past and the future. A great number of persons obtained health of mind or body by her marvellous intercession. At last the servant of GOD, laden with sufferings and merit, left this world in the odour of sanctity, on the eighteenth of the calends of May, in the year of our Lord, fourteen hundred and thirty-three. When her body, then restored to its original beauty, was buried, an enormous number of people were present at her obsequies. Her tomb, over which was erected a chapel adjoining the larger Church, was glorified by numerous miracles.

LECTIO VI.

Post duo fere sæcula, sacello ab acatholicis occupato, ob sanctitatis vero et miraculorum famam virginis memoria cultuque perdurante, sacræ ejus reliquiæ Bruxellas translatæ et ab Archiepiscopo Mechliniensi recognitæ sunt. Majorem partem Belgii gubernatrix, Archiducissa Isabella, Carmilitidum discalceatarum conventui Bruxellensi tradidit; cujus ordinis et conventus moniales, quum deinde per duo iterum cum dimidio sæcula, pretiosum illud depositum fidelissime asservassent et coluissent, Summus Pontifex Pius Nonus, Episcopali

LESSON VI.

After about two centuries, the chapel became the property of heretics, but the renown of the sanctity and miracles of the virgin preserved her memory and her veneration. Her holy remains were transferred to Brussels, and recognised by the Bishop of Malines. The Archduchess Isabel, Governor of Belgium, gave the greater part of the relics to the convent of the barefoot Carmelites of Brussels. The nuns of this order and this convent preserved this precious gift and honoured it with fidelity for two and a half centuries. Then

Harlemensis rogatu, insignes aliquot B. Liduinæ reliquias, e prædicto monasterio in Virginis natalem urbem, ad parochialem S. Mariæ de Visitatione ecclesiam deferri concessit. Quo facto, crescente in dies erga eam devotione, Episcopi Harlemensis, cujus precibus ceteri Nederlandiæ Episcopi una cum Archiepiscopo Mechliniensi suas libentissime preces conjunxerunt, vota suscipiens summus Pontifex Leo decimus tertius Liduinæ cultum confirmavit et in ejus honorem Missam celebrari et proprium officium recitari pro Nederlandiæ regno indulsit.

Pope Pius IX., at the instance of the Bishop of Haarlem, allowed the transportation of certain important relics of B. Lydwine from this convent to the parish church of S. Mary of the Visitation, in the virgin's birthplace. As a result of this concession, the veneration she inspired increased daily, and the Bishop of Haarlem, assisted by other Bishops of the Netherlands and by the Archbishop of Malines, who joined their request very willingly to his, obtained from the Sovereign Pontiff Leo XIII. the confirmation of the veneration of Lydwine. The celebration of a Mass in her honour, and the recitation of a proper office for the Kingdom of Holland, were also granted by the Holy Father.

In III Nocturno.
Lectio sancti Evangelii
secundum Matthæum.
Lectio VII.—Cap. V.
De homilia S. Augustini
Episcopi.
Lib. I de sermone Domini
in monte, c. IV.

At 3rd Nocturn.
Lesson from the Holy Gospel
according to S. Matt.
Lesson VII.—Chapter V. of
the Homilies of S. Augustine,
Bishop, on the sermon on
the Mount, c. IV.

Printed in Great Britain by MACKAYS LTD., Chatham.